Fashion, Progress, Hard Feelings,

Fashion: 'Lucie brings an almost Jon[son]
of his odious characters, and it is a real pleasure to encounter a
work that puts a large number of articulate, maliciously drawn
people on the stage and lets them fight it out in a style that is at
once provocative and wildly funny.'   *Daily Telegraph*

Progress: 'The scene is set for a vicious satirical comedy, as
appallingly funny as anything Mr Lucie has written . . . his
observation is as gruesomely accurate as ever . . . a masterpiece of
comedy.'   *The Times*

Hard Feelings: 'Doug Lucie is suggesting in this pugnacious and
funny play that there is a whole generation around that puts style
before content, fashion before feeling, and show before basic
human sympathy . . . a genuine dramatist alert to the poignancy
of human waste.'   *Guardian*

Doing the Business: 'An impassioned, wholehearted and very
funny dialogue about the corrosive effects of artistic
sponsorship.'   *Guardian*

Doug Lucie was born in Chessington in 1953. He was Resident
Playwright with the Oxford Playhouse Company from 1979–80
and worked as a Visiting Playwright to the University of Iowa,
USA, in 1981. His plays include **John Clare's Mad Nuncle**
(Edinburgh, 1975), **Rough Trade** (Oxford Playhouse, 1977), **We
Love You** (Roundhouse, 1978), **Oh Well** (Oxford Playhouse,
1978), **The New Garbo** (Hull Truck and King's Head, London
1978), **Heroes** (Edinburgh and New End Theatre, London,
1979), **Fear of the Dark** (read by the RSC at the Royal Court
Theatre Upstairs, 1980), **Poison** (Edinburgh Festival, 1980),
Strangers in the Night (New End, 1981), **Hard Feelings**
(Oxford Playhouse tour, 1982; Bush Theatre, London, 1983; BBC
TV 1984), **Progress** (Bush, 1984), **Key to the World** (Paines
Plough, Leicester Haymarket and Lyric Theatre Studio,
Hammersmith, 1984), **A Class of his Own** (BBC TV, 1984),
Force and Hypocrisy (Young Vic Studio, 1986), **Fashion** (RSC,
Stratford, 1987) and **Doing the Business** (Royal Court, London,
1990).

Methuen Modern Plays

Doug Lucie

Fashion
Progress
Hard Feelings
Doing the Business

Methuen Drama

Methuen Modern Plays

This collection first published in Great Britain in 1991 by
Methuen Drama, Michelin House, 81 Fulham Road, London
SW3 6RB and distributed in the United States of America by
HEB Inc, 361 Hanover Street, Portsmouth, New Hampshire
03801.

Fashion first published as a Methuen New Theatrescript in 1987
copyright © 1987, revised 1991 Doug Lucie
Progress first published as a Methuen New Theatrescript in 1985
copyright © 1985 Doug Lucie
Hard Feelings first published as a Methuen New Theatrescript
in1985 copyright © 1985 Doug Lucie
Doing the Business copyright © 1991 Doug Lucie
This collection copyright © 1991 Doug Lucie
The author has asserted his moral rights.

The front cover photograph by Alastair Muir shows Paul
Freeman as Cash in the 1991 Tricycle Theatre, London
production of *Fashion*.
The back cover photo of the author is by Alastair Muir.

ISBN 0-413-65090-1

A CIP catalogue record for this book is available from the British
Library.

Caution

Printed and bound in Great Britain
by Cox & Wyman Ltd, Cardiff Road, Reading

Contents

Fashion

Fashion was first presented by the Royal Shakespeare Company at The Other Place, Stratford-upon-Avon, on 7 April 1987, with the following cast:

Paul Cash	Brian Cox
Liz Scoular	Stella Gonet
Robin Gingham	Akim Mogaji
Stuart Clarke	Alun Armstrong
Eric Bright	Clive Russell
Howard Lipton	David Howey
Amanda Clarke	Estelle Kohler
Dooley	David O'Hara
Gillian Huntley	Linda Spurrier

Directed by Nick Hamm
Set design by Fotini Dimou
Lighting by Ian Loffhagen
Sound by Mo Weinstock
Fights by Malcolm Ransom

The revised version of **Fashion** reproduced in this volume, was first presented at the Leicester Haymarket in 1989 and the Tricycle Theatre, Kilburn, London in 1990, with the following cast:

Paul Cash	Paul Freeman
Liz Scoular	Karen Lewis
Robin Gingham	Paul Battacharjee
Stuart Clarke	Jim Carter
Eric Bright	Robin Soans
Howard Lipton	Robert East
Amanda Clarke	Gillian Eaton
Dooley	Paul Higgins
Gilliant Huntley	Lorna Heilbron
The Voice of Berkowitz	Linal Haft

Directed by Michael Attenborough
Decor Michael Pavalka
Lighting Bill Bray
Fights Malcolm Ransom

Act One

Scene One

6.40 a.m. A plush office on the top floor of a building in a quiet back street in central London. The set is split level. The lower, office level is hi-tech: desk, sofa, chairs, hi-fi, large video screen. The upper level is a modern kitchen and dining area, with a pine table and chairs. To one side of the set is a glass door leading to the lobby where the reception desk is.

On the sofa, we can just make out a blurred shape. It is **Paul Cash**, *asleep, under a duvet.*

A telephone rings once and the answering machine clicks on. All phone calls are amplified round the office on a speaker. When **Cash** *uses the phone, he has one he can use without needing to use the receiver, so he can hold a conversation almost anywhere in the room.*

The voice on the answering machine tape is that of **Liz Scoular**, **Cash**'s *secretary.*

Liz Hello, Cash Creative Consultancy. There's nobody in the office at the moment, but if you'd like to leave your name and number, we'll get back to you as soon as possible. Thank you for calling.

The tone sounds.

Berkowitz Hi, Cash. Berkowitz. New York. Listen, I just finished with McLeish and Harper, and thank God, the landscape's starting to flatten out at last. They bit on Windfall and the TCC promo, but I have to tell you, Gingham's five-part went down like cold cockroach chilli. You see who we're getting in the sack with here. The Guggenheim Foundation it ain't. Anyhow, two for three's an OK strike rate. And hey, listen, Buckley's still chewing me out over the visit. See what you can do, huh? Dinner at Downing Street is top option, but I know how these things are. It'd sure grease the wheels, anyhow. Oh, yeah, you can reach me at the Boston office after tomorrow a.m. OK? Ciao.

The phone line goes off. **Cash** *slowly gets out of the duvet, naked. He sits for a moment, scratching, stretches, stands up and walks across to the answering machine and presses the button to rewind the tape. On the desk are last night's Chinese takeaway containers. He picks up a spoon and eats some cold Chinese food, then goes to the drinks cabinet and pours a mineral water. The* *tape has rewound. He switches it on. As it plays, he takes two hand weights from under the sofa and does lifting exercises and t'ai chi style movement and breathing. The first call is from* **Howard**.

Howard Hello, Paul. Howard. Ten thirty p.m. Tuesday. Sorry not to get back to you earlier. Got stuck in a bloody briefing at Number Ten. Twerp from the *New Statesman*'s got hold of some defence leak. End of civilisation as we etcetera. Honestly, what a bunch of tossers. Of course they'll all be rounded up if there's a nuclear alert, what on earth do they bloody well expect? Still, page and a half in the *New Statesman*, thirty seconds on Channel Four News, total audience figures: two lesbians, a dog and Tony Benn. Anyway, the matter in hand. I have a cautious green light. So see what you and our dusky chum can magic up for me. OK? And listen, it's not entirely a matter of public record just yet, so complete discretion would be appreciated. Right. I'll be popping in lunchtime as arranged so you can meet the Lincoln candidate before we take her through the TV training drill. All right? Over and out.

The tape beeps and goes on to the next call which is from **Eric Bright**.

Eric Paul, it's Eric Bright, returning your call returning my call. Yes, lunchtime tomorrow would be fine. 'Bye.

The tape beeps and goes on to the next call, which is from **Stuart Clarke**. *He is drunk.*

Stuart Cash, you bastard? It's Stuart. Old Clarkie. Listen, you creep, why can't you return my calls? Eh? I've left you three bloody messages in a week. So come on. You know I'm the best director you're going to get. Give me a job. Any job. I'm not proud. Hovis, Andrex, the wonder of sodding Woolworths. I don't care. Just employ me, right? We go back a long way, Cash, so shuffle some of that green folding stuff my way, or I'll come round there and break your teeth. (*Beat. He belches.*) Oh, and Amanda sends her love.

The tape beeps and goes on to the next call, which is from a young Scottish man.

Dooley I know you. (**Cash** *stiffens slightly.*) Yeah. I know you all right. Nancy boy. Nonce. (*Beat.*) Thought it was a secret, didn't you? Well, it's not. 'Cos I know. (*Beat.*) I'll bet you're trying to put a face to my voice now, aren't you? A pretty wee face. (*Beat.*) Well, fret not. You'll get your chance. In the flesh. (*Beat.*) Is it nice up

there in your castle? Eh? Thick carpets? Leather chairs? Money
pasted all over the walls? The smell of lovely money? (*Beat.*) I'm
coming. I'm going to invade your space. Soon. 'Bye 'bye. Darling.
(*He blows a kiss and puts the phone down.*)

The **Berkowitz** *call begins to play back.* **Cash** *saunters over and switches
off the answering machine, opens a desk diary, finds a phone number and
dials. It rings for a long time. Finally it's answered. It is* **Amanda
Clarke**.

Amanda (*half asleep*) Hello?

Cash Amanda, hello, darling.

Amanda What? Paul, is that you?

Cash Yes. (*Beat.*)

Amanda Are you all right?

Cash Fine. (*Beat.*)

Amanda What time is it?

Cash Six-forty.

Amanda Uh huh. (*Beat.*) Well?

Cash Oh, what are you doing for dinner tonight?

Amanda Are you kidding?

Cash No.

Amanda Actually, I'm busy. Maxwell's in town, so my arse has
to be well in gear.

Cash Never mind. Let me talk to your husband, will you?

Amanda Stuart?

Cash That's the one. Unless there's something you haven't told
me.

Amanda I don't know where he is. Last time I saw him, he was
popping out for a drink . . . three days ago . . . oh, hang on, his
coat's here. I'll see if I can find him.

Pause, during which **Cash** *takes out an electric razor and starts to shave.*
Amanda *comes back.*

Hello, Paul?

He switches off the razor.

He's on the sofa with a bottle of Jack Daniels. I've woken him up. What d'you want him for?

Cash I'm just returning his call.

Amanda You bastard. (*Beat.*) I'm going to take a shower, now I'm awake.

Cash Wish I could be there.

Amanda Yeah (*Beat.*) Look, I may give you a ring at lunch, OK?

Cash OK.

Pause, during which **Cash** *starts shaving again.* **Stuart** *comes to the phone.*

Stuart Cash?

Cash *stops shaving.*

Cash Hang on a minute, will you, Stuart? (*He finishes shaving.*) Right. (*Beat.*) How are you?

Stuart For fuck's sake, man, you don't ring me at this time of day to ask how I am.

Cash Never did have much time for the formal niceties, did you?

Stuart Bollocks.

Cash Still the angry young man.

Stuart No, I've matured. I'm now a slightly peeved, middle-aged man. With a terrible fucking hangover. So what is it?

Cash You've been ringing me, Clarke. I don't need this. (*He hangs up, goes over to the duvet and folds it up. The phone rings. He flips the switch on the desk.*) Cash.

Amanda Paul, what are you playing at? You ring at the crack of dawn and hang up . . .

Cash Listen, darling, some of us get up early. That's why some of us are very successful. On the other hand, some of us spend our lives in an alcoholic stupor. Which is why some of us are no-hope ex-movie directors.

Amanda Paul . . .

Cash But, seeing as Stuart's an old friend, and seeing as he's been leaving begging messages on my answering machine, and seeing as I'm screwing his wife behind his back, I thought I might help

him out. Put a bit of work his way. Just like you wanted.
Remember? (*Beat*.) However, when I call him to tell him the good
news about his career prospects, all I get is the usual fucking
mouthful. And so I hang up. (*Beat*.) And I can smell his breath
from here. I thought you said he'd got it under control.

Amanda He had when I last looked.

Cash When was that?

Amanda I don't remember.

Cash Well, you should look more often.

Amanda What? No fear. (*Beat*.) Actually, he had a little bit of
money through, so he went on a bender. (*Beat*.)

Cash Just put him back on, will you?

Amanda OK.

*She goes away from the phone and we hear her call 'Stuart' etc. Suddenly the
lights in the office come on.* **Cash** *doesn't react. We see* **Liz** *going into the
lobby towards the reception desk in her coat. She disappears. She comes back
across by the door, coat in hand, to hang it up.* **Cash** *drops the food container
in the waste bin.* **Stuart** *comes to the phone.*

Stuart Hello.

Cash Let's start again, shall we?

Stuart Yeah. (*Beat*.)

Cash Tell me, Stuart, do you still subjugate your art to your
politics?

Stuart Christ's sake, Cash . . .

Cash What I mean is, do you still refuse to produce work which
you consider to be detrimental to the interests of the proletariat?

Stuart I don't get the chance. I don't produce. Remember?

Cash Well really, Clarkie, a film with an Arab hero is a touch near
the knuckle. A Palestinian Arab hero . . . that's a fucking suicide
note. (*Beat*.) Anyway, I need to know whether you're politically a
little bit more flexible these days.

Stuart Isn't everybody? (*Beat*.) Try me.

Liz *enters with a small bowl, flannel and towel. She puts it on the desk by*
Cash. *They don't acknowledge each other.* **Liz** *goes.* **Cash** *washes and
dries his face through the following conversation.*

Cash What I want to know, Stuart, is if I employ you on a specific campaign, would you allow your personal – sorry, ideological – feelings to interfere with your work?

Stuart Depends.

Cash No. Let's have no grey areas. I want it cut and dried, black and white. Are you a professional director, or a professional liberal?

Stuart I've never been a liberal. You know that.

Cash How very true.

Liz *comes back in with* **Cash***'s clothes for the day. Suit, shirt, tie, socks, underwear. She lays them out on the sofa and goes, taking the duvet.*

Stuart One thing I do know. You've got to be a realist to survive. So, if you want it straight, yeah, I'll do the work, whatever.

Cash Glad to see you've adjusted to the spirit of the time.

Stuart No one said it's going to last for ever. It's not as if we're talking about the thousand-year Reich. I hope.

Liz *comes in and goes up to the kitchen and prepares coffee and orange juice.* **Cash** *opens his diary.*

Cash OK, I want you here this morning. Say ten.

Stuart Oh God . . .

Cash Realism, Stuart . . .

Stuart Yeah. I'll be there. Listen, I think Amanda wants to speak to you. Dinner invite or something.

Cash OK. See you at ten.

Stuart Yeah.

Pause while **Amanda** *comes to the phone.*

Amanda Paul?

Cash Hi.

Amanda Look, I thought, seeing as you'd called, we could arrange . . . (*Beat.*) It's OK, he's gone.

Liz *looks round.*

Amanda (*speaks softly*) So?

Cash He's coming in.

Amanda Thanks. (*Beat.*) I'm sure you can use him. We both know how good he is.

Cash Was, darling.

Amanda You don't lose something that special. (*Beat.*) If you want to meet up tonight, we could always go for a nightcap at the Bluebird.

Cash Sounds good.

Amanda Maybe you deserve a treat. (*Beat.*) Speak to you later.

Cash Bye.

Amanda Bye.

He flips the switch and goes over to his clothes and starts to dress.

Liz Good morning, Mr Cash.

Cash Good morning, Liz.

Liz D'you want toast?

Cash No thanks.

Liz Cereal?

Cash No.

Liz You'll get an ulcer. Or worse. Bowel cancer. That's terrible. And it's really common.

Cash So I hear.

Liz I'll just get you a small bowl, then, shall I?

Cash Why not?

Liz (*doing the cereal*) Don't want you wasting away, do we?

Cash Not much chance of that.

Liz It happens really quickly. Like my dad. He got so skinny you could see the bones. Like one of them concentration camp people. (*She puts the cereal on the desk.*) There. And eat it all up.

Cash Keep me clear till lunch, Liz, Eric Bright should be in mid-morning, and I've got someone coming in at ten.

Liz Right.

Cash And have Robin clear his desk for the day. I'm going to need him.

Liz What about calls?

Cash No domestic. Only New York or Jo'burg. Message if you can. And if Amanda calls this morning while there's anybody with me, definitely take a message.

Liz Uh huh. (*She opens the window blinds. Light floods in.*) It's a beautiful day.

Cash *is dressed. He buttons his jacket and sits at his desk.*

Cash What?

Liz It's a beautiful day. (*Beat.*)

Cash Every day's a beautiful day, Liz. Every day.

She turns and half smiles.

Blackout.

Scene Two

The office, about 9.45 the same morning. It is deserted. Pause. **Robin Gingham** *enters, just arrived for work. He's eating an apple. He goes to the kitchen area and pours a coffee, then comes down to* **Cash**'s *desk and browses through some papers on it.* **Liz** *enters.*

Liz Good morning, Mr Gingham.

He starts slightly.

Robin Oh, hi Liz.

Liz *tidies the papers up.*

State secrets?

Liz *smiles professionally.*

Where's sir?

Liz Popped out.

Robin What? Out of his office? Out of . . . the building? Christ. Have we had the four minute warning, or is his bank on fire?

Liz He's gone to buy a shirt.

Robin The plot thickens.

Liz He spilled coffee down the one he had on.

Robin Ah. (*Beat.*) Liz, do you ever have, like, really silly thoughts?

Liz No.

Robin I thought not.

Liz I'm a secretary.

Beat while he ponders this for a moment. She starts to go. He calls her back.

Robin Liz.

Liz Yes?

Robin Cardinal Richelieu died in 1642. (*Beat.*) Thought you might like to know.

Liz Thank you. Mr Cash wants you to keep yourself free today.

Robin For what?

Liz Work?

Robin Hey, careful, I had a heavy night.

Liz There are people coming in this morning. The Tory Party account, I think.

Robin Ah. Indeed. Work. (*Beat.*) Have we got the account then?

Liz I don't know.

Robin So who's coming in?

Liz I don't know.

Robin What's the only mammal that can't jump? (*Beat.*)

Liz The elephant.

She turns and goes as **Cash** *comes in with his new shirt.*

Cash Rob.

Robin Hi.

Cash (*changing his shirt*) Stan Berkowitz called.

Robin The Beast of the Bronx. What'd he have to say?

Cash They loved Windfall and TCC.

Robin Hacks.

Cash And they found your grand opus . . .

Robin Yuh?

Cash A crock of shit, darling. (*Beat.*) No reason as yet. (*Beat.*) *I* liked it.

Robin Paul, why do we work for these jerks? I mean, that's the third biggie they've nixed.

Cash We'll get there.

Robin Christ, I spent nearly two weeks getting that bastard looking right. And it looks bloody perfect. That promotion's a work of art, for Christ's sake. (*Beat.*)

Cash Rob, I've told you: advertising is the revenge of business on culture. We inform, we entertain, but most of all, we oil the wheels of commerce.

Robin Paul, people are image-sophisticated. They read the messages loud and clear. The most snotty-nosed tower block kid can recognise Russia in a Levi's ad. References stretching back through Le Carre, 'Ipcress', Tarkovsky, 'The Twilight Zone', Dostoevsky, James Dean. Every advert thirty seconds of cinematic purity. Claude Chabrol with Persil in the starring role. People *know*. They're sussed, Paul.

Cash Not so McLeish and Harper. (*Quickly, he doesn't want to have this conversation.*) Look, we've market tested, we've random sampled, we've pinpointed our target group. Now all we have to do is convince the Yanks we can come up with the package to sell to that group. Easy, really. So fuck art. Let's make money.

Beat. **Robin** *smiles.*

Robin Whatever you say.

Cash I'd never have put your idea in if I hadn't believed in it. Honestly.

Robin Yeah. (*Beat.*) I have this fantasy, right? We're filming for a new shampoo, and on the studio floor we've got . . . I dunno . . . Redgrave and Irons, with Menges and Joffe behind the camera, and in the corner, doing a rewrite, there's Stoppard and Shaffer. Don't tell me that wouldn't make money.

Cash Did the British film industry? (*Beat.*) How's the script coming on, by the way?

Robin (*evasive*) How did yours come on?

Cash Got as far as the title page.

Robin I haven't even got that far.

Cash It'll come.

Robin Yours didn't.

Cash I got sidetracked.

Robin Me too. D'you know what I mean? I go back to that nice piece of real estate I call home, and I sit there and I think, right, Robin old son, let's make like Hollywood. Let's do the Putnam shuffle. And I come up with three brilliant ideas, and I pour a nice long writer's drink and I visualise these great movies. They are so good. So I decide I have to tell somebody, go out, get absolutely plastered and end up playing 'Trivial Pursuits' till the sun comes up. I've got visualisation and I've got realisation. It's just the intervening period of creation that's absent.

Cash And I thought you took your *work* home with you.

Robin Bollocks, boss. Ahem, talking of which, what's this Liz tells me about Smith Square?

Cash I'm not absolutely sure yet. I'm just putting some people together, see what happens, see if we can't get a little piece of the action.

Robin Think we'll get it?

Cash How could they resist? We have genius on our side.

Robin Why, thank you.

Cash I meant me.

They exchange a smile.

Anyway, Eric's coming in later. (*He looks at his watch.*) And I've got a director coming in any minute.

Robin Anybody I know?

Cash Could be. So . . . thinking-cap time. I want to see you sparkle.

Robin OK. I'll just make a couple of calls.

Cash Fine.

Robin *goes as* **Liz** *comes in with some letters to be signed.*

Coffee, Liz. (*She goes to the kitchen.*) And can you get on to Rodney, tell him that if Benson keeps stalling we'll have to take him to court.

As he speaks, **Stuart Clarke** *comes into reception. He stands a moment and looks around*

And send him a copy of the figures. Just in case the last set got lost in the post.

Liz I understand Mr Benson has cash flow problems.

Stuart *is thinking about coming into the office.*

Cash This is not an episode of 'Minder', Liz. Mr Benson's chirpy cockney patois will not excuse the fact that he owes me seventeen grand.

Stuart *stands gingerly in the doorway. He takes a deep breath, knocks on the door and strides in very purposefully.*

Stuart Cash, you old bastard.

Cash Stuart.

They greet each other with a warm but tentative handshake.

Long time, long time.

Then **Stuart** *holds out his arms and they embrace, still tentative.*

Cash How are you?

Stuart Great, y'know . . .

Cash Yeah, you've put on weight.

Stuart Idle living.

Cash Couple of games of squash, I'll soon sort you out.

Stuart Make that five card draw and you're on.

Cash Times *have* changed.

Stuart Yeah. They have. (*Beat.*)

Cash Uh, that's Liz. My secretary and saviour.

Stuart Hello, Liz.

Liz Hello.

Cash Is that coffee ready?

Liz Nearly.

Cash (*going to the kitchen*) Strong, black. I'm guessing here . . .

Stuart Spot on.

Cash How's Amanda?

Liz *looks at him.*

Stuart You tell me.

Cash *stiffens.*

I've hardly spoken to her for a month.

Cash Diverging lifestyles . . .

Stuart No, she hates my guts. (*Beat.*) Hey, I have to thank you.

Cash For what?

Stuart For opening my eyes to a new cultural experience.

Liz *has poured the coffee, which* **Cash** *brings down to* **Stuart**. **Liz** *goes.*

Cash I have?

Stuart Yeah. Y'know, before this morning, when you summoned me here for this dawn rendezvous, I had never seen, that is to say, I had gone out of my way to avoid seeing, breakfast television. And now . . . well, what can I say? It's terrifying. Like being locked in a Barratt home with three hairdressers from Cockfosters.

Cash Actually, they're terribly chummy. (*Beat.*) I've been on.

Stuart What, on Breakfast TV?

Cash Yes.

Stuart Fuck me. (*Beat.*) The only bugger I recognised was Clare Rayner, God bless her and all who sail in her, but who in their right mind wants to discuss breast cancer and Inter-Uterine Devices at eight o'clock in the morning? Who in their right mind even wants to be up at that time of day?

Cash The masses?

Stuart Oh them. (*Beat.*)

Cash Here, sit down.

They sit.

Got a lot to catch up on.

Stuart Yeah. (*Beat.*) Sorry about the phone calls.

Cash Not at all. Breath of fresh air.

Stuart No, I was soused.

Cash The way I remember it, you always were.

Stuart No. That was energy. But . . . you get older, the energy flags, the drink talks. (*Beat.*) Cash, I'm up for it. I need to work.

Cash Money problems?

Stuart (*lying*) Not really. I still get a few bob from the old stuff. And Amanda's very good, y'know . . .

Cash Done any work?

Stuart (*laughs*) Home video.

Cash Ah. Let's not talk about that, then.

Stuart Not the hard stuff. Just . . . I dunno, women with no clothes on. Cadbury's Flake without the Flake, if you know what I mean.

Cash Yeah. (*Beat.*) Look, I can't promise on this particular project, it's all up in the air at the moment, but if it doesn't work out, there's other stuff I could consider you for.

Stuart Thanks.

Cash And if it does work out, I'm doing myself a favour. You've been out in the cold for too long now.

Stuart I'm not into a comeback. I just want to work.

Cash I know. (*Beat.*) God, this is funny isn't it? Fifteen, twenty years ago, you were up there. You commanded the heights. People like me . . . well . . .

Stuart You were into money.

Cash I know. The lowest of the low. Completely ruined my sex life. Politics and art were sexy. Money and work were a cold shower. While you were making those movies . . . great movies, I might say . . . and enjoying the fruits thereof, I was on my own, tossing off and dreaming of this.

Stuart And tell me, Mr Cash, when did you *stop* beating your meat? (*Beat.*) Sorry. I'm here for a job. I better shut up.

Cash No. What I mean is . . . things are *very* different now. *This* is sexy.

Stuart You're making me feel old.

Cash No, not old. Old-fashioned.

Stuart Fashions change. Today the miniskirt, tomorrow trouser suits.

Cash Don't underestimate it. The one constant is that it's always there. You were fashionable once. Be grateful. (*Beat.*) Lecture over.

Stuart No, feel free. I seem to remember haranguing you at every available opportunity in the old days.

Cash That's true. You threw me out of the house once.

Stuart God, did I?

Cash Uh huh. Called me a despicable Tory anarchist and shoved me down the steps.

Stuart I remember.

Cash And I shouted: 'Hey, less of the anarchist if you don't mind'.

Stuart I don't remember that.

Cash (*icy*) No. You'd slammed the door by that time. (*Beat.*) I could hear you all laughing inside. Amanda, Maggie, John, Freddy, I think was there . . .

Stuart The three-day week. It was then.

Cash Yeah. Candles.

Stuart One thing about Ted Heath: he knew how to lend atmosphere to a dinner party.

Cash It's more than I did.

Stuart Not true. You provided us with some very entertaining moments.

Cash I *am* glad. (*Beat.*) Anyway, that's all in the past.

Stuart So what's in the present?

Cash Right. I've got a very specific proposition to put to you. It's not definite yet, but if we get it, it's big. If we don't get it, you'll still receive a development fee. Sound OK?

Stuart Why me?

Cash I went down the BFI last week. Had a look at some of your old stuff. Some of that work is incredible. Just the camera work. Brilliant. Incredibly powerful.

Stuart Thank you.

Cash It's true. (*Beat.*) And that's what I need. Something unashamedly manipulative. Emotive.

Stuart In what sort of area? (*Beat.*)

Cash Propaganda. Stuart, I want to make the sort of film that, were he alive today, Goebbels would be making. (*Beat.*)

Stuart I see. And who exactly would be exploiting my talents for this little trip down memory lane? (*Beat.*)

Cash The Conservative Party.

Stuart What?

Cash I've been asked to create a dummy campaign. If they like it, we could be looking at the chance to produce the next series of Tory party political broadcasts.

Beat. **Robin** *comes in.*

Ah, Robin, great. Robin, this is Stuart Clarke. Robin's my chief partner in crime, Stuart. Well, not quite partner yet.

Robin *holds his hand out.* **Stuart** *has stood up. He stares at* **Cash**.

Stuart You absolute fucking toerag. (*Beat.*) You arsehole.

Robin *has withdrawn his hand.*

Yeah. Good game, Cash. I'll be seeing you.

Cash Stuart . . .

Stuart *turns round.*

Stuart Don't mate. Let me go, then you can have your little laugh.

Cash I won't be laughing if you go.

Stuart No?

Cash No. If I wanted to humiliate you, I could do it in a million ways. Sorry, but it's true. I never joke about work.

Stuart *considers his next move.*

Cash Have another coffee.

Cash *nods at Robin, who takes* **Stuart***'s cup to the kitchen and fills it.*

Black.

Robin Hmmm?

Cash The coffee.

Robin *brings* **Stuart** *his coffee.* **Stuart** *takes out a quarter bottle of Scotch and pours some into his cup. He drinks, daring* **Cash** *to say something. He sits again.*

Stuart Right. So what makes you think a socialist director who hasn't made a film in six years is the right person to produce films for the Tory Party?

Cash Simple. I want the best.

Stuart How the fuck d'you expect me to work for the people my whole professional life's been spent trying to expose?

Cash This is work. Not art. Skill. Not passion. (*Beat.*) Look, Stuart, I have a reputation for making things happen. Things people thought were impossible. Come on. Let's do the impossible. (*Beat.*) I happen to find the idea of you making Tory Party broadcasts mind-bogglingly brilliant. (*Beat.*)

Stuart I suppose if I turn this down, I don't get another chance.

Cash That's right, yes. (*Beat.*) It's an interesting team. You won't be the only renegade socialist.

Stuart Oh? Dug up Ramsay MacDonald, have you?

Cash Close.

Stuart Who?

Cash Ex-Labour MP. Now a TV pundit and newspaper columnist . . . (*Beat.*)

Stuart Eric Bright.

Cash On the button.

Stuart Eric sodding Bright. I can't work with that schmuck.

Cash Why not?

Stuart Christ, if we all moved to the right as fast as he did, we'd knock the earth off its axis.

Robin *sighs heavily.*

Stuart Sorry?

Robin Politics is boring.

Stuart Oh, it talks then.

Cash Rather well.

Stuart Does it ever think? Or is *that* too boring?

Robin I don't know what it is, but whenever I encounter a sixties has-been flaunting his political soul, I come over all lethargic.

Stuart This boy of yours any good?

Cash Very.

Stuart He'll have to be if he wants to get away with talking to me like that.

Robin *smirks.* **Stuart** *turns to* **Cash**.

Stuart D'you remember that time . . . God, where was it . . . the Chinese place. That Tory prat. Remember?

Cash Yeah.

Stuart Gave us a lecture on the evils of socialism. Said I should be shot. (*He smiles.*) Looked a bit funny, didn't he, when I broke his nose. (*Beat.*)

Robin Wow. Right on. You break a guy's nose because he has different politics to you. Highly egalitarian.

Stuart No, I broke his nose because he knocked my drink over and refused to buy me another one. See, there's only one thing I hate more than a Tory, and that's a graceless Tory. (*Beat.*)

Cash I want you in on this one Stuart. And I have to tell you, it feels good. (*Beat.*) D'you want a bit of time? Think it over?

Stuart *looks at him glumly and shakes his head.*

Stuart No. No thanks.

Beat. Then he holds out his hand to **Robin**, *smiling.*

Hello, Robin. I understand we're going to be working together.

They shake.

Blackout.

Scene Three

Lunchtime the same day. **Stuart** *is sitting on the sofa, a near-empty bottle of wine on the table, and a half-eaten salad on his lap.* **Liz** *is washing up in the kitchen. She seems half-nervous and half-pitying of him.*

Liz Is there anything I can get for you, Mr Clarke?

Stuart (*drains his glass*) Some more of this stuff, if you've got it.

She goes to the fridge and gets another bottle and starts to uncork it.

I hope it's bloody expensive.

Liz D'you like it?

Stuart Only if it costs. That's the point, isn't it?

Liz Is it?

Stuart That's what I thought. (*Beat.*) Unless I'm out of touch.

She brings the bottle down to him.

Liz Actually, it's £1.99 a bottle. Mr Cash gets a discount.

Stuart I'll bet he does. Tell you what, I'll have a brandy.

Liz Och . . .

Stuart A large one.

Beat. **Liz** *seems to want to say something.*

I've heard it all before, Liz, so don't waste your breath.

Liz I wouldn't bother. I've *seen* it all before.

She goes back to the kitchen and pours a brandy.

Stuart Thanks for the lunch, anyway.

Liz 's OK.

Stuart It was very healthy.

She brings the brandy.

Liz Who is it you're punishing?

Stuart Oh no, please . . .

Liz It's somebody. I know in the long run it's you, but that's not where it started is it?

Stuart Look, I'll only say this once. Mind your own fucking business.

Liz Then get your own fucking brandy.

She takes it back.

Stuart (*laughing, trying to shrug it off*) OK, I'm sorry. Peace?

She puts the glass down in the kitchen and stands defiant.

It's not somebody. It's something.

He goes and gets the glass.

Liz Aye. That's what they always say. (*Beat.*) Why are drunks so predictable? Eh? I mean, you can take a hundred people, all completely different, and then you get them drunk, and they all turn into the same person. (*Beat.*) There was a documentary on the other night. Australian aborigines. They looked incredible, y'know? But they've given them drink, and Coca-Cola T-shirts and cut-off jeans, and now they look like every wino you ever saw in your life before. It was heartbreaking. (*Beat.*)

Stuart Isn't Cash responsible for some lager accounts?

Liz Aye. And vodka, and French liqueurs. (*Beat.*) But Mr Cash usually drinks mineral water.

Stuart Mais naturellement. (*He smiles.*)

Liz You know what happens to alcoholic men? Their breasts swell and their testicles shrink. (*Beat.*)

Stuart What about women?

Liz They've already had the experience.

He pours another drink.

Stuart Don't you have any vices then, Liz?

Liz Oh aye. Men.

Stuart Sorry, can't help you there. I'm a one-woman man.

She gives him a sorry look.

Liz I like Arab men, anyway.

Stuart Ah.

Liz My weakness. (*Beat.*)

Stuart You and . . . what's his name . . . ?

Liz Who? Robin? No way. He's more English than strawberries at Wimbledon. He's just a boy, in any case. I value finesse.

He raises his glass.

Stuart To quality.

Eric Bright *suddenly comes in, cheerful and lively.*

Eric Hullo, Liz. Little bit on the late side, I'm afraid. Couldn't be helped.

Liz Mr Cash is in Mr Gingham's office looking at some artwork. He won't be long.

Eric Smashing.

Liz I'll tell him you're here.

Eric That's smashing.

She goes out. **Stuart** *studies the label on the brandy bottle as* **Eric** *goes to the kitchen and opens the fridge. He opens a bottle of Guinness and pours, lovingly.*

Nectar of the gods. Dublin-brewed. Nothing like it. A glassful of history. Cheerio.

Eric *drinks and smacks his lips.* **Stuart** *studies his glass.*

Stuart French. Over-priced. Somebody else's. A goblet of bile. (*He knocks it back.*)

Eric (*busying himself with his case*) Waiting for Paul, are you?

Stuart Liz does the waiting. I'm a guest. (*Beat.*)

Eric *smiles.*

Eric Yes. But seriously.

Stuart Hmmm?

Eric Are we part of the same affair?

Stuart I sincerely hope not. We haven't been properly introduced.

Eric I sort of assumed you'd know who I was.

Stuart Yes, but I'm a stickler for protocol. (*Beat.*)

Eric Eric Bright.

Stuart We've met.

Eric Really? When?

Stuart Nineteen seventy . . . six. The terrace at the House of Commons. Photocall.

Eric Ah. Photographer, are you?

Stuart No. (*Beat.*) Arts for Labour. I was an artist. For Labour. You were an MP. For Labour.

Eric Don't remind me. (*Beat.*) I'm sorry . . . you're . . . ?

Stuart Stuart Clarke. (*Beat.*) Films. 'Red Sky over Clydeside'? 'The Poacher'?

Eric Of course, yes. I remember. Haven't done a lot this, er, decade, have you?

Stuart I was before my time. Tragic.

Eric Yes, yes. Arts for Labour. I was there, was I?

Stuart In body, at least.

Eric That's right. One of the problems with Labour, isn't it? We could always get Arts for the Party. Demonstrators for the Party, pop groups for the Party. It was *votes* for the Party where we came unstuck. (*Beat.*) Yes, I remember it now. Jim Callaghan was petrified somebody was going to smoke pot like the Beatles at Buck House. In fact, they were a very . . . respectable lot. Crusty even. Yourself excepted, of course. The electorate must have thought they were being asked to return the cast of 'Coronation Street' to Number Ten.

Stuart Instead, they opted for 'Miami Vice'.

Eric And who's to say they were wrong?

Stuart Not you, I'll bet.

Eric This is a democracy. The people made their choice. I merely observe.

Stuart Too modest. You're an example to us all.

Eric I like to think my mind was broad enough to change.

Stuart Don't we all. But, here I am, stuck in this straitjacket of ideals and ideology, of history and experience. I just can't seem to shake it off. If only I could be like you.

Eric Your cloth cap's showing, dear.

Stuart So's your fake suntan, but I'm too polite to mention that.

Pause.

Eric So what brings you to Paul Cash's office? Apart from the brandy?

Stuart Why, my undoubted talents as a film-maker, of course.

Eric Oh? Got the TUC account, has he?

Stuart You wouldn't be here if he had.

Eric That's true. I don't work for losers.

Stuart *pours another drink.*

I feel like I'm being judged here.

Stuart (*smirking*) Doesn't history judge us all?

Eric Oh God. One of the reasons I got out of the Labour Party was to escape from all that bloody council house, second-rate Leninist rhetoric. Or Dennis Skinner, as it's more commonly known.

Stuart *laughs.*

Ah. You were being ironic.

Stuart It's a possibility.

Cash and **Robin** *come in, mid-discussion.*

Robin . . . references, Paul. It's called visual wit. Remember?

Cash It's too prissy. Too bloody fey. Minimum impact. I want the truth about the product. Hello, Eric. (*He pats him on the shoulder.*) We're not pouring cream on, we're getting the cream out.

Robin But what's wrong with moving on to a larger canvas?

Cash Nothing, so long as it's not designed by another art school reject friend of yours.

Robin Get 1989 for Christ's sake, boss.

Cash Rob . . . try again. Dump the artwork. Keep the text if you must. But give me a wonderful experience. Please. And do it now. Sit this one out.

Robin *stares at him.*

We'll bring you in when we've got some basics worked out. OK?

Robin *stands a second then goes out.* **Cash** *presses the intercom buzzer.*

Liz, no calls. (*He pours coffee.*) Jesus, I want something bold and vivid to pass on to the agency, and he's giving me the history of art. OK. You two met?

Eric We're old friends.

Cash Yeah? Good. Sit down, Stuart. Come on, let's get formal. Right, Eric, did you tell Stuart where we are on this?

Eric I didn't really get a chance.

Stuart We were having such fun reliving old times.

Cash OK. Well, Eric and I have been working together since the last election, grooming Tory candidates. We show them the ropes as far as media techniques go, interviews and so on. Now, having got my foot in the door, I've been asked to put together some provisional ideas for party political broadcasts. To do that I need a team.

Stuart And we're it . . .

Cash For now yes. Quite simply Stuart I'm not alone in thinking Tory publicity has been handled very badly. I believe I can do better. I know I can do better. (*Beat.*)

Stuart So. We're all in love with the Tory Party.

Cash Yeah, that's right. For the purposes of this campaign, we are.

Stuart This is all a bit sudden.

Cash Last month I was heavily involved with British Airways. Next month I fully intend to be having a torrid affair with the South African Tourist Board.

Stuart You really put it about.

Cash That's the nature of the beast.

Stuart Mind you don't catch something.

Cash I've had the jabs. I'm germ free. (*Beat.*) Are you familiar with Eric's column Stuart?

Stuart Is that the one in Trafalgar Square . . . ?

Eric *chuckles*.

Cash Don't fuck about, man.

Stuart Well, if you ask me questions like that, it could very quickly be the end of a beautiful relationship.

Cash Come on. Have you read it?

Stuart Yes.

Cash And? (*Beat.*)

Stuart Forgive me, but, it's smug, self-satisfied, lowest common denominator crap.

Eric *chuckles.*

The guy's in love with the starch of Margaret Thatcher's skirts. (*Beat.*) He despises the working-class, because that's where he comes from. He's dangerously nostalgic, a cynic masquerading as a realist. In short, his bank roll's so far down his throat, it's coming out his arse. Oh, and he probably wants to travel and help children. (*Beat.*) Can I go now?

Eric *laughs.*

Eric You see! That's what they say. Grown men and women turn into little playground bullies. It's pathetic. We can nail this in the film, Paul. They don't want a Labour government, they want to take their bat and ball home so people like us won't be allowed to play any more. (*Beat. He's enjoying himself.*) Stuart, have you ever been to a Party conference?

Stuart Once.

Eric Let me tell you . . . the bit I hate most. It's those beady-eyed little fanatics with the badges and the look of the converted. Staring at each other in corners, repeating their mantra: 'Jobs and services, welfare state, jobs and services.' I used to stand there thinking: my dad was a metalworker, you pasty-faced little white-collar shits. He held my hand on the terraces at Old Trafford. He was a shop steward, a full-time union official when there was still something to fight for. And if one of you disordered little twerps had ever dared call him comrade, he'd have wrung your bloody neck.

Stuart So much for the brotherhood of man.

Eric Sexist.

Stuart The only time I went, I can't say as I was as revolted by the rank and file as you obviously were. No, it was the PLP who got up my nose. The sleek patricians of Westminster, with their directorships, their consultancies, their newspaper columns. You lot went into a room, and by the time you came out, something was decided. Because that's how it worked. The poor silly ordinary bastards worked like slaves to get you elected, and from then on you made the decisions. As if it was God's law. Well, I had a good chuckle watching those jaws drop when they realised they were going to have to stand for re-selection. Like someone had just told them the earth was flat.

Eric Re-selection, yes. The revenge of the pygmies. (*Pause.*)

Cash Well. Old wounds don't heal, do they?

Eric Not the oldest wound of all, the Labour Party. It still gushes blood, the poor old thing.

Cash The point is, Stuart, that your attitudes are no longer those of the ordinary Labour voter. You represent, shall I say, a hard rump.

Eric No, don't mention Eric Heffer.

Stuart Christ.

Cash Britain has changed, shifting class barriers, new technology, the environment . . .

Stuart Spare me the Murdoch memorial lecture.

Cash I know you don't want to hear it, but it's where we have to start from. Now somewhere out there is a mainstream critique of Tory policy. Which is beginning to give your ordinary Tory voter the jitters. I want us to identify it, agree on it and counter it.

Stuart Isn't that Bright's job?

Eric Don't look at me. I'm in love with the starch of Margaret Thatcher's skirts.

Cash Don't be shy, Stuart. Put the emotion on hold and let's have the intellect in functioning mode for a change. What are the Tories' main weaknesses?

Stuart How long have you got?

Cash As long as it takes?

Eric It *is* important to agree, *if* we're going to get into bed together on this one.

Stuart I'll keep my trousers on if it's all right with you.

Eric Oh dear. We shouldn't really be part of the same country, should we?

Stuart We're not.

Eric 'Twas ever thus. (*Beat.*)

Cash Finished?

Stuart Look, it's quite simple, Thatcher broke the unions to create a docile workforce, to get people back into a mobile labour market, a commodity, stripped of rights and representation. Also to push down real wages so the new industries could be manned at cheaper rates, making them economically viable for the immediate future. She financed unemployment with the money from North Sea oil, and floated a boom which let international capital alter the structure of British industry to such an extent that it would be impossible to reform it back again. How's that for an obituary?

Eric Right. Economic argument. Piece of cake.

Stuart The Welfare State has to be dismantled, sorry, rationalised, because it's an example of collective security, altruism if you like, which uses money, but, horror of horrors, doesn't make anybody a profit. Cannot make anybody a profit. So, smash it up. Private medicine makes a profit. Taxed benefits get something back at least. Stands to reason, push more and more people into private health care by making the NHS so piss-poor that only the dregs will still be able to *bear* to use it.

Eric (*writing*) Tory health cuts myth! (*Beat.*)

Stuart Down in Lambeth there's a derelict site, one of many, where young Londoners, dressed as New York hoodlums, chased Charles Bronson around for a couple of weeks while the cameras rolled. (*Beat.*) Where this recreation of Yankee social blight was being filmed, had once been a hospital. They knocked down a hospital and made 'Death Wish Three' on the ruins.

Eric Anti-Americanism. Good. (*Beat.*)

Stuart Is there anybody out there?

Cash You bet.

Eric That's really smashing, Stuart.

Stuart *goes to the kitchen and pours a brandy.*

We've got the right man here, all right, Paul.

Howard *and* **Gill** *have come into reception.*

Stuart Were you born a prat, Bright, or do you practise?

Cash Hey, this is work, Clarkie.

Eric Politics, not personalities. Right, Mr Clarke?

Liz *shows* **Howard** *and* **Gill** *into the office.*

Cash Howard

Howard Cash.

Eric *stands, rather sycophantically and holds out his hand.*

Howard Bright.

Eric Hullo.

Howard Still on our side, are you?

Eric Oh yes.

Howard *licks his finger and holds it up to test the wind direction.*

Howard Yes. Still blowing our way, I think. Cash, meet Gillian Huntley.

Cash Hello.

They shake hands.

Howard Gill's going to win the Lincoln by-election for us in a couple of weeks, we hope, so we need to teach her some of your television presentation tricks. Sprinkle some of your fairy dust, Cash.

Cash A pleasure.

Howard Friday week OK?

Cash Yes, fine.

Gill I've heard a lot about your expertise, Mr Cash.

Cash Good, I hope.

Gill Felicity Hammond sings your praises.

Cash Ah yes. We were very successful there.

Gill She won the seat.

Cash And so will you.

Howard Another one in the House. What's the world coming to eh?

Eric Well, you have an excellent example to follow, my dear.

Howard You surely don't mean me.

Eric I mean the PM.

Gill I think she's an example to us all. Including the men.

Howard Hmm. You're right of course. But I draw the line at twinset and pearls. (*Half-hearted laughter.*) Who's the wallah burglarising your best Napoleon, Cash?

Cash Stuart, come and meet Howard.

Stuart *ambles down.*

Howard Come on down, Stuart.

Stuart Why not? The price is right. (*He arrives.*)

Cash Howard, meet Stuart Clarke. Film director extraordinaire.

They shake.

Howard Stuart Clarke? Stuart Clarke?

Stuart Well, it was fun while it lasted.

Howard No, no, old man. Great fan of yours. And the good lady wife. Well, her especially.

Stuart Don't tell me you've seen my films.

Howard Of course.

Stuart And you like them?

Howard Like them? We had money in two of them. (*Beat.*) Bloody good stuff. Politics daft as a brush, but what the hell, it's a free country. Made us a few shillings if I remember. In fact, I think I'm right in saying, your film, what was it . . . something with 'Life' in the title . . .

Stuart 'A Backstreet Life'.

Howard That's right. Well, 'A Backstreet Life' bought us our villa in Greece.

Stuart (*not unfriendly*) So that's where the money went.

Howard 'Fraid so, yes. God, the wife will be so pleased. Listen, you must come to dinner. We'd be thrilled.

Stuart OK.

Eric I didn't know you were a patron of the arts, Howard.

Howard No? Well write it down for future reference. Look, can't really stop, Cash. Just wanted to meet the team. Talking of which, where's our dusky chum?

Cash Shall I get him?

Howard God, no. He makes me nervous. (*Beat.*)

Cash Can I get you anything? Coffee?

Howard Yes. Gill, you'll do that for me, won't you? It's up there in the little pot. Thanks.

She goes to pour the coffee.

OK. Those of you who haven't been down a dark hole for the last few years will be aware that the Conservative Party consists, crudely but accurately, of two factions. Known as the Wets and the Dries. Or Gentlemen and Players as I prefer it.

Gill Milk?

Howard What? Yes. You will also be aware –

Gill Sugar?

Howard No thank you. Also be aware that I'm not especially aligned with either party. Which is to say that I once served Heath loyally and prayed to Keynes every night, and I now serve Thatcher loyally. No prayers, you will observe, in conviction politics.

Gill *gives him his coffee.*

Thank you. Now, there has emerged, recently, a grouping which wishes to steer a middle course between these two opposites, wet and dry. We, they, see it as vital that we present a package to the electorate which stresses the strengths of the Party as a whole. In short, a balanced ticket. The Prime Minister obviously has great appeal for many people, but it is important that we don't allow our ability in depth to be swamped by just the one personality. So, some of us on the presentational side of things are keen to come up with a few examples of balanced, but effective, publicity. Not, I might say, without some opposition from both sides. I fear without it, we may lose the next general election. And HMS Britannia will be steering a course for the nearest bloody great iceberg. (*Beat.*)

Stuart Sort of a 'Did Six Million Really Die' exercise.

Howard In a way.

Stuart Were Four Million Really Unemployed?

Howard Not on our bloody figures they weren't! (*He laughs.*) Cash, you know the form. Get me something good.

Cash Commitment to excellence. That's our promise, Howard.

Howard Good. (*Beat.*) Well, we must be off. I've promised this young lady lunch somewhere she can throw bread rolls at Roy Hattersley. Adios.

Gill Goodbye.

They all say goodbye etc. **Howard** *and* **Gill** *go.*

Stuart So. It's not even the Tory Party we're working for here. It's the Eton and Harrow Tendency. (*He laughs.*)

Eric In my experience, you throw a bread roll at Hattersley, he just eats it. (*Beat.*)

Cash I know Howard's a bit of a smoothie, but believe me, he delivers. He got me the candidate training account against some of the big boys, and that pays a lot of bills. (*Beat.*) If we get this right, it could do us a lot of favours.

Eric I'm with you all the way.

Stuart Is that an election pledge? Because your track record's not overly impressive on that score.

Eric This is the *real* world, Mr Clarke. (*Beat.*)

Cash Last time of asking, Stuart. No going back. Are you in?

Stuart In? I wouldn't miss it for the world. (*Beat.*)

Cash I'll have Liz draw up a contract.

Amanda *comes into reception.*

Eric Time I was off. Mr Murdoch wants three thousand words on popular capitalism by Thursday. Can't disappoint him. When shall we three meet again?

Cash I'll call you. See if you can draft out a few ideas for next time.

Eric No problem. Oh, don't forget I've got a week's freebie in Montserrat coming up.

Cash It's in the diary.

Amanda *comes in.* **Liz** *is behind her, but she gives up and goes back to her desk.* **Amanda** *sees* **Stuart** *and is taken aback.*

Eric Goodbye then. (*He goes.*)

Stuart What are you doing here?

Amanda Come to take my husband to lunch, what else? Assuming there's maybe something to celebrate.

Cash I'm just waiting on his references. Amanda, how are you? Long time no see.

They kiss formally.

Amanda You haven't changed much since I last saw you.

Cash Some things never change.

Stuart I've *had* lunch.

Amanda Liquid, by the look of it.

Stuart Salad. We can go to a boozer. I'll just take a leak. (*He goes.*)

Cash I thought you were busy today.

Amanda I've got an editorial board meeting at three. It could be very long and very bloody. I'm sorry. I thought Stuart'd be gone by now.

Cash You mean you came to see me?

Amanda Of course. I'm not the Sally Army. I don't follow him around like a soup kitchen. I gave that up years ago.

Cash It's a bit risky. I'm going to be seeing rather a lot of your husband.

Amanda Good. That means you can see more of me. (*Pause.*) Sod this. I want to kiss you. On the mouth. I want to lick your tongue.

Cash I'd like that.

Amanda You like everything. You're undiscriminating.

Cash It's this lust for life. I can't help it. (*Beat.*)

Amanda What about this evening?

Cash What about it?

Amanda Are you free?

Cash I could be.

Amanda Don't fuck me about Paul. You're not so hard to get.

Cash Ring me after lunch. (*Beat.*) I may be busy.

Amanda I could come late. Do it on your desk. Mess up your papers.

Cash How come we never do it on your desk?

Amanda Open plan office, darling. I may be many things, but an exhibitionist isn't one of them. Some things I keep to myself.

Stuart *comes back in.*

Stuart Right.

Amanda Did you wash your hands?

Stuart Shove it.

Amanda Anybody'd think you just *lost* a job.

Stuart I just lost *some*thing. Fuck knows what. (*Beat.*) Come on. (*They turn to go.*) Propaganda, Cash. That's what you said.

Cash That's right.

Stuart Pretty pictures. You're on.

Stuart *and* **Amanda** *go.* **Cash** *sits at his desk.* **Liz** *comes in.*

Liz D' you want some lunch?

Cash No thanks. (*Beat.*)

Liz I like him.

Cash Stuart?

Liz Aye.

Cash He's an easy guy to like. Or he used to be. (*Beat.*) He was nearly killed, you know. In Ulster.

Liz I didn't know.

Cash Yeah. (*He starts to smile.*) He was going to make a film. Pro IRA. Silly sod got caught in one of their city centre bombings. Complete accident. (*Laughs.*) Sorry. But you've got to laugh.

She stands for a second then picks up some papers from his desk.

Liz Are these signed?

Cash Yeah.

She goes. **Cash** *smiles to himself.*

Blackout.

Scene Four

About ten o'clock that night. The office is quite dark. **Cash** *is stretched out on the sofa. After a moment's pause, a young man,* **Dooley**, *comes in. He's drying his hands on a paper towel. He crosses the room and throws the towel into the waste bin.*

Dooley So. Paul. Are you often to be found in the Moulin Cinema Complex, Great Windmill Street? (*Beat.*) Are you?

Cash Occasionally. (*Beat.*)

Dooley Tell me, was it 'Ranch of the Nymphomaniac' or possibly 'Erotic Exploits of a Sexy Seducer' which drew you to this place? Or were you merely in out of the cold?

Cash It's a warm night. (*Beat.*) 'Prisoner of Paradise' was the film that particularly caught my eye.

Dooley The overtones of confinement, was it? You were expecting perhaps, bondage or some such? (*Beat.*) You should see the one with the Queen in it. 'Detained at Her Majesty's Pleasure.' (*Beat.*) I'll have that drink now.

Cash Help yourself. It's in the fridge.

Dooley One for yourself?

Cash I'll have a Scotch.

Dooley I hate the stuff. (*He takes a beer out of the fridge and pours a Scotch.*) Y'know, people say it's Scotch that makes the Scots the way they are. Well, I'm the way I am and I hate the stuff. (*Beat.*) Personally, I find the deletion of the erect male organ a great disappointment, don't you? (*He hands* **Cash** *his drink.*) In the films. I mean, we get to see every nook and cranny of the girls. The camera would appear to be fearless in its probing of the female extremities. But where are the throbbing willies? I sometimes feel like shouting out: 'Where are the cocks?' Y'know?

Cash You'd get thrown out.

Dooley What, by those wee Pakistani fellers?

Cash They carry knives. (*Beat.*)

Dooley Maybe that's where all the cocks have gone, eh? The Pakistani fellers slice them off and put them into samosas.

Cash Maybe.

Dooley Nah. It's a wee little Englishman somewhere who decreed that we were not to be allowed sight of the aroused male member. Has to be. It's so typically fucking English, that. (*Pause.*) I like cocks.

Cash You've told me.

Dooley Did you decorate this place yourself? Nah, course you didn't. I expect you had a firm of interior designers do it all for you.

Cash That's right.

Dooley I knew it. And d'you know how I knew it? It's like a public lavvy in here. That's how I knew it. (*Beat.*) A very nice public lavvy, but all the same . . . Do you ever go home?

Cash Not very often. I don't like going outside very much.

Dooley That's why you favour the erotic cinema, I suppose.

Cash No. (*Beat.*)

Dooley It's weird, is it not? That you never go home, though you have one, and I'm sure it's very nice, not like a public lavvy at all, and I don't have a home but would very much like to go there. If I had one. Is that not weird? That definitely says something to me.

Cash What?

Dooley Hey, I'm no philosopher. Which is just as well. Can you see one of them bastards sleeping in a cardboard box under the arches? No, you cannot.

Cash Why not? George Orwell did it.

Dooley Who?

Cash Orwell. Wrote '1984'.

Dooley Aye? Shite film. Fucking depressing. The music was OK. I like the Eurythmics. That Annie Lennox, she's worth a poke, eh? (*Beat.*) You've not got a clue who I'm talking about, have you?

Cash I have the Eurythmics on compact disc, as a matter of fact.

Dooley What, in your cheesy home you never go to?

Cash That's right.

Dooley Maybe I should burgle you. Steal Annie Lennox off you.

Cash Be my guest. I'm insured. (*Beat.*) Crap in the bed. Whatever it is you do. (*Beat.*)

Dooley You really wouldn't mind?

Cash Not in the slightest.

Dooley Don't you want all the things you own?

Cash I don't know what I want. All I know is, what I get isn't enough. (*Beat.*) What do *you* want?

Dooley Me? Fucking everything. I want a house, a couple of cars, flash, with stereo speakers and tinted windows. I want an American Express card. A video. Loads of coke. An Armani suit. And I wanna be on Wogan.

Cash (*genuine*) So? Do it.

Dooley Oh aye . . .

Cash Why not? It's there. You can have it.

Dooley Gonna give it to me, are you?

Cash No, it's easier than that. You just walk in and take it. (*Beat.*) If you weren't so bloody terrified of success, you could have it.

Dooley I'm not terrified of nothing.

Cash Wise up. You're all the same. You hang around Piccadilly Circus all day because you want to. You enjoy sleeping in a box. It's easy. You know that to go out and get what you want means standing on your own two feet. And that's something you never learned. Well I'll tell you, it's easier than spending your life whining on about how you're never going to get it.

Dooley If I get it, I'm depriving somebody else of it, am I not?

Cash So?

Dooley And you, at this very moment, are in fact depriving me of what is rightfully mine.

Cash But I'm sharing it with you.

Dooley Not sharing. Bartering. I'm allowed to dip my wee toe into your pool on the understanding that at some point I may agree to play with your erect member. Or allow you to play with mine. Or put it in my mouth. Or worse. (*Beat.*) You've bought me. Is that not right?

Cash In a sense. But in a sense, we're all bought and sold.

Dooley Aye. Except how come when I'm bought and sold I feel like a Filipino or a twelve-year-old Bangkok virgin?

Cash That's your speciality. That's your area. (*Beat.*) Anyway, who said anything about sex? (*Pause.*)

Dooley I'll help myself. (*He goes to the kitchen and gets another beer.*) Like I said, I like cocks. (*He smiles, thinking he may have gone too far.*)

Cash Do you have many friends?

Dooley No. Do you?

Cash (*Beat*) No. I don't.

Dooley Is that why you're talking to me?

Cash No. (*Beat.*)

Dooley What's your speciality, Paul? What's your area?

Cash I tell lies for a living.

Dooley Are you good at it?

Cash One of the best. It's a very crowded market these days, but I like to think I've carved out my own little niche.

Dooley Who do you tell these lies for?

Cash Whoever pays me.

Dooley And who do you tell them *to*?

Cash Everybody. You. All the people who can't afford to pay me.

Dooley Have you been telling me lies tonight?

Cash Who knows? (*Beat.*) Why have you been following me? Why did you leave threatening phone calls on my answering machine? (*Beat.*)

Dooley You must have somebody else in mind. I never met you before tonight. Halfway through 'Warm Nights, Hot Pleasures' at the Moulin Cinema. The bit where the young girl found herself alone in the kitchen with the chauffeur and the gardener. (*Beat.*) And then the governess came in.

Cash Why?

Dooley I believe she was interested in some form of perverted sex. I missed the crucial next section as you engaged me in conversation. Something to do with how much of the film had you already missed. Lucky, really, that you didn't turn up ten minutes earlier. Ten minutes earlier I had my hand in the pocket of a middle-aged gentleman, performing executive relief for the price of the cinema ticket. If you were after more of the same, I was going to have to ask you to change sides as my left wrist was flagging just a wee bit. The right's much stronger. Practice, y'see.

The doorbell in reception suddenly rings. They freeze. It rings again, more insistent. **Cash** *gets up and goes to the window. He looks down.*

Cash Shit. You have to go.

Dooley Now?

Cash Yes. (*He ushers him to the door.*) Go into the office on the right, and as soon as it's clear, get down the stairs and let yourself out. I'll meet you tomorrow. Same place. OK? (*Beat.*)

Dooley OK.

The doorbell rings again. **Dooley** *goes out.* **Cash** *goes to the intercom and speaks into it.*

Cash Hello . . .

Amanda Paul? It's me, Amanda.

Cash Oh, hello darling. Hang on. I'll let you in.

He presses the buzzer and goes to the office and arranges his desk to make it look as if he's been working. Then he sits and picks up a pen. He notices an empty beer can, gets up and puts it in the bin. He sits again. After a moment, **Amanda** *comes in with a bottle of wine.*

Amanda Help me drink this. Please.

He gets up and kisses her and takes the bottle and goes to uncork it.

Guess why Maxwell's back in town early. (*Beat.*)

Cash You're sacked?

Amanda No. Re-organisation.

Cash Sacked sideways.

Amanda Not even that. Sacked upwards. (*Beat.*) My salary's been raised by four thousand, my department's been enlarged, and I feel like I've been sacked. (*Beat.*) Of course, I've got a couple

of placements in the department that weren't exactly my idea.
Daughters of friends, that sort of thing. But, what the hell? I can
cope. Nevertheless, there's a nasty smell of nepotism in the air.
Also, a smell of impending reshuffle. (*Beat*.) Paris was mentioned.
And New York.

Cash I see.

Amanda It's been mentioned before. Nothing ever came of it.

Cash Sounds like you're being given a trial.

Amanda It does, doesn't it?

Cash Is it what you want?

Amanda Yes. I suppose. (*Beat*.) At this rate, I'm never going to
have kids.

Cash I didn't think you wanted any.

Amanda I don't.

Cash Well then.

Amanda (*she runs her fingers through his hair and kisses his face*) Mess
up the papers?

Cash Darling . . . I've got to work. I'm behind on McLeish and
Harper. And Robin's been playing silly buggers with the artwork.
If I don't get it sorted a.s.a.p. we'll lose it.

Amanda Uh huh.

Cash I know it's a bastard, but what can I do?

Amanda I don't know. (*Beat*.) Shit, I'm miserable. (*Beat*.)
Post-anxiety depression, most probably. What I need is to get
zonked and roll in the hay.

Cash I am sorry.

She sits. He is not happy.

Amanda I think I'd prefer Paris to New York. The language is
easier. (*He smiles*.) How was Stuart?

Cash Oh, you know . . .

Amanda No . . .

Cash He was a bit . . .

Amanda Prickly?

Cash That I can handle. It's just a very funny situation. Me employing *him*.

Amanda Somebody's got to.

Cash But he hates my guts. Always has done. (*Beat.*) Still, playtime's over. After all these years, Stuart's had to grow up.

Amanda You're enjoying it. (*Beat.*)

Cash Yeah. I'm helping the guy out, but . . . I guess revenge is sweet.

Amanda Very in tune with the times.

Cash What is?

Amanda Oh, revenge. (*Beat.*) Anyway, I'm glad it worked out. I've been on at him for months. In fact, I think *he* sees it as getting revenge. He likes to think you can't live without him. We both know you can, but you boys, you have to have your illusions.

Cash Why so keen to get us together?

Amanda Christ, Paul, haven't you ever heard of symmetry? (*Beat.*)

Cash You don't, by any chance, want to have your cake and eat it?

Amanda Don't be silly.

Cash Or maybe it's a way of softening the blow.

Amanda What blow?

Cash Letting one of us down easily. (*Beat.*)

Amanda I love you, Paul.

Cash And you love Stuart.

Amanda Not in the same way.

Cash How many different ways are there?

Amanda Hundreds. Look, don't get jealous, for Christ's sake. (*Beat.*) What am I saying? I'm telling my lover not to be jealous of my husband. Something's wrong here. (*Beat.*) Stuart and I have been together for a long time. We gave up bothering to love each other properly years ago. But I love you. (*Beat.*) We'll never have the same sort of relationship as I had with Stuart. I mean, I think once in a lifetime is enough for all that stuff. In fact, I don't think

I'm capable of it any more. I'm too proud now to become a couple again.

Cash So, basically, I'm your little bit on the side.

Amanda I like the sound of that. (*Beat.*) It's all there is. Take it or leave it.

Cash I'll leave it for tonight, if that's OK with you.

Amanda Sure. (*Beat.*) Paul, when I say I love you, that's what I mean. I don't mean I want to marry you and have your children and go all starry-eyed when you walk in the room and sing your praises to your boss and . . . look after you. I want someone to do that for me. And if they can't, then the occasional bout of lovemaking will do just as nicely thank you. I've got a job and a life to look out for. And it's a dirty job, but somebody's got to do it, and if it isn't me, then it's not going to be any other bugger.

Cash Yeah. (*Beat.*) I should have made my pitch for you nearly twenty years ago.

Amanda No way. You were foul. Then.

The phone rings.

Cash It's OK. It's on the answering machine.

Cash *and* **Amanda** *start to kiss.*

The machine clicks on. **Liz***'s voice speaks.*

Liz Hello, Cash Creative Consultancy. There's nobody in the office at the moment, but if you'd like to leave your name and number, we'll get back to you as soon as possible. Thank you for calling.

The tone sounds. It is **Stuart**.

Stuart Hi, Cash, uh, Paul . . . yeah, it's Stuart.

Cash *and* **Amanda** *look at each other, then kiss again and start to undress each other.*

Look, I just wanted to say . . . thanks. I hope I wasn't too much of an arsehole today . . . I'm a bit out of practice, that's all. (*Beat.*) I've started doing some research. Got some good ideas. If you want to give me a ring, I'll go over them with you. (*Beat.*) Hey, don't worry about Bright. He's a spiv. I know all about them. (*Beat.*) It'll be great to get behind a camera again. There's a lot of things I'm learning to do again. (*Beat.*) Listen mate, strictly

between us . . . I made love to Amanda for the first time in months
this morning. After you called. You're obviously a bigger turn-on
than we ever thought, Cash.

Amanda *closes her eyes.*

Anyway . . . it's, uh, good to be on board. Yours for a great
Conservative campaign and a Labour victory. Bye.

The line goes off. Pause. **Cash** *stands.*

Amanda Don't you dare give me a hard time for sleeping with my
husband. (*Beat.*)

Cash I really have to get on with this. (*Beat.*)

Amanda Yeah. (*She stands and stares at him.*) Yeah.

She picks up her bag and goes. **Cash** *stands, hands in pockets, for a second,
then finishes undressing. Finally, naked, he sits at his desk and finishes his
Scotch.* **Dooley** *comes back in.*

Dooley But, as I soon became aware

Cash *starts.*

. . . you weren't in the market for executive relief of the kind only I
can give in the stalls of the Moulin cinema. So you engaged me in
idle chat and I thought to myself, this wee man's just a wee bit
lonely. Company. That's all he's after. Am I right? (*Beat.*) I
didnae leave, as you can see. I'll go if you want.

Cash No. That's all right.

Dooley I was browsing through your man's desk in there . . . (*He
paces around, taking off his clothes as he goes.*) . . . and I was taking a
look at some of the crap he had in there. Heavy. Intellectual stuff,
no doubt. But surely you don't have to have a degree to lie to
people. Maybe it helps. I dunno. But low, animal cunning must
play a large part in this charade. And I am blessed with that
particular commodity by the bucketful. I have a very resourceful
nature. So.

He stands, naked, by **Cash**. *After a pause,* **Cash** *stands.*

Dooley I want to be employed. (*Beat.*)

Cash I want to be loved.

Beat, then **Cash**'s *hand goes out to* **Dooley**.

Blackout.

Act Two

Scene One

Mid-morning a week later. **Cash** *is in the kitchen, leaning against the table drinking a cup of coffee.* **Robin** *is in the office setting up the video camera tripod.* **Liz** *enters with some papers and goes to the desk.*

Cash Is that the Benson stuff?

Liz And the Windfall contracts.

Cash Good. Liz, see if you can raise Billy at Machin and Drew for me, will you? If he's in court, leave a message. Say it's the Benson file.

Liz Uh huh. (*She goes.*)

Robin Windfall's definitely going through then, is it?

Cash You bet. They're convinced they can get a bigger share of mind now we've shown them how to unlock the strengths of the product.

Robin A two-year-old could have done that.

Cash But a two-year-old didn't. We did. Actually, I hate to say it, but your idea of putting them with Ronnie at the Tate agency was brilliant. Sticking with Todd's was flogging a dead horse. I'm eternally grateful.

Robin So give me a rise.

Cash See my lawyer.

Dooley *comes in with a portable video camera. He now wears a smart suit, shirt, and has a trendy haircut. He takes the camera to the tripod.*

Dooley This is a real beauty. Light as a feather. Feel that. Weighs nothing at all.

Robin I know.

They start setting it up.

Dooley I wouldn't mind one of these for Christmas. Hire myself out for weddings and that. Bar mitzvahs. Orgies. Make a fortune. That's how Spielberg started, y'know. Aye. I was talking to a guy in a pub, from one of the film companies in Wardour Street, and he said that Steven Spielberg started with home movies.

Robin Fascinating.

Dooley That's what I thought.

Cash *has come down and is looking through the papers on his desk.*

Cash You can set this up, can't you?

Robin Yeah.

Cash *goes out to talk to* **Liz.**

Dooley What's all this in aid of, then?

Robin If you were meant to know, somebody would have told you.

Dooley Well, I'm asking you. (*Beat.*) Is it your toy? Is that it? (*Beat.*) Well, the whole fucking place can't be your toy, now can it? (*Beat.*) Say something, even if it's only fuck off.

Robin Fuck off.

Dooley *laughs.*

Dooley You're fulla crap, you know that?

Robin Oh, just get out of my face.

Dooley *lights a cigarette.*

Dooley Pardon me for breathing, pal. Excuse me for polluting your air space. But I work here, much as you dislike it, I know. I am on the payroll. On the books. Official. So don't give me a hard time.

Robin Look, I know why you're here. I don't like it, but there you are.

Dooley You're breaking my heart.

Robin I know you're just a ponce. You'll be gone soon. To ponce off someone else. So it's no skin off my nose. Just don't get in my way, that's all.

Beat, then **Dooley** *grabs him by the collar.*

Dooley You smooth little bastard. Does it get that far up your nose, eh? Seeing someone like me in your place? (*He lets go.*)

Robin Just move on somewhere else.

Dooley I'm staying, pal. It's you who'll have to do the moving.

Robin I know it may be quite an effort, but think for a minute.

I've been here nearly two years. I know this business. I'm
qualified. I'm fucking good. You've been here a week. You're a
gofer. A nobody. You don't know the business. You don't know
shit. (*Beat.*) Now, the first sign of unpleasantness, who do you
think abandons ship? Got it? You. You're trash. The suit doesn't
hide that. Pal.

Stuart *comes in to look through the videos.*

Stuart Ay ay. What's all this in aid of, then?

Robin Interview drill. Cash teaches the candidates not to pick
their noses on 'Panorama'.

Stuart Really?

Stuart *has the video he was looking for.*

Cash *comes back in.*

Cash Cut the chat, boys. Let's see some work around here.

Dooley Sorry, Mr Cash.

He goes out to reception where **Liz** *gives him an envelope which he goes out
with.*

Stuart Hey, Cash, I think I've come up with a slogan.

Cash Hit me.

Stuart 'Nobody with a conscience ever votes Conservative.'

Cash Snappy. But stick to the pictures.

Stuart Whatever you say. (*He goes out.*)

Cash Rob?

Robin What?

Cash Come on. Meditate on your own time. Is that thing ready to
go?

Robin Yeah. (*Beat.*) I think we should talk.

Cash About what?

Robin About the company. About Young Lochinvar.

Cash Ho ho. How long did it take you to think that one up?

Robin Get smart, boss. He's a user.

Cash So am I. So, for that matter, are you. It's good for business.

Robin He could be very bad for business. Unless you want to be known as Rent Boy Limited.

Cash OK, shut up.

Robin No. And what's more, when do we get round to discussing making me a partner? It *was* part of the deal. (*Beat.*)

Cash First, I didn't notice anybody making any derogatory comments when I took you on –

Robin Well, Christ, at least I've had some formal education –

Cash Oh pardon me. Private school and Polytechnic of North London. I forgot you were so well connected.

Robin I mean, at least I have some qualification for the work.

Cash He's got the best qualification you can get. He wants it. I can turn him into anything. You'll always be an arty bastard, good for some things, but dodgy on the big stuff. You'll make a great living, no doubt about that, but you'll never take the world by the throat.

Robin And he will?

Cash No, I will. But he'll be there. (*Beat.*) And I'll think about making you a partner when you straighten out McLeish and Harper.

Robin What's wrong with it now, for Christ's sake?

Cash Nothing much. It could be better, that's all. Show it to Dooley. See what he thinks.

Robin You are joking, of course.

Cash No. (*Pause.*)

Robin OK, Paul, you've made your point. I'm sorry. Ideas above my station, etcetera. But please . . . ditch the rough trade. It's you I'm thinking of.

Cash I'm touched. (*Beat.*) If you weren't so precious, you'd understand. He's useful. To that boy, nothing is sacred. That's what I want. So for now, I'll let him run errands, hang around, upset you, I'll pay him, because one day, I'll open the box and there he'll be, fully formed. Ready to be unleashed on an unsuspecting world. And let's face it, the world saw *you* coming a mile off. We can't afford to stagnate, Robin, my old mate.

Howard *comes into reception.*

Robin You're going to fall flat on your face, you know.

Cash I got here by taking risks, not by worrying about my image.

Howard *comes in.*

Howard. Hello.

Howard Morning. No sign of Miss Huntley?

Cash Not yet.

Howard (*looking at his watch*) Good God. A fault. At last. I was beginning to think she could walk on water.

Cash Think about what I said, Rob. OK?

Robin Oh, yeah. Say goodbye, Rob. Goodbye Rob.

He goes.

Howard Is Bright in on this one?

Cash Yes.

Howard He's terribly good, isn't he? Terribly clever.

Cash Yes.

Howard I loathe him, though. Can't help it. Him and his kind, they're all the same. Stab their own in the back, then come over to us and start preaching the gospel. The fanaticism of the convert. (*Beat.*) Still, they're as nothing compared to this new breed of woman we keep getting. Clones of 'Herself'. Heads on one side, the voice of sweet reason, they're like a lot of little girls at a talent competition. All impersonating the same woman. One day, they'll be standing there in front of the voters, and suddenly the penny will drop. And the people will laugh. With every copied bloody mannerism the laughter will grow and grow until they all run from the podium screaming and crying, never to be seen again. (*Beat.*) I've been shafting her, you know.

Cash The Prime Minister?

Howard No, bloody fool. The Huntley woman.

Cash Oh.

Howard Back to her hotel after lunch, you know . . .

Cash Is this wise?

Howard No, it bloody well isn't. Don't know what came over me. Just have to hope she was too pissed to remember. Hasn't mentioned it since. But she's been behaving . . . as if she had something on me.

Cash Well she does. Not exactly in the job description, is it? I mean, candidate training doesn't usually involve sleeping with Party whips.

Howard No, not since matron took over. (*Beat.*) God, why are we always sexually attracted to danger areas?

Eric *has come into reception.*

Cash I'll take a raincheck on that one, Howard.

Eric *comes in.*

Eric Good morning.

Cash Morning.

Eric Where's the suspect?

Cash Not here yet.

Eric Black mark. Note that down, Howard.

Cash Sorry, let me get you something to drink. (*He speaks into the intercom.*) Liz. Coffee, please.

Eric Had dinner with Paul Johnson last night. We're going to be working together on the box.

Howard Crackerjack?

Eric (*chuckling*) No, Howard. New discussion programme on Channel Four. Politics and morality. (*Beat.*)

Howard Well. They certainly picked the right two there.

Eric Thank you.

Liz *comes in and goes to get the coffee.*

Cash It's good to see someone other than redbrick Marxists talking politics on the box. It's about time the Left orthodoxy was booted off our screens.

Eric Slow process, Paul. Slow process. But yes, it's happening.

Howard I won't believe it until the BBC's cleaned up.

Eric Privatisation. It's got to come. Then they won't have a rock to hide under. Daft middle-class Oxbridge Trots. Let them try and make a living in the real world.

Liz *puts a tray of coffee down and goes. They help themselves.*

Howard Tell me, Bright –

Eric Call me Eric, Howard, everybody does.

Howard Yes, Eric. How does it come about that someone with such an implacable hatred of all things middle-class finds himself on our side?

Eric Oh, Howard, didn't they tell you?

Howard What?

Eric The Tory Party's gone populist. Surely you'd noticed.

Howard But we haven't gone anti-middle-class.

Eric No, we're on the offensive against the trendy middle-class. The Left middle-class. The ones who consider themselves the natural allies of the proletariat. Islington. Lambeth. The ones who want to nanny the working-class. Who want them under-privileged. (*Beat.*) Unfortunately for them, whole swathes of working people vote Tory. You see them, horny-handed sons of toil with the *Sun* in their back pocket. Superhod. The brickie with the Roller. Holidays in Spain. Youth mobilised not against Fascism. Youth mobilised for Sangria and a suntan. And patriotism, that good old working-class virtue, is back in fashion. Pride, self-reliance. Working-class values, Howard. Many years ago, I joined the Labour Party because I thought it was a radical party. But it's a sheep in wolf's clothing. Margaret Thatcher's Tory Party is the true radical force in this country today. That's why I support you. This government has delivered what Labour promised. A genuine revolution. (*Beat.*)

Howard This is all most disorientating.

Eric You don't have to apologise for being rich any more, Howard. It's a bright new day. (*Beat.*)

Stuart *enters.*

Stuart Excuse me, is this the right room for the two-girl assisted sauna?

Cash Come in, Stuart. I've asked Stuart to sit in, Howard.

Howad Fine. Should raise the tone somewhat.

Stuart We aim to please.

Cash How d'you want to run things, Howard?

Howard Same as usual. We'll do the interview, you come up with any presentation stuff, Paul.

Eric Smashing.

Howard Just one thing . . . she's up against a pretty tough opponent in the election, majority's only a couple of thou, and the media are having a mid-term field day. So, let's not make it easy for her. OK?

Gill *comes in to reception.*

The rougher the ride, the more she'll benefit. Try to pierce the exterior. I want to see if she'll crack.

Liz *shows* **Gill** *in.*

Gill I'm most terribly sorry, My taxi was late, and then we got caught up in a demonstration. Honestly, the sooner we clear the streets, the better, in my view.

Cash Liz, another coffee.

Liz *goes and gets a cup.*

Gill It's monstrous that in a city as busy as London these people are allowed to march wherever the fancy takes them.

Stuart Have you ever tried to circumnavigate Buckingham Palace when there's a garden party on?

Howard Not to worry, Gill. Have a coffee and relax for a minute. Do you know everyone?

Gill Yes, Mr Cash, hello. Mr Clarke. And Mr Bright, of course, I know from his excellent television programme.

Eric You're too kind.

Gill I always make sure the whole family are watching. We gather round the television set every Sunday, all together.

Eric You make me sound like the abdication speech.

Gill (*laughing humourlessly*) Really, Mr Bright, nothing so dreary. (**Liz** *has poured her coffee.*) Thank you. That's very kind.

Cash Would you like to sit down?

Gill Thank you

They sit. **Liz** *goes.*

Cash Howard's explained all this set up to you, has he?

Gill Thoroughly.

Cash Good. Have you ever performed in front of cameras before?

Gill I was interviewed once. On a council matter.

Cash So it's not a completely new experience?

Gill Not completely.

Cash Fine. Eric will be conducting the interview with, I'm sure, some valuable guidance from Howard.

Howard *smiles at him.*

Stuart and I'll be watching the screen. Afterwards we can watch the video and take you through the interview again. Possibly suggest one or two ways you can present yourself more positively. If that's the case.

Gill I'm sure I'll be very rough.

Cash It's much easier than you think. Right. Let's get started.

They all stand and **Cash** *sits* **Gill** *on an uncomfortable chair in front of the camera.* **Eric** *and* **Howard** *sit just out of shot.* **Gill**'s *face is up on the screen.*

Gill Will questions be specific? Or. . . ?

Eric I expect we'll roam around all over the place.

Gill Jolly good.

Howard For the purposes of the test, assume us to be hostile.

Gill I'm sorry?

Howard 'Newsnight'.

Gill Got you.

Cash All right, then. In your own time.

Long pause while **Eric** *and* **Howard** *rake out sheets of prepared questions and flick through the pages.* **Cash** *settles down on the sofa with a pad and pencil, kicking off his shoes and watching the screen.* **Gill** *becomes uncomfortable.* **Eric** *suddenly breaks the silence in best interviewer style.*

Eric Gillian Huntley. Hello.

Gill Hello.

Eric May I first broach the thorny subject of the economy?

Gill Please.

Eric Very well. It is generally accepted that the economy is in trouble. The question is, just how bad is that trouble? On the definition that two straight quarters of declining national output constitute a recession, some economists would indeed claim that we are already in recession. Business confidence is slumping; many forecasters are anticipating falls in investment next year; the housing market is very clearly in recession. (*Beat.*) Of course, the Chancellor will say this is all fine, no need to panic, because it means domestic demand is slowing down, and this is good for our disastrous balance of payments figures. However, it also means, unfortunately for the Chancellor, that *supply* is also showing. That is: output which can be sold abroad is slowing. And that is very bad news indeed. (*Beat.*) Now, here we all are, strapped into our seats, going through a little turbulence, and oh dear, one of the engines appears to be on fire. Pilot Lawson has availed himself of the ejector seat. Where will Pilot Major take us? Will it be a soft landing? Or will it be a crash landing? (*Beat.*) Miss Huntley?

Gill I have to say, uh, that your original statement was, uh, incorrect . . .

Eric Which statement? That the economy is in trouble?

Gill No, well . . .

Eric Because I want to be very clear on this.

Gill No, the bit about . . . recession. I mean . . . that's incorrect.

Eric I see.

Gill It is quite incorrect to say that we –

Howard No no no. Sorry to interrupt, Paul, Eric. Miss Huntley, when a questioner says something you know to be an untruth, you tell him so. What he said was not incorrect, it was wrong! Wrong! Plain and simple. Clear as a bell. Murder is wrong. Terrorism is wrong. Labour is wrong. Got me?

Gill Yes. Yes.

Howard All right. Do go on. (*Beat.*)

Gill Well, er . . . I'm not too sure about the . . . details. What I do know is: as a nation, we had been paying ourselves far too much for far too long.

Slightly stunned silence.

Eric Yes. If I may move on? Perhaps we'll come back to that one. Now then. The welfare state. Mrs Thatcher told us the health service was safe in her hands. The health service tells us it's dying the death of a thousand cuts. That august body, the British Medical Association, has been forced to set up a publicity campaign against Kenneth Clarke's NHS reforms. Reforms which he intends to foist on the nation in the face of near-unanimous criticism.

Gill Well . . .

Eric Please . . .

Gill Thank you. The Health Secretary's ambition is a very simple one. He wants to make the National Health service serve its customers better. We can't afford to cut and run now in the face of the BMA or the rest of the chorus of institutional wailers opposed to change, especially when the plain fact is that this government is spending more money, in real terms, on the health service today than at any time since its inception.

Eric All right, you've made yourself admirably clear on that one. What about education? The teachers tell us that they are at their most demoralised. Lack of basic facilities, books for heaven's sake, run-down classrooms, low wages, the list goes on. Here we see another of the traditionally moderate professions alienated, it would seem, by the government's antagonistic social policies.

Gill Well, you know, all we ask of the teachers is that they accept that they have responsibilities to the service in which they work. A service which will seek out those who are inefficient, those who abuse their position for political ends, those who are responsible for the breakdown of discipline in our schools.

Eric But the teachers say that this is all a smokescreen, a decoy behind which you keep their salaries down.

Gill I think anybody who has ever agonised over the plight of the young in our society will feel, as I do, that you cannot measure dedication in terms of financial reward. Goodness knows, we all want to respect and look up to our teachers, but, I ask you, how can we when they refuse to supervise dinner breaks, extra-curricular activities and so on, when they introduce the tactics of industrial anarchy into our classrooms?

Eric What about the principle involved? The Opposition have criticised you on just those grounds, that you have created two nations, with one set of workers being asked to accept a fall in their living standards while others are allowed pay rises way above the level of inflation.

Gill I don't think there's very much the Opposition can teach us about principle, do you? After all, they left us with rising inflation, debts, an economy in which we paid ourselves too much while not producing enough. Do you remember the winter of discontent? I do. And I never want to see another winter like it. And we have not. Since this Government came to power, the realism of our objectives has ensured stability and growth.

Stuart Unless you happen to be unemployed.

Gill We care passionately about the unemployed. We want to see Britain back at work. But we want to see real jobs, not feather-bedding and over-manning, practices which lead to disaster. Take the miners: they have realised now that the future of their industry lies in work, not in strikes, in hard work. There will have to be closures, naturally, because as pits become exhausted, so they have to close. That has always been accepted. We are simply applying the harsh remedies demanded by a competitive world market. (*Beat.*)

Eric Thank you. You've made yourself very clear. Now. The years of this Conservative Government have seen, have they not, a general rise in the level of lawlessness, real and perceived, as well as a sense of disillusion and cynicism about society as a whole. There is a feeling, correct me if I'm wrong, that we are on the whole a less happy nation. Litter on the streets, sewage on the beaches, dirt and infestation in the water, potholes in the road, schools without teachers, hospitals without nurses, an epidemic of crime and lawlessness, and a government that doesn't care.

Gill But, Eric, disorder, lack of discipline, lack of respect for authority are all things engendered in the young by that generation which grew up without benefit of guiding moral principles. The youth of the 1960s were encouraged to rebel, to profane, for no other reason than to annoy. At the same time, they were indoctrinated with decadent and anti-establishment ideas. These people now produce our television programmes, our films, our plays. They teach in our schools, they run many of our councils. They write for Left-wing magazines. They are people who try to use freedom to destroy freedom. They have encouraged the young, already under pressure from social circumstances bequeathed to us by successive Labour governments, under pressure from waves of immigration, to adopt the nihilistic pose so fashionable in the sorry sixties. Children are *encouraged* to worry about nuclear arms which have kept the peace in Europe for over forty years. They are positively encouraged to fear and worry about their future. And in so doing, they are made unreachable by reason and good common sense. They are no longer taught respect for private property. They are taught envy and greed. They are no longer taught to have pride in their country. Instead, they are given politically biased so-called accounts of our imperial past as if it were something to be ashamed of. They are taught 'peace studies'. Policemen are no longer allowed into our schools. But any crackpot black is invited, yes invited, to stir up racial hatred and hatred of authority. Is it any wonder, then, that these children steal, rape, riot, even murder, since without the restraint of civilisation and authority, that is human nature? (*Pause.*)

Eric Thank you. Most comprehensive.

Gill *relaxes as if the interview were over.*

Howard Miss Huntley. Just a couple of points.

Gill *tenses again.* **Howard** *is furious but in control.*

You're a librarian, I believe.

Gill That's right.

Howard And you live with your parents.

Gill Yes.

Howard You're engaged to be married.

Gill I am.

Howard What does your fiancé do for a living?

Gill He's a farmer.

Howard I see. (*Beat.*) And you were educated locally at a private school.

Gill Yes.

Howard And you studied English and Philosophy at St Andrew's University. (*Beat.*) You don't come from a very heavily industrialised area, I think I'm right in saying.

Gill No, it's very peaceful.

Howard I'm sure. And you've never worked in industry, or business.

Gill Neither has Neil Kinnock.

Howard Quite. (*Beat.*) You see, I'm just a little puzzled as to where you get your certainty from. I mean, it all sounds very familiar, it has the ring of truth about it, but . . . how do you know? (*Beat.*)

Gill I talk to people. I read. Books. Newspapers.

Howard Yes, of course, but forgive me, I detect a sense of something rather unpleasant in what you say.

Gill The truth often hurts.

Howard God yes, but I detect something other than the truth. I detect, pardon me for saying it, a fear, an underlying prejudice against your fellow Britons.

Gill If you mean I don't like socialists, you're quite right.

Howard No, I don't mean that. After all, not all teachers can be socialists, or all doctors, or nurses, or hospital administrators . . .

Stuart . . . or even miners for that matter . . .

Howard I mean, speaking as a fellow Briton, I get the impression that you feel we're just not good enough. We fail to measure up to some abstract standard you have for . . . attitude, behaviour. We're just not good enough, and you're jolly well going to do something about it! (*He smiles.*)

Gill I believe that is what politicians are for. (*Beat.*)

Howard Forgive me, but that is the most preposterous, dangerous nonsense it has ever been my misfortune to hear.

Eric *finds something fascinating to do in his case.* **Cash** *reclines with his eyes closed.*

I have been in politics all my adult life. I have known people who came into politics to further their business careers, to boost their egos, to fill an otherwise dull life, to fulfil the family tradition. I have even known people come into politics because they believe they have something useful to offer the nation. But I have never known anybody come into politics because they despise their country and wish to exorcise their fear and loathing with a good dose of corrective medicine. That is not political drive. That is psychological disorder. (*Beat.*) Please don't make the mistake of thinking that we want an army of steel-jawed, flaxen-haired warriors against all things decadent. Our leader is a one-off. She can't go on forever. She is useful in the short term for enabling us to do what we do best: running the capitalist economy. But in the long term, she is just another servant of the Party. (*Beat.*) I just don't think we need any more like you. (*Beat.*) I'm sorry, Miss Huntley, if one day you put your little foot outside Mother and Father's ivy-covered cottage and saw lots of frightening things. I'm sorry if you didn't understand what all those horrible big grown-ups were doing, in their factories, their offices, their pubs, their bedrooms. I'm sorry they called you nasty names, and swore and didn't go to church very often; they did things Mummy and Daddy said weren't very nice. (*Beat.*) But I've got news for you. They've been doing it since the dawn of creation, and they're going to go on doing it whether you stamp your little foot and tell them to stop it or not. (*Beat.*) It's not society that has the problem, Miss Huntley. It's not society that's deviant. It's you. (*Beat.*) My advice would be to marry your farmer, produce your incredibly heavily EEC subsidised crops, have a couple of children, go to church regularly and quietly shrivel up in the peaceful English countryside. That, after all, is what it's there for.

Gill *stands with a look of distress and betrayal and goes out. They watch her go.*

Cash Well, Howard. (*Beat.*) You shouldn't have messed around like that. You should have really let her have it.

Howard Cash, I've seen the future. And it freezes my water.

Eric *chuckles.*

What?

Eric I was just thinking. You're in the wrong party, old fruit.

Howard No. I'm not. She is.

Eric *laughs.* **Howard** *joins in.*

Cash Anybody need a drink?

Howard Please.

Cash *goes to the kitchen.*

I'll tell you what.

Cash What?

Howard I don't know why I'm laughing.

Cash No?

Howard No. Because if Miss Huntley opens her mouth, I'm going to be up to my eyeballs in shit.

He roars with laughter. **Eric** *laughs.* **Cash** *looks seriously at* **Howard**. **Liz** *enters.*

Liz I'm sorry, there's a phone-call from Central Office for Mr Lipton.

Howard Ah. I'd better take it outside.

He goes outside with **Liz** *and uses her phone.*

Stuart Anybody get the feeling there's something we're missing?

Cash Such as?

Stuart Such as: your man there may just not be a true believer.

Eric I would say that is a very definite possibility. (*Beat.*)

Cash So what the hell's he up to?

Eric And where do *we* fit in?

Stuart 'I think we should be told.' (*Beat.*)

Cash I need to talk to some people. Pronto.

Howard *comes back in.*

Howard Right. Now, where's that drink?

Blackout.

Scene Two

Later that day. Mid-afternoon. **Stuart** *is alone in the office, watching a video of Grosvenor Square or demonstrations, making notes.* **Liz** *comes in.*

Liz I'm sorry. Still no sign.

Stuart 's OK, Liz.

Liz It's not like him. I mean, he doesn't even usually go out for lunch. A quick sandwich at his desk and that's it. I practically have to force-feed him.

Stuart You look after him, don't you?

Liz That's my job.

Stuart Being mother?

Liz Comes naturally. (*Beat.*)

Stuart Is he a good boss?

Liz Well, he expects a lot, but then he pays above the average. And he's very considerate sometimes. Let me go for a fortnight when my dad died. Even sent some flowers to the funeral.

Stuart That's nice.

Liz Yes, it was. Can I get you anything?

Stuart A Perrier. I'll get it. (*He goes to the kitchen.*) Does Cash have many women friends?

Liz I wouldn't know.

Stuart Oh, come on. You keep his diary. (*Beat.*) Between you and me, we used to think he might be gay. Not because of anything . . . specific. I suppose he was just a bit of a loner.

Liz He still is, then.

Stuart Fancy him yourself, do you?

Liz No! (*Beat.*)

Stuart I guess all his drive goes into this.

Liz Yeah. I guess so.

Stuart What a waste.

Liz I think he's very proud of the company.

Stuart He'd have to be.

Dooley *comes in, a bit drunk.*

Liz And where the hell d'you think you've been?

Dooley Fret not, hen. I've been engaged on important business. Company business.

Liz In the pub.

Dooley Christ, that's where deals get made.

Liz You're lucky Mr Cash is not back yet. Otherwise you'd be making a deal down at the broo.

Dooley Och, well, if he's no back yet . . .

He goes to the kitchen and gets a beer from the fridge.

Liz You put that back, Dooley.

Dooley Go fuck yourself.

Stuart Dooley . . . (*Beat.*)

Dooley Yes? (*Beat.*)

Stuart Don't talk to Liz like that. She's only doing her job.

Dooley Her job is to type out wee letters and post them. Her job is to make the tea and wipe the boss's bum for him when he has a shite.

Stuart And don't get smart with me, lad.

Dooley *snorts.*

Dooley What are you going to do about it? Going to teach me a lesson are you? Old man?

Stuart No.

Dooley That's right. No. (*Beat.*)

Stuart Look, lad, you'll be out on your arse if Cash comes back.

Dooley I won't be out on nothing.

Stuart Don't screw up. (*Beat.*)

Liz Come on, Dooley.

Robin *comes in.*

Dooley Oh fuck. It's the Bisto Kid.

He laughs and goes out with **Liz.**

Robin You've met the office yob?

Stuart Yeah.

Robin Everyone has to have one. Keeps the unemployment figures healthy.

Stuart What, is he on a scheme?

Robin No. Cash has taken him under his wing, so to speak.

Stuart Oh aye?

Robin Oh aye. (*Beat.*) So, how's it going with you, then?

Stuart Pretty good. You?

Robin Could be better. (*Beat.*) Look, I'm sorry we got off on the wrong foot.

Stuart Forget it. I have.

Robin Yeah. Uh . . . would you do me a favour?

Stuart If I can.

Robin Well, see, I've written this . . . film script. It's not finished or anything, not properly. I wondered if you'd have a look at it for me. Tell me if I'm doing it right.

Stuart What's it about?

Robin Uh . . . basically, it's about two guys who open an off-licence, then a cocktail bar, then a club. One guy's black, one's white. It's sort of a love story. (*Beat.*)

Stuart Yeah, I'll read it.

Robin Great I'll go and get a copy . . . if that's OK.

Stuart Sure.

Robin *goes out.* **Stuart** *looks amused and takes the video out of the machine.* **Liz** *comes in.*

Liz I'm sorry, Mr Clarke. Dooley's quite new.

Stuart You can say that again.

Liz Gives us Scots a bad name, him and his kind.

Stuart I've known enough Scots to be able to tell the difference.

Robin *comes in with the script and gives it to* **Stuart**.

Robin Here. No hurry. Just . . . I dunno. Let me know what you think.

Stuart This is the first script anybody's given me to read for over four years. I'll be very careful with it.

Cash *comes in looking harrassed.*

Cash Hi everyone. Stuart, I'm sorry, we said two-thirty, didn't we?

Stuart Not to worry.

Cash Liz, coffee, please. I'm drowning in bloody brandy. Why is it that some people only seem to think you're serious if you can down half a vat of brandy after lunch? Rob? Do something for you?

Robin No.

Cash OK, then. Off you go.

Robin Maybe if I wore a kilt, I might get a please.

Cash I don't have time, Robin. Just get out and come when I buzz you. Understood?

Robin Crystal. (*He goes.*)

Cash Jesus. Why is everybody a prima donna today? Liz, where's Dooley?

Liz I sent him out.

Cash Shit, why didn't you wait till I got back? (*She brings coffee.*) I want to send him over to Tate's for some artwork.

Liz He won't be long. I'll tell him as soon as he gets back.

Cash He should be here now. Wait until I'm back next time.

Liz I will. (*She goes.*)

Cash What a sodding day.

Stuart Actually Cash, the reason she sent him out was that he'd obviously had one too many for lunch and was being an obnoxious little git.

Cash Why didn't she tell me that?

Stuart Because she's a pro. (*Beat.*)

Cash Oh, fuck . . . (*He presses the intercom.*) Liz. Sorry. (*He releases without waiting for a reply.*) OK, Stuart.

Stuart Shall I tell you what I've got?

Cash First the bad news. I've just had lunch with . . . an old friend in the know vis-a-vis the to-ings and fro-ings of the Conservative and Unionist Party hierarchy. You were right. Howard has been a little naughty with us. This cosy little deal we're part of is news to everyone at Smith Square. I come out looking very bad. Not to mention more than a little silly.

Stuart That's how they are. You stab my back, I'll stab yours.

Cash It's worse than that. We, apparently, are part of a long-term campaign by Howard and friends to discredit the leadership in favour of their chosen successor.

Stuart Oh dear . . .

Cash Right. It's a full-blown bloody conspiracy. And it's all going to come out.

Stuart I'll clear my desk then, shall I?

Cash Not yet. We carry on. Only this time, we're bidding for the official campaign. (*Beat.*) I gave it my very best shot. We're in with a chance.

Stuart Nice one. And Howard?

Cash Backbench obscurity with any luck. Fuck him. Let him die. (*Beat.*) This is my life we're talking about. So I'm not playing softball.

Stuart Well. We're in with the big boys now.

Cash Too right. (*He indicates* **Stuart**'s *glass.*) Perrier?

Stuart You need a clear head when you're working for Fascists.

They smile.

Cash I'm glad you're with me. And Bright. He'll be setting the record straight this Sunday, in Fleet Street code.

Stuart Even rats have their uses.

Cash Not nice.

Stuart I know he's not.

Cash You could get to like him.

Stuart I could get to like ulcerative colitis. But I won't. (*Beat.*)

Cash OK. What have you got? Talk to me, baby.

Dooley *comes in.*

Dooley, run that over to Tate's.

He gives him an envelope.

Dooley What, the noo?

Cash Yes, 'the noo'.

Dooley *sways.*

And then go home. Take the afternoon off.

Dooley *stands there.*

What?

Dooley I'll need a key.

Stuart *pretends not to hear.* **Cash** *gives a key to* **Dooley** *who goes.*

Stuart Right, the idea I have here, very much planning stage at the moment, is that we concentrate on the opposition. Because I'll be perfectly frank, Cash, I hate the bloody sight of Thatcher. And I reckon so does a goodly portion of the nation at large. Her material's thin. She needs to be used sparingly.

Cash Yes, but we *do* need to use her. Particularly now. Forget the balanced ticket. Think you can handle it?

Stuart Oh yes. I can handle it.

Cash Good. (*Beat.*)

Stuart Anyway, I've had a whale of a time, going through archive stuff, and I've come up with a potted history of the Labour movement in revolt since about 1965. Now, to me, this stuff is beautiful. There's the miner's strike. The three day week. Arthur looking great. Heath looking like a twat, not difficult to find, that one. All the Vietnam stuff. Lots of coppers getting booted. Winter of discontent. Strikes, marches, punch-ups. And d'you know what's most beautiful about it? It's in black and white. It's the fucking ark! What is black and white? Black and white is Old, it's depressing, it's the Past. Now, you intercut pictures of today's opposition leaders, also in black and white, with appropriate quotes, but, every time you mention this fucking awful Government's record, you switch to colour, fists, blood, blah-blah, black and white. New technology, sunrise industry: glorious colour. Trade unions, strikes, power failures: black and white. Home ownership, the Falklands: living bloody sensurround. (*Beat.*) I hate it. But I love it.

Cash Sounds good. Sounds very good.

Stuart You ever been on a picket line Cash?

Cash Stuart, please.

Stuart OK, so imagine it. Get the image. What d'you see? (*Beat.*)

Cash Strikers, banners . . .

Stuart Yeah . . .

Cash Police . . .

Stuart Where?

Cash Hmmm?

Stuart Where are the police?

Cash Oh. In front of me.

Stuart Between you and the pickets.

Cash Yeah.

Stuart Protecting you, right?

Cash If you like.

Stuart It's a simple point. Can you ever remember the camera making you feel a part of the picket line? That those people around you were protecting you, your job?

Cash No. But then, that wouldn't be objective, impartial reporting, would it? (*He smiles.*)

Stuart I'm a film-maker. I know the camera's never neutral. The public's so-called objective position is with the police, the bosses, the government, capital. The camera has given the silent majority its politics. The Politics of the State. (*Beat.*) That is what I want to exploit in this broadcast. It'll be very good. You can trust me, I'm a doctor.

Cash So the whole thing'll have a newsy, documentary feel to it.

Stuart Totally. Make it like a news broadcast. Use news pictures. Tap that deep-rooted response. Labour is violence, chaos, fear.

Cash We're not talking major subtlety here, I take it.

Stuart No.

Cash What about sound? Voice over?

Stuart Authoritative. Doom-laden. Get the bloke who does the nuclear warning. And music. Grand and heavy. Scare the public shitless. (*Beat.*) You said think Goebbels.

Cash I didn't know you had it in you. You're not just selling out. You're having a grand closing-down sale.

Stuart Yeah. Everything must go. (*He's down for a moment.*) What d'you reckon?

Cash I like it. A lot. I think you've cracked it. Well done. We'll run it by Eric, then I think we might go with it.

Stuart I've still got loads of archive stuff to go through. Between you and me, I'm trying to turn up a shot of Bright at a miners' gala.

Cash You'll be lucky. When d'you think you can have a mock-up for me?

Stuart Couple of days, tops.

Cash That's great. (*He pours a coffee.*) Coffee?

Stuart No thanks.

Cash How are things at home? How's Amanda?

Stuart OK. (*Beat.*) OK? It's a fucking shambles. (*Beat.*) Cash . . .

Cash I'm not being funny, mate, but . . . not in office hours, eh?

Stuart (*beat*) I reckon . . . I'm pretty certain . . . she's been having an affair. (*Beat.*) I know she's not happy. With her job, with me. (*Beat.*) Every now and again I try to make contact again. Go on the wagon. Be nice. Be whoever it is she wants me to be. It never lasts. I get the feeling sometimes that she doesn't actually like me. Me. Who I am deep down. I mean, I don't always like myself. I let me down a lot. But I always find I have a sneaking residual regard for myself. (*Beat.*) I'm not a bad man.

Cash Maybe just not good enough.

Stuart Yeah. I want to make it work. I don't know how.

Cash You're asking the wrong man. I'm not exactly a paragon of family virtue. (*Beat.*)

Stuart What's it like, being on your own?

Cash It has its moments. Its compensations.

Stuart I don't think I could face it. (*Beat.*) That's why I'm doing this, y'know. For Amanda. That's why I want it to be good.

Cash It's a good enough reason.

Stuart It's the best.

The intercom buzzes.

Liz Mr Cash. Miss Huntley's here to see you.

Cash Oh right. Ask her to come in. (*Beat.*) I hope it works out.

Stuart So do I, mate. Because if it doesn't . . .

Gill *enters.*

Cash Gillian, hello.

Gill Hello.

Cash Just keep at it then, Stuart.

Stuart Yeah. (*Beat. He smiles.*) Right-wing thinking. It ought to carry a government health warning. (*He goes.*)

Cash Hard to believe, but he's the nearest thing to a genius I've ever met.

Gill He doesn't seem very happy.

Cash They never are. That's left to us ordinary mortals. Can I get you anything? Drink?

Gill No, I like to . . . keep a clear head. Nothing, thanks.

Cash OK.

Gill I hope you don't mind me just turning up like this.

Cash Not at all. As a matter of fact I left a message at your hotel. Didn't you get it?

Gill No, I, er, haven't been back there yet.

Cash Ah. (*He offers her a seat.*) I'm sorry we never got a chance to go through your interview.

Gill So am I.

Cash Howard's behaviour was unforgiveable. I'm sorry.

Gill That's all right. He'll pay. (*Beat.*)

Cash Yes. (*Beat.*)

Gill One hears whispers.

Cash Oh?

Gill All very malicious, probably. (*Beat.*)

Cash Right. The interview. I just want to give you some presentation points. Nothing to do with substance, that's not my area.

Gill Don't you have any political beliefs, Mr Cash? (*Beat.*)

Cash Oh yes.

Gill What are they?

Cash Not far removed from yours. More . . .

Gill What?

Cash I was going to say: more ruthless, perhaps.

Gill Oh, don't let my sex fool you. I'm as ruthless as any man.

Cash You'll go far. (*He smiles.*)

Gill Let's hope so. (*She smiles.*) Have you ever thought of standing for office?

Cash Often.

Gill Then why not? Not lack of ambition, surely.

Cash Far from it. My problem is I don't think I could keep up the public face. I think I might look like I was enjoying myself too much. I might look a little . . . smug. Cruel, even. Something a politician can't afford.

Gill I understand.

Cash That's something you have to look out for.

Gill It's difficult, though, when you know you're right, don't you find?

Cash I do. But I'm not after people's votes. And that's the name of the game. Making yourself attractive and credible to the voters.

Gill Mr Cash, you're a cynic.

Cash Probably. But I'm right.

Gill I must think about it. (*Beat.*) I suppose it would be asking too much for you to come to Lincoln next week.

Cash Well . . . I am very busy.

Gill I know . . . I just hoped . . .

Cash But it might be possible. (*Beat.*)

Gill I'd be very grateful. I'm just not sure who I can trust.

Cash I want to see you win. You can depend on that.

Liz *appears at the door.*

Liz Sorry. I've got Mr Benson on the line.

Cash Damn. Uh, look . . . get his number, tell him I'll get straight back to him.

Liz OK. (*She goes.*)

Cash Damn.

Gill I'm sorry, if I'm . . .

Cash No, it's just somebody I've been trying to track down.

Gill Look . . . why don't we meet up again? Somewhere more relaxed. (*Beat.*)

Cash Lunch? Dinner?

Gill Dinner would be nice. (*Beat.*) Why don't you call me at the hotel?

Cash Yes. I will. (*Beat.*)

Gill I think we'll find lots to talk about. There's a lot I want to learn.

Cash I'll do my best. (*He stands.*)

Gill I'm a very determined woman, Mr Cash.

Cash I admire that.

Gill Good. I'll be off, then.

Cash Right.

Gill Goodbye.

She goes. **Liz** *comes in. She gives him a piece of paper. She stands and gives him a look.*

Cash What?

Liz I don't like her.

Cash (*smiles*) I know. Isn't she absolutely bloody awful?

He laughs. **Liz** *goes.* **Stuart** *enters.*

Stuart Sorry, forgot the video.

Cash Help yourself.

Stuart Last time I saw that look on your face Harold Wilson had just resigned. (*He goes to the door. Stops. Turns.*) What did Shirley Temple want?

Pause.

Cash The lot, matey. (*He smiles.*) She wants the lot.

Blackout.

Scene Three

Evening, a week later. The kitchen table is spread with buffet food. There are bottles of wine and champagne. In the lobby are **Cash**, **Liz**, **Robin**, **Gill**, **Eric** *and* **Amanda**, *drinks in hand, looking at the pictures on the wall and talking.* **Stuart**, *in the office, pops a bottle of champagne. He's a bit drunk.* **Amanda** *comes in. She too is slightly drunk.*

Amanda (*seeing* **Stuart**) Oh God. (*Beat.*)

Stuart What? (*Beat.*) I don't know why he doesn't just write a cheque for ten grand, frame it and stick it up on the wall. There's no need to bother with all that paint and canvas. Messy bloody stuff. A good crisp Barclay's cheque. That's all he needs.

Amanda *pours a drink.*

After all, he has the artistic appreciation of a brain-damaged two-toed sloth.

Amanda How do you know?

Stuart We go back a long way. We're old muckers.

Amanda You didn't know Cash twenty years ago and you don't now. You never bothered.

Stuart D'you blame me? (*Beat.*) Have you ever looked into his eyes? Which are the windows of the soul? Have you? I have, I peered in and saw all these pricey pictures and nobody home.

Amanda I thought you weren't going to drink.

Stuart Celebration, isn't it? Thanks to me, Cash got the account. And thanks to Cash, there's another bloody Tory woman in Parliament. Anyway, you're pushing it back.

Amanda I'm allowed. I'm not an alcoholic. (*Beat.*)

Stuart D'you know what he was telling me about the other day? Banking. Advertising jargon and banking. D'you know what a high net-worth individual is? I didn't. Well. A high net-worth individual is a rich bastard. Yeah. And, d'you know what they call banking for people who aren't high net-worth individuals? People who are, in fact, poor? D'you know? It's called cloth-cap banking. (*Beat.*) Don't you just love it? (*Beat.*)

Amanda Stuart. Behave. Please.

Stuart Why?

Amanda I don't know. When in Rome?

Stuart Bollocks. When in Rome, act like a cunt.

Eric *comes in.*

Talking of which . . .

Eric Letting it all hang out, Clarkie?

Stuart In short, yes. Brightie.

Eric Well you deserve it. You did a very professional job of work. (*Dialling the phone, to* **Amanda**.) I love this man. A joy to work with. Never a dull moment.

Stuart That's what you think. I had a few, I can tell you. The dullest has got to be Brightie giving me the gen on popular capitalism. How it's the saviour of Great Britain and all who sail in her. That was dull. Very, very dull.

Amanda You, of course, are never less than riveting.

Eric *is speaking on the phone.*

Stuart Hey, less of the smut if you don't mind. (*Beat.*) Who you calling, Brightie? Eh? Heavy breathing to the blessed Margaret? A bit of insider trading?

Eric *puts the phone down.*

Eric Minicab, actually.

Stuart Minicab? I had you down as a Roller man. Merc at the very least.

Eric Can't leave the Rolls in the car-park at Heathrow, can I? It would only get vandalised by a disaffected member of the progressive class.

Stuart With any luck.

Amanda Where are you flying?

Eric Montserrat. Fact-finding freebie for the Colour Supp.

Stuart He likes to keep his ear close to the ground. Find out what the chap in Club Class is thinking.

Amanda It's supposed to be beautiful there.

Eric I hope so.

Stuart I don't. I can't imagine you with a real tan.

Amanda We've never been anywhere like that, have we?

Stuart (*thinking hard*) I don't know. Is it anything like Barnsley?

Eric Not especially.

Stuart Well then, I don't think we've been anywhere like that.

Amanda No.

Stuart I took you to Derry. Ungrateful bag.

Amanda (*looks upset*) Yes. I forgot. Thanks.

Stuart *raises his hand in a gesture of apology but says nothing.* **Liz** *comes in.*

Liz Everyone OK?

Amanda Fine, thanks.

Eric I'd love a Guinness.

Stuart Me too. Sabrina. That's the one I'd like.

Amanda Oh God . . .

Liz I thought you were reformed, Mr Clarke.

Stuart This isn't really happening. It's a nightmare. Nothing is real.

Liz That's all right then. (*She gives* **Eric** *his drink and goes.*)

Eric Nectar of the gods. Dublin-

Stuart -brewed. Nothing like it. (*Beat.*) You got shares in Guinness or something?

Eric Yes. (*Beat. They both laugh.*) See. We *can* get on.

Stuart I haven't got the energy to hate you, Brightie.

Eric That's good.

Stuart Is it?

Amanda You're all the same. Get a couple of drinks inside you and it's all chaps together. The saloon bar brotherhood. Bloody men.

Stuart My wife's hatred, on the other hand, knows no bounds. She can hate. My God, how she can hate. Bring down a man at a hundred paces with her hatred, she can.

Amanda Most men seem perfectly capable of bringing themselves down, thank you very much.

Stuart (*bitter*) But you just love to give us a little nudge.

Eric Do I detect a whiff of cordite in the air?

Stuart No. Just the embers of a fire that went out.

Again, **Amanda** *is visibly upset. She goes out and joins the others in the lobby.*

Eric Tell me, Clarkie, pre-brewer's droop, were you a whips and chains man?

Stuart Do what?

Eric The black leather hood. Manacles in the cellar. Fag butts on the chest.

Stuart You feeling all right?

Eric Mas-o-chism. (*Beat.*) You do seem to enjoy a good frolic in the broken glass.

Stuart Oh. I dunno. (*Beat.*) Fuck it.

He goes and opens another bottle of champagne. **Robin** *comes in.*

Robin Art fatigue already?

Stuart What Cash knows about art could be written on the back of a cheque stub. In fact, probably is.

Robin But he knows what he likes.

Stuart I wonder.

Eric Why is it that people like Cash and myself attract such venom from the left-wing, artist class? Is it because we achieve? Grammar-school boys in a comprehensive world? Because we make money? Fine for the print worker, not for the journalist? Because we don't swallow the old orthodoxies? What? What is this heinous crime we've committed?

Stuart You're a couple of mercenary shitbags.

Eric God, is that all?!

Stuart Yes. That's all.

Robin Whoah, time out. Left-wing, artist class, moi? Nyet, comrades. What you see before you is the new man. No-wing, hedonist, post-industrial, post-modern –

Stuart Post-early-for-Christmas.

Robin (*mocking*) Style. Dancing on the ruins. It's a hit and run culture. Bizarre connections. Stop making sense. Death to syntax. Long live the slogan. I'm talkin' 'bout my generation, daddio.

Stuart *guffaws and comes down to* **Robin**.

Stuart (*putting his arm round* **Robin**'s *shoulder*) Oh, I love this boy. He means it, he really means it. He reckons his jacket is a political statement. And d'you know what, Brightie? He's not afraid to put his money where his designer boxer shorts are. This boy has given me a film script. This cultural buzz-saw has written a piece for the modern cinema. Post-modern cinema, sorry. A love story! About two blokes, agreed, but that's not exactly risque in these days of Sodom and Gomorrah, is it? I was expecting Fellini, Bukowski, Burroughs, Buñuel at the very least. And what did I get? A polyunsaturated Colin Welland. An absolute beginner! (*Beat.*) And we're going to make the film, aren't we?

Robin (*smiling*) That's right.

Stuart I love him!

Stuart *plants a smacker on Robin's forehead as* **Amanda** *comes in.*

Amanda Now that is grounds for divorce.

Stuart You don't want to divorce me. It's too much fun watching me twitch around with my wings pulled off.

Amanda Fun? Now there's a novel concept. (*Beat.*) C'mon, Paul wants your opinion on something.

Stuart *Paul* wants *my* opinion?

Amanda All right then, *I* want your opinion. Your company. Your presence.

Stuart My balls.

Amanda I've got 'em.

Stuart Yeah.

Amanda C'mon.

Stuart *goes off with* **Amanda**, *taking a champagne bottle.*

Eric You say you're making a film. Is that for real?

Robin Yuh.

Eric You've got finance?

Robin Yuh. TV tie-in.

Eric Well, good luck with it. (*Beat*.) And it's about two blokes, is it?

Robin Yuh.

Eric Interesting. (*Beat*.) You don't get a lot of films like that.

Robin Oh, I don't know.

Eric Well I don't see many like that.

Robin Obviously you don't go to the right places.

Eric Obviously. (*Beat*.) It's a shame you aren't in on the campaign with us. It would have been nice to work together.

Robin Politics isn't exactly my strong suit. I'm easily bored.

Eric Oh, absolutely. That's why I gave up Parliament. I mean, everybody seems to think I did it for money, but it's not true. Not entirely. I did it because it was so boring. The shiny trouser seats. The dandruff on the collars. The shabby, boring ritual of democracy: a lot of middle-aged men reeking of mothballs and stale whisky; a total sham. So I made my excuses and left. (*Beat*.) All the interesting folk have gone. There's only the bores and the lonely left. (*Beat*.) I find the real world so much more stimulating.

Robin Yuh. Me too. (*Beat*.)

Eric Listen, Robin. When I get back from Montserrat, what do you say we meet up. Dinner maybe. I know some very interesting people from your point of view.

Robin Uh . . .

Eric TV, films. All very necessary if you want to go big time.

Robin Sure. Look, Mr Bright . . .

Eric Eric . . .

Robin Eric . . . about the film. The two blokes thing.

Eric (*laughing*) Robin, Robin, don't say what I think you're going to say.

Robin I just don't want any misunderstanding.

Eric What's to misunderstand?

Robin Well, if you write about a gay theme, people sort of assume . . .

Eric I never assume. Assumptions are the death of spontaneity. (*Beat.*) So. Don't worry. I'm not assuming you're gay.

Robin Oh no, it's not that. It's just . . .

Eric What?

Robin Well . . . I don't fancy you. (*Beat.*)

There is a noise from the lobby. **Dooley** *lurches into the room, followed by* **Cash** *and* **Liz**. *He goes straight for the champagne.*

Dooley You cannae have a party without Dooley. I am vital to the smooth running of any social function. Am I no right, boss?

He swigs from the bottle. **Cash** *smiles, trying to placate him.*

Cash Yes, but you have to keep it nice.

Dooley Nice? Fucking nice? Get to fuck . . .

Cash Because if you don't, you get your bottom smacked.

Dooley Ooh, I am all aquiver.

Eric (*amiable*) Trouble with the staff?

Cash Over-exuberance.

Dooley Bollocks to that. I'm on drugs, you bampot.

Liz Dooley . . .

Dooley What is it, hen? You want a good shagging?

Cash OK, that's it.

Dooley Don't you come anywhere fucking near me. I am not your property.

Cash You're fired.

Dooley You did that already.

Cash I'm just reminding you.

Stuart, Amanda *and* **Gill** *come in.*

Stuart Cash, who sold you that bullshit?

Cash It was a commission.

Stuart You actually paid someone to paint it? Jesus. I didn't know you were involved in charity for the blind.

Cash It's an investment.

Stuart Then put it in the bloody bank. Get it out of sight.

Gill I think it's rather good.

Stuart Are we speaking artistically or financially here?

Gill I would say it conforms to certain traditional rules, and as such, is pleasing to the eye.

There is a general frisson at this. **Stuart** *giggles.*

Gill Yes, I know you'll mock, but that's what I feel.

Stuart And you obviously feel things very deeply.

Gill Some things, yes.

Eric Surely it's all in the eye of the beholder.

Stuart Christ, Brightie, with a penetrating and original mind like yours, how come when you ratted on Labour, you never joined the SDP?

Eric I'm not principled enough.

Stuart You said it.

Liz *is bringing round a tray of food.*

Stuart God, Liz, don't wait on me. I hate it.

Liz It's what I do. It's what I'm paid for.

Stuart Well don't do it at me.

Cash Don't you find your social conscience a bit of a millstone, Stuart?

Stuart It's nothing to do with conscience. It's demeaning.

Gill But everybody has to work. Somebody has to do the waiting.

Stuart You do it, then. Or let's see Nigel Lawson's daughter cleaning toilets. Mark Thatcher washing cars for a quid an hour.

Eric Oh Clarkie, you're so tribal. So socialist.

Amanda Huh.

Stuart What's wrong with that? It's not illegal, yet.

Eric Everything's wrong with it. It's what's wrong with the whole bloody country.

Gill Hear hear.

Eric I mean, you're an intelligent man, Stuart. A talented man. Yet you waste your talent desperately trying to dupe the people into swallowing your idiotic vision of a New Jerusalem. I've seen your vision. It's grotesque. It's sentimental. It's a bloody lie. (*Beat.*) Christ, how can a country ever progress if a whole group of people like yourself explode with apoplexy at the injustice of the class system every time they're offered a canape? It's not rational.

Stuart Neither is exploitation.

Eric *laughs.*

Eric Leaving aside the fact that I disagree, look at Liz, Stuart. Does she look exploited?

Liz *gives him a fierce look.*

No, she doesn't. She's simply doing a job of work.

Amanda She's not a specimen, Eric.

Liz I can speak for myself.

Amanda Well, excuse me.

Eric She sells her labour. We all do. It's nothing to be ashamed of. She's hard-working and loyal. Those are virtues. Not things to be sneered at.

Stuart I'm sure you've never noticed, but that's what socialism's all about.

Eric Oh God. Not socialism. *Again.* If only we could wave a wand, make it disappear. Chant a spell, or something. Socialism's irrelevant.

Cash It's also destructive.

Eric Absolutely. It *is* an alien ideology. The majority of people neither understand nor want it. It hangs over us all like a black cloud, desperately kept aloft by the huffing and puffing of the activists. Oh, the activists. The great fat cuckoos in the Labour nest. A nice left-of-centre party, with sensible managerial policies, totally hijacked by a combination of the sentimentally gullible, yourself, and the beady-eyed fanatics, the revolutionaries. Let's face it, socialism's not on the agenda, old fruit. It's history. The people are scared to death of it.

Amanda You, of course, would know all about the people and what they want. With your intimate knowledge of them. From

your Channel Island tax haven and your pied-à-terre in
Bloomsbury. I think, if you were to be completely honest, you'd
have to say that you're making educated guesses based on
self-interest and innate prejudice. Oh, I know those are the perfect
qualifications for membership of your little club, the Sunday
pontificators, but they're sod all to do with the real world. God,
we used to go to church to be preached at and told what was
wrong and what was right. Now we just open the paper and up
pops the pulpit and there's little Eric Bright telling it how it really
is. You and your little chums, all barking away together. D'you
know what you make me think of when you're on your soap box?
D'you know what I see? I see good lunches. Fine wine. And great
fat cigars. (*Beat.*) You're the self-appointed loudhailers for a
government that's turned this country into a land fit for Rupert
Murdoch.

Gill What an utterly absurd statement.

Amanda Oh . . . naff off. It amazes me that you'll all give
credence to this dim-witted country cow, who, by some freak of
nature, is now a Member of Parliament for Christ's sake, and yet
you pour all the shit you can on the idea, just the idea, of
socialism. Well, it's not the people who are scared of socialism, it's
you. Because it would drop your lovely lunch in your lap, and
stick your great fat cigar up your arse.

Gill Is this what passes for politics where you come from?
Foul-mouthed abuse?

Amanda You want politics, sister? I'll give you politics. Not my
husband's soggy labourist crap. That's just Tory paternalism
with a collectivist face. Thanks to their silly soft-centre deference
we still live in one of the most class-ridden, tradition-bound
societies in the modern world.

Eric Don't tell me your wife's a Trot, Clarkie.

Stuart I don't know.

Amanda No, you bloody don't. (*Beat.*) Socialism hasn't failed
Britain. It's never been tried.

Eric Someone's been reading her *New Left Review*.

Amanda I used to write for it, you condescending shithead.

Cash Amanda . . .

Amanda I'm sick of it. Your little parliamentary game. Your boys' club with its crappy rules and its honorary men. Pretending to be alternatives to each other. Well, you're all petrified. Every last one of you. Petrified of anything that'd shake you out of your cosy embrace.

Dooley *swings round with the video camera in his hand.*

Dooley I cannae understand a word you people say. You make a lot of noise, but I don't get any meaning from it.

Robin For once, we agree.

Cash It's called conversation.

Eric Cut and thrust.

Dooley Oh aye? Well the only cut and thrust I know is with a broken bottle.

Gill Really . . .

Dooley *goes over to her.*

Dooley Really . . . Who are you? *What* are you?

Dooley *points the camera at* **Gill***. Her face comes up on the screen.*

Are you a very important person? A VIP?

Beat. He points it at **Amanda***.*

And you? What are you?

Amanda Oh go away.

Dooley Ooh, I like you.

Beat. He points the camera at **Cash** *and then at* **Robin***.*

Well, I think we know all about you two.

Beat. He points it at **Eric***.*

You. I've seen *you* on the box. Yap yap yap. I've seen you. But . . . I don't know what you *do*. I mean, Leslie Crowther, I know what he does. He gives people suites of furniture and mopeds. Les Dawson, he gives them a Blankety Blank cheque book. But *you*. What do you give away?

Eric Nothing.

Dooley Then what the fuck are you doing on my television set?! (*Beat.*) When I lived at home with my family, I used to watch the TV all day. And I can tell you what good television is. It's where they give you something. You wave your arms about and act like a prat and you win a prize. Fucking great, eh? Well, where's my prize? I've come all the way to London to win something and all I've got is a cardboard box to sleep in and a lot of men playing with my willy. Somebody tell Bob Monkhouse. Tell him what it's really like. (*He turns the camera on himself.*) Look, I'm on TV. Look, there I am. Ask me a question. Ask me where I'm from. What do I do for a living? Actually I'm unemployed at the moment. Aaah. No, I'm not married, Cilla, but I wouldn't mind poking you, eh? I like windsurfing and I fuck dogs. Now, gimme a prize. I'm on. I want something. *You owe me* something! (*Beat.*) I'm on . . . you bastards.

Cash *takes the camera from him and hands it to* **Robin**.

Dooley You've got everything, you, and you won't give me a prize.

Cash *turns round suddenly, giving* **Dooley** *a backhanded belt across the face.* **Dooley** *goes flying. The others gasp etc.* **Cash** *picks* **Dooley** *up, blood round his mouth.*

Mind the fucking suit . . .

Cash It's mine. I paid.

He throws **Dooley** *onto the sofa. People are shocked. Nobody does anything.*

Liz Mr Cash . . .

Cash Job training, Liz.

He picks **Dooley** *up and thumps him in the stomach.*

Stuart Stop it, Cash . . .

Dooley (*hardly able to speak*) It's not even my own clothes I'm bleeding on.

He laughs. **Cash** *hits him in the face again.*

Amanda Make him stop.

Cash *lifts him up.*

Cash I owe you nothing! Nobody owes anybody else a thing. Got me?

Dooley (*laughing*) Lend us a fiver . . .

Cash *is about to hit him again.* **Liz** *suddenly steps in and grabs* **Dooley** *away.* **Robin** *rushes out.* **Stuart** *helps* **Liz** *lift* **Dooley**. **Cash** *goes to the* *kitchen and pops a bottle of champagne.* **Eric** *has looked at his watch and out of the window.*

Eric Is it written on tablets of stone somewhere that minicabs will always be late?

Beat. **Gill** *goes to* **Cash** *and fills her glass.*

Stuart You really believe it, don't you, Cash? Nobody owes anybody else a thing!

Cash Having studied all the available evidence, yes.

Stuart You've studied nothing. You're working from instinct. Lust. That's why you're such a vicious bastard.

Cash I operate, Stuart, that's all. Nothing new, nothing special in that. But it means I don't have time for the emotional garbage people like you carry round. I won't be trapped like you. I won't let you trap me. I'll just operate. And screw the cost.

Stuart It'll come back to you. It always does.

Cash Not if you keep moving.

Stuart It'll get you. Even if it's just one night where you wake up, and the dark frightens you.

Cash I'll sleep with the light on.

Stuart Very smart.

Cash I like to think so. (*Beat.*)

Stuart You'll never understand, will you? You haven't got the humanity to understand.

Gill (*pointing at* **Dooley**) Are we supposed to understand that?

Stuart Yes!

Amanda Patronising bastard.

Stuart Not now. Please. (*Beat.*)

Liz *stands* **Dooley** *up. He's in a bad way.*

Liz Come on . . .

Stuart Need a hand?

Amanda Don't you run out now.

Stuart He's in pain, for Christ's sake.

Amanda Well, you're not going to stop that. You'll only be making yourself feel good.

Liz Fuck you . . .

She walks **Dooley** *out.*

Stuart Doesn't hide it, does it? All the high-tech. It's still a fucking jungle.

Cash What did you expect?

Stuart Oh, God, I dunno. What did I expect? Nothing, I suppose. (*Beat.*) What did I want? (*Beat.*) Love. (*Beat.*) This . . . ruthlessness. It's not human, that's all.

Cash You see, that's your mistake. It is human. Quintessentially bloody human. You're a freak of nature. You've forgotten you're an animal.

Stuart Yeah. It's what's known as civilisation.

Amanda *sits by him.* **Howard** *suddenly appears, very upset.*

Howard Ah. (*Beat.*)

Cash Howard.

Eric *looks out of the window.*

Eric At last. (*He gets his bag.*) Can't stop, Howard, my cab's here. I'll call you next week, Paul.

Cash OK.

Eric's *almost gone.*

Howard You're a treacherous bastard, Bright.

Eric *stops, half-turns and looks as if he's going to reply, then he smiles.*

Eric Yes, see you then. (*He goes.*)

Howard And as for you two . . .

Cash What can I do for you, Howard?

Howard Take the knife out from between my shoulder-blades.

Cash Oh, come on . . .

Howard *takes out a photo wallet.*

Howard Look. My wife. My children. Do you know what you've done to them?

Cash Frankly, no.

Howard Joint effort, was it? The two of you cook it up together?

Cash Who?

Howard You and the wicked witch here.

Cash Gill? What's she got to do with it?

Howard Oh Jesus, spare me that one, please. OK, Cash, you get a better offer, fair enough, do some politicking of your own. That I can take. That, I possibly even expect. But why, dear God, why drag me all the way down?

Cash I changed clients, that's all. You hadn't been exactly honest with me, Howard. In fact you could have ruined me.

Howard So you ruined me.

Cash I changed clients. And Eric wrote a small piece. Hardly treacherous.

Howard And what about the fact that I am now officially branded a criminal? (*Beat.*)

Cash Sorry, Howard, not with you.

Howard I'll draw you a bloody map, shall I? I have just been forced to offer my resignation. Due to ill health. Didn't know I was ill? No, it came as a surprise to me as well. I was accused of an abuse of my position. I was accused of a criminal offence. To stop it going public, I had to resign. That was the price. I am no longer a Member of Parliament. I'm now an irrelevance. Finished.

Cash But why?

Howard God, because this woman accused me of raping her. (*Beat.*)

Cash Ah.

Howard Is that all you can say?

Cash Well . . . (*Beat.*)

Howard And so, they're rid of me. Opposition y'see. They know it's a lie.

Gill I beg your pardon, but they do not know that it's a lie. Because it isn't a lie. You're a filthy animal who takes advantage of his power to compromise women Party members in order to secure sexual favours. I risked great harm to my personal and

professional reputation to expose you. However, I felt it was
something I had to do, if only to protect other women like myself.

Howard For Christ's sake, somebody switch her off! (*Beat.*)
Listen to me you tart, you disgusting automaton, I'm going to do
everything I can to ruin you. My life is shattered, all for the sake of
an afternoon in the sack with a whore on the make. For that, I've
lost everything. (*Beat.*) I've got a wife at home who hasn't stopped
crying for two days. Three children who are going to have to live
the rest of their lives with whispers and innuendoes about their
father. You don't do that to somebody and expect to get away
scot-free. I'll drag you down. I have friends. People with
influence. I'll see to it that nobody in the party will ever trust you.

Gill You're a bad loser. That's a flaw in a politician.

Howard I think I have a right to be a bad loser, considering I've
lost everything.

Cash Come on, Howard, that's not strictly true. At last count you
had, what, four company directorships, a thriving family
business, and homes on three continents. Hardly destitute.

Howard And the disgrace?

Cash What about it? Probably do your reputation good in some
quarters. (*Beat.*) You thought you were invincible. You
underestimated the stakes. Fatal. Old boy. (*Pause.*)

Amanda I'm sure it won't hurt for very long. Have some
champers.

She holds the bottle up. **Howard** *starts to cry.*

Oh God . . .

Howard My whole life . . . gone . . .

Stuart You're only out of a job.

Amanda Now you know how it feels.

Beat. **Howard** *looks at them and goes out.*

Gill What a pathetic individual.

Amanda You should know.

Cash Did you shop him?

Gill Yes, of course.

Cash Harsh.

Gill You think so? (*Beat.*)

Cash No.

Gill Good. (*Beat.*) I have to go. My fiancé's picking me up at the hotel. We're driving back to Suffolk.

Cash Give him my regards.

Gill I will, thanks. (*She kisses* **Cash** *on the cheek. To* **Amanda** *and* **Stuart**.) I hope you can come to terms with what we're doing.

Stuart Or else?

Amanda Up against the wall.

Gill I don't think so. Well. Wouldn't be very English, would it? Goodbye. (*She goes.*)

Amanda Stuart . . . oh God . . . I want to confess something. (*Beat.*) I've had an affair. (*Beat.*) I'm sorry.

Cash *stares straight ahead.*

Stuart Had. Is it finished? (*Beat.*)

Amanda Oh yes.

Cash *stands and goes out.*

Stuart It hurts.

Amanda I know. (*Beat.*)

Stuart What do we do now?

Amanda Christ, I don't know.

Stuart Do we have another go?

Amanda I don't really know what I want any more. I just feel drained, and angry.

Stuart What can you do about it?

Amanda I don't know. (*Beat.*)

Stuart Between the two of us, we don't know very much at all, do we?

Amanda Nothing that's of any use. (*Beat.*) Let's . . . 'have another go'.

Stuart OK.

Cash *comes back in with some papers.*

Cash Might as well get on with some work.

Robin *comes in and gives* **Cash** *an envelope.*

What is it?

Robin Resignation.

Cash Why?

Robin *shrugs.*

Another job?

Robin Sort of.

Stuart It's my fault, Cash. He gave me a script. I showed it to David at Channel Four. We go into production in March.

Cash You finished it.

Robin It was finished all the time. (*Beat.*) I've got a couple of commissions as well.

Cash Well done. (*Beat.*) Well. (*He extends his hand.*) Good luck.

They shake.

Robin See you in the movies.

He goes. **Stuart** *stands.*

Stuart Sorry I won't get to do the broadcast.

Cash You've done all the work. I can get a hack in.

Stuart Well. It's been really real.

Cash You don't have to go.

Stuart (*looking round the room*) Oh . . . I think I do. (*To* **Amanda**.) Fancy a meal?

Amanda Japanese?

Stuart You're paying.

Amanda OK. (*She stands.*)

Cash Take some champagne.

Stuart No. You keep it. For a celebration.

Cash There's still work for you, if you want it.

Stuart I'm gonna be a bit busy, as a matter of fact.

Cash Sure.

Stuart Thanks.

Cash Nice to see you again, Amanda.

Amanda Same here.

Cash Keep the faith.

Amanda What else is there to do? (*Beat.*) C'mon.

They go. **Cash** *surveys the room.* **Liz** *comes in and starts clearing up.* **Dooley** *comes in holding his stomach.*

Cash Did I hurt you?

Dooley (*trying to smile*) Get tae fuck.

Cash You can take it.

Dooley Aye. (*He takes a bottle of champagne and curls up on the sofa.*)

Cash Leave it, Liz.

Liz It's got to be done.

She starts washing up. **Cash** *sits at his desk.*

Cash First thing tomorrow, I want to chase Benson. (*The phone rings.*) And don't forget I'm at Smith Square in the afternoon. (*The answering machine goes on.*) So, anything urgent, you can get me there.

Cash *switches the answering machine speaker on.* **Liz***'s message is just finishing.* **Cash** *gets up and pours himself a glass of champagne.*

Liz . . . as soon as possible. Thank you for calling. (*The machine beeps.*)

Berkowitz Cash, hi. Berkowitz, New York. Things are really starting to happen, pal. I lunched Forbert like you said, and the guy is jumping without a parachute. His tongue is so far up my ass he's licking my lips. I don't know what you did over there, Cash, but you've got Buckley and the whole crew creaming themselves. You better think about opening up over here. Better still, get yourself down to Heathrow and come see us. I mean it. So. Call me. And let's bust this thing wide open, OK? They need you. They love you. So come and explore, you hear?

Beat. The machine goes off. **Cash** *raises his glass.*

Cash You got it.

Blackout.

Progress

Progress was first presented at the Bush Theatre, London on 2 July, 1984, with the following cast:

Ronee, *33 years old. She is an administrator of a South London Community and Arts Centre. A tough, articulate woman.*   Lindsay Duncan

Will, *34 years old. Ronee's husband. He is a Current Affairs researcher at Channel 4. Very much Ronee's male equivalent, though he is slightly in awe of her.*   Gregory Floy

Oliver, *31 years old. A crafts stallholder. He is small and very talkative, particularly when drunk.*   David Bamber

Martin, *29 years old. He is supposedly Oliver's bisexual live-in companion. He is witty and superficially callous.*   Kevin Elyot

Bruce, *32 years old. A barman. He cultivates a quiet, rather macho image. He is shy, with a stammer.*   Struan Rodger

Ange, *20 years old. A young wife staying with Ronee and Will, having left her husband after he beat her. Shy and reserved, though with a tough streak.*   Sharon Maiden

Lenny, *21 years old. Ange's husband. He is a car mechanic, conventionally inarticulate, but with animal cunning and an evil sense of humour.*   Perry Fenwick

Mark, *32 years old. He is Ronee's and Will's tenant, a journalist on the Daily Express. Outspoken, a constant stream of fairly tasteless jokes being his trademark. He is already going to seed, but regards himself as irresistible.*   David Cardy

Directed by David Hayman
Designed by Geoff Rose
Lighting by Bart Cossee
Sound by Annie Hutchinson

Act One

Scene One

Monday morning, 10 a.m.

Ronee *is at the table eating muesli and fruit for breakfast.* **Will** *is standing in his dressing gown, rubbing his hair with a towel. She's leafing through the* Guardian *while on the stereo a tape recording of* **Oliver**'*s voice plays.*

Oliver . . . To see him like that. Terrible, just terrible. (*Beat.*) And he denies it, y'know? He can hardly stand up. And he looks me in the eye and says, 'Ollie, on my mother's grave, I haven't touched a drop.' (**Will** *goes off.*) And when I point out that Gran was cremated and therefore doesn't have a grave . . . (*Pause.*) And the next thing. 'All right, Ollie, I admit it. I might have had one or two'. One or two. The amount of vodka he gets through, he's single-handedly keeping the Russian economy afloat. And then it's tears. He breaks down. Y'know? Your own father grovelling around on the floor, begging you to forgive him. I mean, Christ, it hurts. (*Pause. The sound of a drink being poured.*) And, like, my kid brother, it cracks him up completely. He drinks himself senseless. It gets the whole family. My mother doesn't speak to any of us, hardly, any more.

Ronee Clever girl.

Oliver And that's the point. It's her I feel most sorry for. Thirty-five years married to the guy, and he turns out a jerk. What can you say? Tough luck, Mum? (*Pause.*) She's in the WI, y'know. She's not exactly a sister, if you know what I mean. (*Pause.*) I hate him for what he's done. But he is my father. (**Will** *enters, partly dressed.*) Can anybody give me any idea what I can do?

Ronee Switch that awful little twerp off, will you?

Oliver I need help.

Will *switches off the tape.*

Ronee How many hours of tape have you got with that drunk going on about his father?

Will It's not always his father. There's also non-aggressive football supporting, coming to terms with a bisexual nature, and the problems of getting your non-patriarchal leg over. (*Beat.*) He does need help though.

Ronee He needs a psychiatrist, not a men's group.

Will Ronee, love, we're trying.

The phone rings.

Ronee I'll say. (*She answers the phone.*) Hello. Oh, hi. Wie geht's? (*Beat.*) Ja, richtig. Das werden fabulos sein. (*Beat.*) 'The Poison Girls.' Feminist Gruppe. (*She laughs.*) Liar. Du verstehst. (*Beat.*) OK. Sechs Uhr. Ja. (*She glances in* **Will***'s direction. He's leafing through the paper.*) Ich liebe dich. OK. Tschuss. (*She puts the phone down.*)

Will My clipping got in 'Naked Ape'.

Ronee I saw.

Will Spelled my name wrong, though.

Ronee I saw that too.

Will How's Andrea?

Ronee Fine.

Will She hasn't been round for ages. I'd love to see her. Why don't you ask her to dinner some time? (*Pause.*) It'd just be nice, that's all I mean.

Ronee No.

Will It's not very fair. She's not your property.

Ronee I saw her first.

Mark *enters. He looks as if he's been up for hours, though he hasn't.*

Mark Yo. (*He goes straight to* **Ronee** *and points at her nipples, which are showing under her t-shirt.*) Is it cold in here, or are you just glad to see me?

She starts to go.

That was fantastic last night. Best ever. Don't let on to Will, though. Don't want to make him jealous.

She's gone.

Morning, brother.

Will Good morning, Mark. I'm trying to read the paper, so shut up.

Mark That rag? Call that a paper? This is a paper. (*He holds up the* Daily Express.) And I should know. (*He opens it up.*) Oh, yes. I like it. Look at that. (*He spreads the paper out on the table.*) All my own work.

Will *stares at it.*

Will Mark, tell me, what exactly *is* a love nest?

Mark Depends. In this case it's a council house where a dypso has-been DJ lives on the dole with a very tasty social worker.

Will And you don't think maybe he'd like to be left alone?

Mark Bollocks. He loved it. He's making a come-back, see?

Ange *comes in. She's wearing a see-through blouse over which she's about to put on a jumper.* **Mark** *points at her breasts.*

If you're selling those puppies, I'll have the one on the right with the brown nose.

She quickly puts the jumper on.

Spoilt a lovely view.

Will Hi. Make yourself some breakfast if you want.

Ange Ta. (*She goes out to the kitchen.*)

Mark You dirty dog.

Will Mark . . .

Mark I don't suppose she wants to make an old man very happy.

Will Her name is Ange. She's staying here for a few days on account of her husband keeps using her for a sparring partner and she doesn't box. She doesn't need you breathing down her neck.

Mark It's not her neck I want to breathe down.

Will Give it a rest.

Mark Rest? Bloody hell, rest's about right. Last night I picked up this nymphomaniac . . .

Will I don't want to hear.

Mark . . . Went back to her place, I was done in by midnight. And she kept farting non-stop. Had to scrape the duvet off the ceiling.

Then this morning, I woke up, I felt so rough I had to have a wank to get my heart started.

Ronee *appears at the door.*

Ronee See you.

Will What time'll you be back?

Ronee Late. We've got a social tonight.

Will I could drop in . . .

Ronee Women only.

Will Ah.

Mark A woman's place is in the oven, that's what I always say.

Ronee If you could be late with the rent just once, so I could kick you out.

Mark You love it, really.

Ronee Oh, get cancer.

She goes. He shouts after her.

Mark Don't forget to leave the window open. I'll be up that drainpipe. (*A door slams.*) Here, this fella's walking down the street, sees an old mate. He thinks, funny, he looks like a woman. So he says, 'What's happened to you?' Fella says, 'I've done it, I've had the operation.' So this bloke says, 'Didn't it hurt?' Other bloke says, 'No.' He says, 'What, not when they give you tits?' He says, 'No.' He says, 'Not when they, y'know cut it off?' He says, 'No.' Then he says, 'I'll tell you what did hurt, that's when they shrunk my brain and widened my mouth.' (*He laughs.*)

Will Jesus. You should see someone, y'know. Get professional help.

Mark I've got it. Swedish massage in Brewer Street.

Ange *comes in with a bowl of cereal.*

Hello again.

Ange 'Lo.

Mark I'm Mark. I live in the attic.

Ange Oh.

Mark If you ever feel like coming up to see my etchings . . .

Ange Don't think so.

Mark The door's always open.

Will Have a bit of tact, will you?

Mark Most tactful man in Fleet Street, me.

Will This isn't Fleet Street.

Mark Don't you believe it. We get everywhere. (*Beat.*) Talking of which, I'd better get to work. I'm after some woofter pop singer today.

Will God . . .

Mark Horrible little fudge-packer.

Will Just go, will you?

Mark I'm on my bike. (*To* **Ange** *as he goes.*) Hey, don't forget to leave your window open tonight. I'll be straight up that drainpipe.

Will D'you know what time you'll be back?

Mark No idea. Tell you what, if I'm not in bed by twelve, I'll come home.

Will Don't come barging in if I've got people here.

Mark You should let me in. I'm great fun at orgies.

He goes.

Will That was supposed to be a joke.

Ange Eh?

Will Orgies. You look worried. (*Pause.*) Sit down, make yourself at home. (*She does.*) He's all mouth and trousers.

Ange He's creepy.

Will Sitting tenant, I'm afraid. Comes with the house. Our resident damp patch. (*Pause.*) Hey look, while you're here, treat the place like your own. Don't feel . . . inhibited or anything. (*She nods.*) It's rough for you, I know. Anything we can do, just say.

Ange Ta. (*Pause.*) Cup of tea? I made a pot.

Will Yeah, lovely.

She gets up and goes to the kitchen. He stares at her and takes a deep breath and raises his eyebrows, or does something to indicate he finds her attractive.

He goes over to the stereo and turns on the tape quietly. We can't make out what's being said. **Ange** *comes back in with two cups of tea. He takes his tea and sips.*

Great. Worker's tea. Ronee always makes the perfumed stuff. Earl Grey. Me, I'm an unashamed PG Tips man. (*Pause.*) What I call worker's tea. (*He switches off the tape.*)

Ange What's that?

Will It's a tape of the men's group that meets round here. (*She looks blank.*) We talk about things . . . Try to understand and come to terms with sexism, relationships, that kind of stuff. We're trying to change our attitudes by being open and supportive without resorting to traditional, hierarchical structures. (*Beat.*) Trying to prove that not all men are monsters.

Ange Oh.

Will Y'know, like your husband.

Pause.

Ange He's just a rotten git.

Will Yeah, well . . . (*Pause.*) I can never understand a man hitting a woman. I don't mean that in a sexist way, chivalry, all that crap. I mean, it seems such a pointless thing to do. So negative.

Ange Well, I did hit him with the frying pan.

Pause.

Will Why?

Ange Tried to put my head through the window, didn't he?

Will When it was shut?

Ange 'Course.

Will Not very nice.

Ange No. He's a rotten git.

Will Then he hit you, did he?

Ange Yeah.

Will Poor kid. (*Pause.*) This is great tea. You can come again. (*Pause.*) Well, I better stroll into work, I suppose. (*He puts on his socks, shoes and jacket.*) D'you work?

Ange Only down the Centre.

Will Right. Ronee told me.

Ange Lenny don't like the idea of me going to work.

Will Bit prehistoric, your Lenny. Drags you around by the hair as well, does he? (*She shrugs.*) Maybe he should join our group.

Ange He's got his mates. He goes out on the piss with them. Right rotten lot, they are. Do some rotten things. (*Pause.*) D'you know what they done? Last year?

Will Shock me.

Ange They went camping down Cornwall. Before we was married, this is. And they was at this disco, and they got Bobby – he's the nice one, that's why they call him Bobby, out of Dallas – and they stripped him naked, nude, y'know, and they handcuffed him to this girl in the disco. And Bobby and this girl had to go all the way back to the campsite to get the key. And they wouldn't let her go. They never done nothing to her, but they kept here there. And they all thought it was dead funny. Then her boyfriend came and got her, but he couldn't do nothing 'cause there's like eight of them. I mean, and they thought it was dead funny.

Will Sad, very sad. (*He's dressed: t-shirt, jeans, Kickers.*) Right. Well, look, I'll see you tonight. Help yourself to food and anything else. Ronee gave you a key, did she?

Ange Yeah.

Will OK. I'll see you later. Take care.

He goes. She looks round the room, ending up at the stereo. She turns on the tape, picks up the two cups and goes to the kitchen as **Will**'s *voice plays on the tape:*

Basically, what we're talking about, I suppose, is understanding our own maleness.

Fade.

Scene Two

Monday lunchtime.

Ange *comes into the room with a sandwich and a cup of tea. Radio One is playing on the stereo. She sits on the sofa and flips through a copy of* Spare Rib. *The doorbell rings. She looks up. It rings again. She gets up and goes* *through to the front door. Pause.* **Lenny** *appears.* **Ange** *follows him in, and turns off the radio.*

Ange I never said you could come in.

Lenny I'm in now, ain't I?

Ange This ain't your house.

Lenny Ain't yours, neither. (*Pause.*) Bit tasty, this, innit?

Ange What you want?

Lenny Come to look at the drains, ain't I? What the fuck d'you think I want?

Ange Don't start swearing.

Pause.

Lenny Don't I get a cup of tea?

Ange No. (*Pause.*) How'd you know I was here?

Lenny I asked down the Centre. (*Pause. He takes a piece of paper out of his pocket and gives it to her.*) Here.

Ange What is it?

Lenny Open it up. Find out.

She does.

Ange Oh, God . . .

Lenny Read it, then.

Ange Don't want to.

Lenny Why not?

Ange 'Cause I don't.

Pause.

Lenny I wrote it for you.

Ange I didn't think you wrote it for the milkman.

Lenny Read it.

Ange I've read your poems before.

Lenny It's a different one though, innit? It's a new one. Go on.

She gives it a cursory reading.

Ange Yeah. Lovely.

Lenny You never read it.

Ange I did.

Lenny You never. Takes longer than that. Read it properly.

Ange I have read it properly.

Pause.

Lenny Rotten cow.

Pause. She reads it again.

Ange There.

Lenny Like it?

Ange Dunno.

Lenny What d'you mean? Dunno?

Ange I mean, I dunno.

Lenny Don't be stupid. Either you like it or you don't.

Ange I like it.

Lenny Good. (*Pause.*) How come I don't get a cup of tea?

Ange 'Cause you ain't staying.

Lenny Says who?

Ange I do.

He takes a packet of sandwiches out of his overalls pocket.

Lenny I've got to have something to wash me dinner down.

Ange What d'you think you're doing?

Lenny It's me dinner. This is me dinner hour so I'm gonna have me dinner.

Ange Not here you ain't.

He stuffs a sandwich in his mouth.

Lenny Bleedin' well am.

Ange You horrible pig. (*Beat.*) Who made them, then?

Lenny Me mum. (*Beat.*) Egg and cress. Lovely.

Ange You don't like egg.

Lenny I do the way me mum does it.

Ange You can't do nothing with egg, 'cept boil it.

Lenny She mashes it up. With salad cream. Tasty.

Ange Get food poisoning if your mum made it.

Lenny Dead tasty.

He eats. She goes to the kitchen. He looks round the room. He picks up the Spare Rib *and reads it. She comes back in with a cup of tea.*

What the fucking hell d'you call this?

She snatches it off him.

Ange I call it a magazine. What d'you call it?

Lenny Pile o' crap, I call it.

Ange It's nothing to do with you.

Lenny Load o'bollocks. (*Pause.*) Here, Dink and Wobbler had a scrap last night. Down the Duke. Dink bust his finger. (*Beat.*) Pretty good scrap, they reckon.

Pause.

Ange Kids.

Lenny Eh?

Ange Nothing.

Lenny What?!

Ange Kids! You are. Bloody scraps. Bloody stupid nicknames. You're supposed to grow outa that sorta thing when you leave school, y'know.

Pause.

Lenny They're *my* mates.

Ange You can have them.

Pause.

Lenny Right. When you coming back?

Ange You what?

Lenny I got the motor outside. You can dump your gear in it now if you like. Don't matter if I'm a bit late back. (*Pause.*) You ain't making a lot of noise here, doll. (*Pause.*) C'mon. You've usually got enough rabbit for both of us.

Ange 'S not true. I can't say nothing, case you don't like it.

Lenny Only when you're talking crap.

Ange Yeah. Which is most of the time, according to you.

Lenny Well, you ain't exactly Mastermind, are you?

Ange Which university did you go to, then?

Beat.

Lenny I asked you a question. When you coming back?

Ange Dunno.

Lenny Don't know fuck all, you. (*Pause.*) Listen, I ain't got time to muck about. Get your stuff. (*Beat.*) C'mon.

Ange I ain't going nowhere. Not yet.

Beat.

Lenny Ange. 'Case you've forgotten, you're my wife.

Ange 'Case you've forgotten, I ain't a punch-bag.

Lenny You're my wife.

Ange Makes it all right, does it?

Lenny You ain't s'posed to piss off every time we have a bit of a barney.

Ange What *am* I s'posed to do?

Beat.

Lenny What other women do.

Ange What, like Rose?

Lenny Like Rose what?

Ange Your rotten brother breaks her nose and won't even let her go to the hospital, 'case the Old Bill do him for it. I ain't standing for nothing like that.

Lenny When'd I ever break your nose?

Ange Had a bloody good try.

Lenny 'S just a little tap. Anyway, you hit me.

Ange You hit me first.

Pause.

Lenny Look . . . I won't. All right? I won't hit you again.

Ange Pigs might fly.

Lenny I won't. (*Beat.*) I never knew you was gonna leave, did I? Wouldn't have hit you if I did.

Ange What do you expect me to do? (*Pause.*) Eh?

Lenny I dunno. (*Pause.*) Me mum never left me dad when he hit her.

Ange I ain't your mum. And I ain't gonna end up like her, neither.

Lenny What you mean?

Ange You know what I mean. You can end up like your dad if you want, but I ain't ending up like your mum.

Lenny I dunno what you're on about.

Ange Don't you?

Lenny No.

Beat.

Ange Comin' home from work, and if your dinner ain't on the table shouting your head off and kicking the poor bloody dog's what I'm on about. Not letting my mates in the house is what I'm on about. And if they do manage to get past the front bloody door, telling us to shut up 'cause you're watching 'Crossroads' is what I'm bloody on about.

Lenny Well, you sat there jabbering on. Drives me fucking mad.

Ange And you sat there, like bloody God in front of the bloody telly. Drives me mad.

Lenny What's wrong with watching the telly all of a sudden? I work bloody hard all day, I wanna come home and relax.

Ange With your flies undone.

Lenny You what?

Ange You always undo your trousers, soon as you get in that chair.

Beat.

Lenny What's that got to do with anything?

Ange I hate it.

Lenny What? Me undoing me trousers?

Ange Yeah. It's gross. (*He looks puzzled.*) D'you know what I'm talking about?

Lenny I ain't got a fucking clue.

Ange That's it, innit? You ain't. You don't understand nothing I say 'cause you never listen. (*The door slams.*) Oh, Christ, now I'm for it.

Mark (*from the hallway*) Lock up your daughters, 'cause . . . (*He enters and sees* **Lenny**. *Pause.*) How do.

Lenny Wotcher.

Pause.

Ange 'S Lenny. My husband.

Mark Oh, right. Pleased to meet you. (*They shake.*) Thought perhaps you were a burglar. (*Feeble laugh.*) Mark. I live in the attic. (*Beat.*) Uh . . . I forgot my address book. Had to pop back and get it. (*Beat.*) Upstairs.

He goes.

Lenny Who's that then?

Ange I dunno. I just met him this morning. He's a creep.

Lenny Yeah? Looked a bit glad to see you, didn't he?

Ange How should I know?

Pause.

Lenny Where you kipping, then?

Ange You what? Upstairs.

Lenny Yeah, in the attic?

Ange Bloody hell. You're cracked you are. I only met him this morning.

Lenny So what's he doing here now?

Ange He lives here, for God's sake. And he said, 'forgot his address book,' didn't he?

Lenny What, you think I just stepped off the banana boat?

Ange Wish you'd step off a bloody cliff.

Lenny (*standing*) Ange . . .

Mark *reappears.*

Mark Here we are, then. (*He holds up his address book.*)

Lenny Do us another cup of tea, will you?

Ange *goes to the kitchen.*

Mark That's OK. I haven't got time. (*He puts the book in his case.*) You patching things up?

Lenny What's it to you?

Mark Me? Sod all. (*Pause.*) None of my business, pal. I just live here. Tenant, that's all I am. I don't have any say in who comes in and out. That's all down to Will and Ronee. Well, Ronee.

Lenny She the bint from the Centre?

Mark Yeah. Miss Bra Burner of sixty-eight. Mind you, he's no better. Can't say a bloody word round here without getting your head bitten off. Trendy lefties. About as much fun as a plane crash.

Lenny You can always move.

Mark Do us a favour. NW6, highly des. res.? Twenty-five quid a week? I wouldn't move if we had Brezhnev in the basement. Which, for all I know, we might very well have. (**Ange** *comes back in and gives* **Lenny** *his tea.*) Anyway, I've got to go stake out some woofter pop singer. (*They look confused.*) I'm a journalist.

Lenny Yeah?

Mark God's gift to the gutter press. Don't you believe it. So, I'll see you.

Lenny See you.

Mark *goes.*

Journalist, is he?

Ange That's what he said.

Beat.

Lenny This tea's rotten.

Ange Hard luck.

Lenny Trying to poison me, are you?

Ange If you don't want it . . . (*She goes to take it.*)

Lenny Leave off . . .

Ange If it's so bloody rotten . . . (*He snatches it back from her and spills some.*) Oh, you pig. (*She rushes out. He smiles and slowly starts to pour more on the floor. She comes back with a cloth.*) What you doing?

Lenny It's good for the shag pile.

Ange You bloody pig. (*She goes down on all fours and rubs the carpet.*)

Lenny (*laughing*) Fucking look at you.

Ange What's funny?

Lenny Mrs Fucking Mop. Got you skivvying for them, have they? Doing the dishes?

Ange No. Fuck off. (**Lenny** *laughs again. Pause.*) I'll have to shampoo this . . .

He suddenly goes down on his knees behind her and holds her hips tightly. She freezes.

Lenny You coming home?

Pause.

Ange No.

Blackout.

Scene Three

Monday. 7 p.m.

Bruce *is sitting in one of the chairs. He is gripping a wrist strengthener. A door slams off stage.* **Ronee** *enters and puts her bag on the table.*

Ronee Hello, Bruce. (*He raises his hand and gives a half-smile.*) Where's Will?

Bruce Uh . . . probably, I think . . . In the kitchen, maybe.

Ronee He's not cooking, is he?

Bruce Yeah, well . . . He mentioned . . . something, uh, Chinese.

Ronee Delia Smith, eat your heart out.

Bruce Spare . . . ribs in, uh, black bean sauce. I think.

Ronee Sounds ridiculous enough.

She goes out and upstairs.

Bruce Uh, yeah.

He starts clenching again. **Will** *enters.*

Will Did I hear Ronee?

Bruce Yeah.

Will *goes to the door and shouts upstairs.*

Will Ronee?

Ronee (*off*) What?

Will What are you doing?

Ronee (*off*) Getting changed.

Will Oh, right. D'you want some food?

Ronee (*off*) I've eaten.

Will Ribs in black bean sauce.

Ronee (*off*) I've eaten.

Will OK. Sometimes I think my wife doesn't like my cooking.
Help yourself to a drink, Bruce.

He goes. **Bruce** *goes to the drinks. He pours a vodka, holds the glass up and
downs it in one. He puts the glass down and takes a can of beer. As he sits
and opens it,* **Ronee** *enters, changed, and gets her bag. As she goes she calls
to* **Will** *in the kitchen:*

Ronee Don't wait up for me.

She goes.

Will (*off*) What? (*He appears.*) What?

Bruce Don't wait . . . up for me. She said.

Will Jesus, she could have waited.

Pause.

Bruce Uh . . . Maybe she . . . needs space . . .

Will (*pouring a glass of wine*) Ollie and Martin are late.

Bruce (*looking at his watch*) Six . . . minutes.

Will Yeah. (*Pause. They are not very comfortable together.*) You had any joy with the flat-hunting?

Bruce I saw a . . . flat at the, uh, Oval?

Will Any good?

Bruce Great.

Will Problem settled, then.

Bruce Uh, no.

Will How come?

Bruce Like . . . Uh, it's got three . . . skinheads squatting in it.

Will Ah. Slight problem.

Bruce Right.

Pause.

Will Is it council?

Bruce Yeah.

Will They'll evict them, won't they?

Bruce Well . . . Yeah, but . . . Really heavy . . . Police and everything . . . Lot of hassle . . .

Will I suppose it would be.

Bruce So, uh . . . I guess something'll . . . Come up.

Will Best of luck.

Bruce (*taking some small bottles out of his bag*): Want some . . . Vitamins?

Will No. Thanks. (**Bruce** *takes some.*) Eat healthy food, you don't need them.

Bruce They're just, y'know . . . A boost.

Will Sure.

Bruce And . . . I don't enjoy it, uh, cooking, a lot . . .

Will I love it, I really do. It's a hobby for me and it liberates Ronee.

Bruce Sort of . . . reversal of, uh, roles . . .

Will Yeah, sort of. (*Beat.*) And it's so bloody easy, y'know. Take this thing I'm knocking up now. When I first read the recipe, I thought, Jesus, stroll on, back to the drawing board. But then I made it a couple of times and now, I can do it from memory. Chop the garlic, ginger, onion, soak the black beans, mix it all together with sherry, soya sauce and water, fry the ribs for five minutes, drain off the oil, put in the black bean mixture, stir fry for half a minute, cover and heat for ten minutes, put in cornflour, water and sugar, stir fry very hot, hey presto. No sweet and sour and a number ninety-three to go, please. This is the genuine article.

Pause.

Bruce I, uh . . . can't . . . wait . . .

Will You'll have to, till Ollie and Martin get here, I'm afraid. Help yourself to drink.

He starts to go.

Bruce I'm OK . . . Thanks.

Pause. **Will** *goes.* **Bruce** *goes to the drinks and pours another vodka and downs it in one. The doorbell rings.*

Will (*off*) Get that, will you, Bruce?

Bruce *goes to the door. As soon as he opens it, we can hear* **Oliver** *talking, very fast, very agitated.*

Oliver Hi, Bruce. Sorry I'm late. Fucking Martin. (*They enter.*) He's not here by the remotest bloody chance, is he? No. 'Course he isn't. Where is he? Your guess is as good as mine, mate. That man is a walking bloody disaster area. I haven't seen any trace of him since last night. Lunch today? No show. Help me out on the stall this afternoon so I can go and see the bank manager? No bloody show. Meet at six in the Dragon? Ha. And where is he? Check missing persons. It's your best bet. I need a drink. (*He pours a huge glass of red wine.*) He could be lying headless in the Thames mud for all I know. I mean, I need this, y'know? I really need this.

Will *enters.*

Will, I'm sorry. Fucking Martin. I'd've been here hours ago, except he didn't show up. I've been hanging on.

Will No bother.

Oliver What does he think he's up to? Ask him. If he ever turns up. You ask him. 'Cause he won't tell me. Might as well talk to the trees for all the information I get out of fucking Martin.

Will Calm down, mate. We've got all night.

Oliver But it's not fair, though, is it? I mean it's not fair to me, it's not fair to you. I'm really going to give him a piece of my mind this time. He's completely buggered up my day. (*Beat.*) I know it's negative but I am bloody furious.

Pause.

Bruce Would you . . . like some vitamins?

Oliver Peace of mind, Bruce, that's all I need. A little bit of mental tranquillity is what I'm after.

Will *pours another glass of wine.*

Bruce But apart from that . . . Mrs Lincoln . . . What did you, uh . . .

Oliver Think of the play.

Bruce Think of . . .

Beat.

Oliver It's the way you tell 'em, Bruce.

Slight discomfort.

Will No point starting without Martin, is there, really?

Oliver Will, I don't know if he's still even in the country, let alone anywhere near the vicinity of North West London. Start if you like.

Will Let's give it a few minutes. (*Beat.*) Hey, I might have something quite interesting for us tonight.

Bruce (*to* **Ollie**) Spare ribs . . . in . . .

Will No, not the food.

Bruce Oh.

Will One of the women from the Centre's been staying here. Her husband's been bashing her about. Ronee brought her back last night. You should see her, poor kid.

Oliver That makes my blood boil. What sort of man does that?

Will Anyway, I thought if she was up to it, we could maybe talk to her.

Oliver I don't know . . .

Will I don't mean give her the third degree. I mean talk. Constructively. Positively. Y'know, show support.

Oliver Probably frighten her to death.

Will Well, obviously, if . . .

Bruce It's the husband . . . we should . . . talk to.

Oliver The thing is, Will, we're supposed to be helping ourselves, right? The group is for us to examine ourselves. (*Beat.*) It's pornography tonight. That's what I've come to talk about. Pornography. I've been working on it all week.

Pause.

Will Sure. OK. Pornography it is.

The doorbell rings. **Will** *goes out.* **Ollie** *pours another drink. Voices outside.* **Will** *and* **Martin** *enter.*

The prodigal returns.

Martin Hi, gang. Sorry I'm late. Will, I could severely molest a G and T, if that's OK.

Will Sure. (*He pours it.*)

Martin Didn't start without me, did you?

Will No.

Martin Good. (**Will** *hands him his drink.*) Thanks. Everybody have a good day?

Will So-so.

Martin Bruce? Good day?

Bruce I . . . saw a film.

Martin Good film?

Bruce Uh . . . No.

Beat.

Martin Ollie? Good day? (*Beat.*) Ollie?

Oliver What?

Martin Did you have a good day? (*Silence.*) You do like to keep us guessing, don't you?

Oliver I had a fucking awful day.

Beat.

Martin Uh-huh.

Pause.

Will What about you?

Martin Me? Well, one day's very much the same as another, really, I tend to find. They all sort of merge. I'm never quite sure where one ends and another begins. So today was . . . another day. Didn't exactly register on the Richter scale or anything.

Oliver God . . .

Martin *looks at him. Pause.*

Will I've still got a couple of things to do in the kitchen. Won't be a minute. (*As he goes, he touches **Bruce** on the shoulder.*)

Bruce I want to, uh, see . . . how he does it . . . Chinese . . .

He goes.

Martin My God, how bloody polite. (*Pause.*) OK. Let's have it, Ollie.

Oliver Martin, you've no idea how disappointed, how let down, I feel.

Martin Don't be daft. Of course I have.

Oliver Then how can you . . .? (*Pause.*) What did you do last night?

Martin Oh, I went to a party.

Oliver Whose?

Martin Piers and Molly. You know Piers and . . .

Oliver I don't know Piers and Molly.

Martin I'm sure you do.

Oliver I do not.

Martin I thought you met them at Sandra's that time . . . (*Pause.*) Maybe not.

Oliver No.

Martin I'll invite them round. You'd love Molly, she's a scream.

Oliver Where?

Martin Where is she a scream?

Oliver Where was the party?

Martin Oh. At Piers and Molly's.

Oliver Which is where?

Pause.

Martin Let me get this right. You're asking me these absurd questions because you think what?

Oliver Where were you?

Martin Because you think I was . . . What?

Oliver Where?

Martin I was what?

Oliver Screwing around!

Pause. **Martin** *starts to laugh. He gets up and looks round the room.*

Martin (*opening a cupboard*) No. No one there. (*He looks under the sofa.*) No. The room is empty. Apart from us. (*Beat.*) So. Who's it for? Who are you trying to kid?

Oliver You were going to look after the stall this afternoon.

Martin (*genuine*) Ah, I forgot. Honest.

Oliver Why?

Martin I don't know. (*Beat.*) I'm sorry.

Oliver Martin, believe me, you tear me apart sometimes. (*Pause.*) D'you know what I'm saying?

Martin Yes.

Oliver We've both made a commitment. We've both got to keep it up.

Martin I really did forget. (*Pause.*) So, did you get to the bank?

Oliver How could I?

Pause.

Martin I'll do the stall all day tomorrow. How's that?

Oliver It's something.

Martin Take the day off. Have fun or something.

Oliver Yeah.

Martin Look, don't let's fight.

Oliver OK.

Pause.

Martin Perhaps I ought to let Will and Bruce know we're . . .

Oliver I'll do it. (*He starts to go.*) I need you, mate.

Martin I need you too.

Ollie *goes.* **Martin** *breathes out loudly and gets another drink as* **Bruce** *comes in. They look at each other. Pause.*

All sorted out.

Bruce *nods. He goes to the drinks, pours a vodka and drinks it down in one.* **Martin** *smiles. They look at each other.* **Martin** *throws a glance at the door and turns back. They kiss.* **Bruce** *sits down as* **Will** *and* **Ollie** *come back in.*

Will . . . No, light soya sauce you use more with fish or chicken. In South East Asian food, mainly.

Oliver Oh, I see.

Will Talking of which, did you get to that Malayan place I told you about?

Martin No, not yet.

Will Well, don't forget. You'll thank me.

Martin We could try it tomorrow, couldn't we, Ollie?

Oliver Yeah, why not?

They all settle.

Will OK. Why don't we get started?

Oliver Whose turn is it to chair?

Will (*setting up the tape recorder*) I did it last week.

Oliver So . . . alphabetically . . . It's Bruce's turn.

Martin Will – by the way, how's Ronee?

Will Busy. Very busy.

Martin She's an amazing lady.

Will I know.

Oliver I believe we covered the use of the word 'lady' in our first meeting, didn't we?

Martin Deliberate irony, Ollie.

Oliver Sloppy consciousness, Martin. Very sloppy.

Martin I know. 'Chick, bint, skirt, tart, crumpet, tail, little woman, wifey, bit of stuff'. These words will never again pass my lips.

Oliver Or 'lady'.

Martin You really are becoming a little commissar, you know that?

Oliver It's important. It's what this is all about. What's the point of changing the way we behave if we don't change the way we speak? Y'know?

Martin Right on.

Beat.

Will Tape's running. OK, Bruce.

Bruce Right, Uh . . . Pornography. Shall we . . . do it as normal . . . ?

Martin Beg your pardon?

Bruce I mean . . . Like we . . . Someone start off and . . . Y'know . . .

Oliver I think we should start by talking about our experience of pornography. As men. Be honest about it. OK?

Martin Off you go, Ollie.

Beat.

Oliver OK. I've used pornography. In the past. I'm ashamed to say it, but it's true.

Will Why are you ashamed to say it?

Oliver Because I feel I've exploited fellow human beings. Namely, women. Merely to satisfy selfish male desires. And, I mean, it doesn't stop there does it? Once you've seen one picture of a woman offering herself to you, that's it. The mind automatically makes the connection: all women are like that. Because it appeals to immaturity. We've all got that bit of us that's still four years old, the bit that made us fumble around in bushes and school toilets, finding out what bodies were like. That's the bit of us that's brought into play when we use pornography.

Martin That's the bit of you that's brought into play.

Oliver OK. So, I'm generalising. But isn't it true?

Will I think we should define what we mean by pornography, and what we mean by 'using' pornography.

Oliver All right. I've got us off on the wrong foot.

Martin Again.

Oliver OK. I apologise.

Bruce Doesn't matter.

Will So. Definitions.

Oliver Well, I agree with the feminist argument that all pornography is based on violence against women.

Will Even 'Zipper'?

Oliver Gay porn, obviously, is different. Maybe we can discuss that separately.

Martin Separatism, so soon?

Oliver Try and keep it serious, please, Martin.

Will Look, there are many different types of porn. There's straightforward *Mayfair* crotch shots, there's the gynaecological crotch shot. There's spanking, bondage, SM, TV, lesbianism . . .

Oliver For a male audience . . .

Will Agreed. There's straight couples, groups, animals, paedophiles. All catering to different people, to different needs. So. Do we lump them all together, and say they're all based on violence against women? Or do we try to understand if and how they differ, in content and function? And then explain if and how they may be relevant to our own lives.

Beat.

Oliver Are we supposed to sit here and discuss each variant in sordid bloody detail?

Bruce Well . . . yes . . .

Will *gets up and takes a carrier bag from the cupboard.*

Will They're all in there. I bought a selection.

Oliver God's sake, Will . . .

Will Why not? If we're going to discuss it, we might as well know what we're talking about.

Oliver We do know . . .

Will And most important, if we're going to try to influence other people's rights to use porn, then we most definitely have to know. Otherwise we're just Mary Whitehouse. We must argue from experience, not prejudice.

Pause.

Oliver I find them offensive.

Will So do I. Some of them.

Oliver Then why do we have to look at something we know we find offensive?

Will Some of them, I said. (*Beat.*) I'll get the food on.

He switches off the tape and goes.

Oliver Do you two go along with this?

Martin Why not?

Bruce Sure.

Oliver Bloody absurd. I don't need to look at these.

Martin Seen it all before, eh?

Oliver Piss off.

Martin You're embarrassed, aren't you?

Oliver No.

Martin You can't fool me. (*He looks through the bag.*) Oh . . . My
. . . God. He really went to town on this one. What d'you fancy,
Ollie? 'Burning Butt' or 'Hot Ass Nurses'?

Oliver (*more to himself*) Lose all sense of dignity. Self respect.
Those things, they cheapen your soul.

Martin Do wonders for your other bits, though.

Oliver Fuck off!

He goes out. **Martin** *is a bit shaken by* **Oliver**'*s reaction.*

Martin He's got a stash at the flat y'know. He thinks I don't
know. Keeps them at the bottom of a suitcase. (*Beat.*) How do I
know? I went through his things.

Bruce What's he . . . into?

Martin Copulating couples. (*He laughs. Pause.*) You know what I
don't like about Ollie? He has 'Him' and 'Zipper' on the
bookshelf, and he hides the het sex at the bottom of an old
suitcase.

Ollie *comes back in.*

OK? Not hyperventilating, or anything?

Oliver (*mock cheerful*) No, no. Just took a deep breath and counted
to ten. Works every time. Now then. (*He takes out a magazine.*)
'Lesbian Lasses.' (*He flicks through it.*) Uh huh. Women pretending
to cavort together for the benefit of the male viewer. Uh huh.
(*Beat. He holds it up for them to see.*) What's missing?

Martin Sorry?

Oliver What all-important object is missing from that picture?

Beat.

Martin Dunno. Toothbrush? (*He and* **Bruce** *laugh.*)

Oliver No. (*Beat.*) Can't spot it? (*Beat.*) The phallus. That's
what's missing. Women forced into a faked impersonation of
male/female sex. Forced into behaving like men. Two women,
and it's all about penetration. All it lacks is the phallus. Which is
what the male reader supplies.

The door opens. **Ange**, *her lip now cut and swollen, comes in.* **Ollie** *is still
holding the magazine up.*

Jesus . . . (*He puts it in the bag.*) I'm sorry, I wasn't . . .

Ange I was upstairs . . .

Beat.

Oliver Yeah. (*He goes to the door.*) Will? You got a minute?

They look at her. **Will** *appears.*

Will Oh, Ange, hello . . . (*He sees her face.*) Bloody hell. Sit down, c'mon. (*He sits her down.*) When did you do that?

Ange I . . . didn't do it.

Will Your husband, was it? Ange? Was it your husband?

Ange Lenny done it.

Will Here? He came here?

Ange He came round . . . It was his dinner hour . . .

Oliver For Christ's sake, he comes round in his dinner hour to beat his wife up.

Will Yeah, OK, Ollie. Ange, is there something I can get you? That's a nasty cut.

Ange And he . . .

Will What?

Ange After . . .

Will After what?

Ange After he hit me . . . He . . .

Will What did he do after he hit you?

Beat.

Bruce D'you think . . . Maybe he . . . raped her . . . or something?

Oliver No, dear God . . .

Will Is that it, Ange? Did he? Did he rape you? (*She breaks down.*) Someone get a brandy, will you? (**Oliver** *does.*) Here, drink some of this.

Oliver Should be bloody castrated.

Will Someone ring the centre, tell Ronee. Number's by the phone. (**Oliver** *goes to the phone and dials.*)

Oliver We can report him, y'know. To the pigs. Get her seen by a doctor. They can put him away.

Will (*to* **Ange**) Have you been upstairs all this time? Have you? (*She nods.*) You should have come down, you daft kid.

Ange I's frightened.

Will No need to be frightened of us.

Oliver (*into the phone*) Hello, Johnson Place? (*Beat.*) Yeah, can I speak to Ronee? (*Beat.*) Thanks. (*To* **Will**.) They're getting her. (*Beat.*) Hello? Ronee? It's Oliver. From the men's group. I'm at your house. Look, I think you'd better come home. The girl who's staying here –

Will Ange.

Oliver Yeah, Ange. Her husband's beaten her up again, and we think he might have raped her. (*Beat.*) She's in a terrible state, we don't know for sure. (*Beat.*) OK. Good. (*He puts the phone down.*) She's coming straight back.

Will Ronee'll be here soon, Ange. You're going to be all right. (*Beat.*) Oh fuck.

Martin What's the matter?

Will The ribs. They'll be bloody ruined. (*He goes out.*)

Oliver (*next to* **Ange**) It's OK. You'll be OK. (*She pulls away.*) We're your friends. (*She pulls away.*) No one's going to hurt you.

Ange Leave me alone.

Oliver Hey, c'mon. We're friends of Will's.

Martin Ollie . . .

Oliver We can help.

Ange Leave me alone.

Oliver Please.

Martin Ollie.

Oliver What, for Christ's sake?!

Bruce *puts his hand on* **Ollie**'s *shoulder.*

Bruce Best, maybe, leave her alone.

Martin C'mon, Ollie.

Ollie *pulls violently away from* **Bruce**.

Oliver All right, all right.

Will *comes back in.*

Will Food's fucked. Sorry.

Bruce 'S OK.

Martin Look, why don't we go?

Bruce Yeah . . .

Will I think it's best. Sorry and all that . . .

Martin Oh, come on. This is more important than our meeting. (*Pause.*) Ollie?

Oliver Yeah.

They get their things.

Will I'll call you tomorrow, work out another time.

Oliver (*indicating the magazines*) Burn those bastard things, Will.

Beat. They go.

Will (*to* **Ange***, who has curled up*) 'S OK, mate. Ronee won't be long. (*Beat.*) What d'you want to do? Have a sleep? (*She nods.*) I'll cover you up.

He puts his jacket over her and sits down. She closes her eyes. He goes and gets a drink and sits again.

Ange?

She seems asleep. He takes out one of the magazines and sits facing away from her. She opens her eyes and looks at him.

Fade.

Scene Four

Monday evening, 11 p.m.
Will *is sitting in the same chair reading* Mastering the Art of French Cooking. **Ronee** *comes in and pours two drinks. She takes one and goes out.*
Will *carries on reading. She comes back, takes the other drink and sits down.*
Will *puts the book down and looks at her. She's very tense.*

Will Well?

Beat. **Ronee** *doesn't seem able to say what she wants to say.*

Ronee Sod it. There are times . . . (*Beat.*) Yes. He did. And you don't have to be a doctor to see it. 'Injuries consistent with forceful sexual intercourse' is how they describe it in court. (*Beat*.) And she won't do anything about it. She won't report him.

Will For crying out loud . . .

Ronee I know. But she's scared to death of him. And who wouldn't be?

Pause.

Will How is she now?

Ronee She keeps waking up. That's the worst thing. It keeps coming back, apparently. (*Beat*.) It's a bloody good job Andrea's here. She knows all about it. From personal experience. (*Pause*.) She's staying tonight. (*Pause*.) You don't mind sleeping down here, do you?

Will No. (*Meaning yes*.)

Pause.

Ronee (*after a nervous laugh*) I just don't know if Ange could handle it. If she woke up. And saw a man . . .

Will It's OK. It really is.

Pause.

Ronee All in all, this has been a bastard day. Two kids had a fight at the Centre. Girls. Using those Afro combs, y'know. (*Beat*.) I tell you, I despair sometimes.

Will Don't.

Ronee I'm tired. That's all.

Will You sure?

Ronee What d'you mean?

Beat.

Will Are you *just* tired?

Ronee I don't understand.

Will Neither do I. (*Beat*.) Sorry. I didn't mean to lay that on you.

Ronee Forget it. (*Pause*.) I know I've been a bit . . . distant lately. I can't help it. Work and everything . . .

Will And Andrea . . .

Ronee Yes. And Andrea. (*Pause.*) Don't forget you encouraged me. It was actually your idea.

Will It wasn't my idea that you'd have a completely independent affair.

Ronee No, what you wanted was a happy little set-up where you got your kicks whenever you felt like it, without any involvement. And I can't do that. I have to invest a piece of *me* in people I sleep with. I can't just do it and – I dunno – tape record it and play it back. I'm not that detached.

Will I wanted to try something a bit radical. I'm sorry you couldn't handle it.

Ronee There's nothing radical about a harem.

Will Bullshit, Ronee. That's not what I wanted. I wanted to try other ways of keeping a relationship alive.

Ronee Our relationship wasn't dead.

Will And it is now?

Ronee I don't know. (*Beat.*) You're forever meddling with people. You're never content just to be, and let other people be. You have to keep fiddling about, trying new things. And it doesn't work.

Pause.

Will And your little lesbian affair isn't 'fiddling about'? That works, does it?

Ronee Don't say 'little lesbian affair' like that. You were happy enough when we let you in. And yes, it does work. Now that you're not involved, it works. Like a dream.

Pause.

Will This is political lesbianism we're talking about, isn't it? It's nothing to do with sex. You'd prefer to keep sex right out of it. Because sex can be dangerous. You can't always control it. Sometimes it turns wild on you. And you don't go too near things you don't understand, do you? 'O Lord, spare us the unpredictable.' That's your prayer.

Ronee Unpredictable? You? You inflict a few dippy ideas on me and Andrea, a few dusty clichés you've got hanging around from the sixties and that's supposed to indicate a wild, dangerous nature, is it? You: a progressive free spirit? (*Beat.*) Well, the reason we exclude you is that it had become a cliché. There's nothing wild or dangerous about a live sex show, although you might disagree. And that's all we were. You put your penny in the slot, and we'd perform. For you. For your entertainment. We got absolutely nothing from it, except the growing realisation that if you weren't there, then there was maybe something we could find together. For ourselves. Just ourselves. (*Beat.*) You're right. It was unpredictable. It was dangerous. For you. (*Pause.*) You wanted cheap thrills, and you got 'em. But you paid. (*A door slams.*) I'm very tired, Will. I'm sorry.

Mark *puts his head round the door.*

Mark Yo. All right if I come in?

Will Yeah, I want to have a word.

Mark (*coming in*) Christ, have I had a day. I finally collared this fella, this singer, and I said, 'Given that you've denied in print that you're a screaming woofter, how d'you account for the little Filipino back-door boy you've had in your trendy mews flat all night?' And he says 'Are you pulling my plonker! I don't know what you're on about.' At which point, said Filipino bum-bandit tries to make it away out the back. Well, immortalised forever by the process of photographic impression, isn't he? So, man with the golden tonsils cracks up, rings his manager and agrees to exclusive interview in which he admits that he may just have indulged in some male willy-stretching in the dim and murky past, but that's all behind him, 'scuse the pun. And anyway he's thinking of becoming a Christian. (*Beat.*) Mission accomplished. Am I a reptile, or what?

Ronee You're disgusting.

Mark (*smiling*) Mmm. (*Pause. To* **Will**.) Hey, ask me how many feminists it takes to screw in a lightbulb. Go on. Ask me.

Will Get lost, Mark.

Mark Come on. How many feminists does it take? Ask me.

Beat.

Will (*reluctantly*) How many feminists does it take to screw in a . . .

Mark (*mock strident, pointing his finger*) That's not funny! (*He laughs.*) Heard that one today.

Will *stands.*

Will (*to* **Ronee**) I'm going for a walk. Get some chips. You can tell him . . .

Ronee Yeah.

Will *goes*.

Mark Just you and me, eh? Cosy.

Ronee Shut your sexist trap for two seconds, will you?

Mark I love it when you talk dirty.

Ronee Like banging your head against a brick wall . . .

Mark I'm not fussy. Brick wall, chandelier, wardrobe, you name it, I'll bang against it.

Ronee Stop! While I talk to you, I'll be brief. I won't overtax your powers of concentration, I promise. I just want your undivided attention for two seconds, OK?

Mark What are you doing for the rest of your life?

Ronee OK?

Mark Fixed up for breakfast, are you? (*Pause.*) All right.

Beat.

Ronee Did you meet Ange? She stayed last night.

Mark Told you, has she?

Ronee Told me what?

Mark That she finds me irresistible.

Ronee You've met her, then?

Mark I should cocoa. Blood pressure's been up all day. Amongst other things.

Ronee Sometime today her husband came round and . . .

Mark Yeah, I met him.

Ronee When?

Mark Lunchtime. I came back for my address book. Seemed a nice enough fella.

Ronee What was he doing?

Mark Er . . . having a cup of tea.

Beat.

Ronee Well, I presume after you'd gone your nice enough fella beat up and raped his wife.

Mark Get away.

Beat.

Ronee Bloody hell, you're sympathetic . . . Anyway, the thing is, she's in a dreadful state, so: one, be as quiet as you can, and two, don't give her any of your hilarious scatalogical badinage. Cut the sexist crap, all right?

Beat.

Mark Never entered your head, has it, that all this linguistic and ideological purity – don't forget I've got a degree too – is just a little bit arrogant?

Ronee If you weren't so crass I wouldn't have to keep telling you.

Mark And if you didn't keep telling me, then maybe I wouldn't be so crass. (*Beat.*) Think about it.

Beat.

Ronee I've got someone else staying the night, too. A friend of mine. Pinch her bum and she's likely to cut your throat. You think about that.

Mark I don't pinch bums. I admire them.

Ronee Whatever.

Pause. She gets blankets and a pillow from the cupboard and spreads them on the sofa.

Mark Well, really, I'm not that kind of boy. (*No response.*) You wind yourself up any tighter, you're going to snap. (*Beat.*) G'night. And don't forget to leave that window open . . .

He laughs and goes. She takes a deep breath and finishes making up the bed. Then switches out the main light. As she's about to go, the doorbell rings.

Ronee Why didn't you take your keys . . . ?

She goes. We hear talking and suddenly **Lenny** *appears with* **Ronee** *following. He's totally legless.*

Lenny Where you got her? Eh?

Ronee I said out! Now!

Lenny Upstairs, is she? With that bloke? That cunt?

She shuts the door.

Ronee If you go out of this room, it's to go out the front door, OK?

Lenny Listen, you fucking cow, I wanna see Ange.

Ronee You can't. She's not here.

Lenny Fuck off.

Ronee She's where you put her. In the hospital.

Lenny What you talking about? Get fucked. I wanna see my wife. (*Pause. He sees the drinks and takes a bottle of gin and swigs from it.*)

Ronee You've had enough to drink.

Lenny I've only had eleven fucking pints. (*He takes a huge swig. As he drinks, we see him quickly become less and less capable.*)

Ronee If you don't go, I'm calling the police.

Lenny Fucking try it.

Ronee I'm warning you.

Lenny Shove it up your middle class fucking arsehole, fucking bitch. (*He takes a huge swig, then takes a bottle of scotch and drinks from that. He takes his poem out of his pocket.*) Hey, listen. This is what I wrote. Didn't think I could fucking write, did you? Well I can. Listen. 'When I look up at the sky / And the clouds are floating by / I think about you / And the things you do. When the sun comes out / It makes me want to shout / Your name out loud / To the passing crowd. When it starts to rain / I can feel the pain / That's going to come / Now that you're gone.' Yeah. I fucking wrote that.

Ronee Yeah. Very nice . . .

Lenny But I've written another one. 'Cause I reckon that one's fucking stupid. This one's better. (*He reads.*) 'When I get my hands on you / I'm gonna put my fingers round your throat / And squeeze till you go blue. I'm gonna write on your face / With a razor blade / I'm Lenny and I love you. I'm gonna slice your tits / And slash your fanny / And cut your tongue out too. I'm gonna drop you in the river / With your head cut off / And a note saying I love you.'

He takes a swig and stands staring at the floor, completely preoccupied.
Ronee *goes to the phone and picks it up. He moves towards her, and, as she*

puts the phone down, raises his arm to give her a backhander. As his arm comes down, she blocks it karate style and hits him hard in the stomach. He drops, retching, throws up and passes out. Door slams. **Will** *enters, puts the light on, and sees them. He's eating a bag of chips.*

Ronee Will, Lenny. Lenny, Will.

Beat.

Will Hello, Lenny.

Beat.

Ronee Passed out.

Will Mmm. (*Beat.*) Fancy a chip?

Blackout.

Act Two

Scene One

Monday morning, 10 a.m.

A week later. **Ange** *is lying on the sofa.* **Mark** *is at the table reading the paper, eating toast and drinking coffee. They're ignoring each other.* **Ronee** *enters.*

Ronee What bright spark left the hot tap running in the bathroom?

Mark *looks at her then at* **Ange**.

Ange . . .

Ange What?

Ronee Love, try to get it together, will you? Please?

Ange I never left it on.

Ronee Taps don't turn themselves on.

Ange I never.

Ronee OK . . .

Mark *stands with his cup.*

Mark Round the bloody twist.

He goes.

Ronee You going to make it to the Centre today?

Ange Dunno.

Ronee I wish you'd try. (*Pause.*) I'll wait if you want to come now. (**Ange** *shakes her head.*) Look, we'll have a talk. You can't go on like this.

Ange I have talked.

Ronee I know.

Ange Fed up with talking.

Ronee It's for your own good. (*Beat.*) You've got to get back into it. You can't stay here indefinitely.

Ange Why not?

Beat.

Ronee Look, Will and I are having some problems. We need to sort ourselves out. And it's not very easy . . . Y'know.

Ange 'Cause of me.

Ronee No, not because of you.

Ange What about Andrea?

Ronee What do you mean?

Mark *enters with a cup of coffee.*

We'll talk about it later. See you.

She goes.

Mark Give me half an hour, I could sort all your problems out. (*Pause.*) Milking it a bit, don't you think? (*Pause.*) You like it here. I can tell. I wonder why? (*He goes over to her.*) What are you after?

Ange Nothing.

Mark Think I'm stupid, do you?

Ange Yeah.

Mark Be making a silly mistake, you go around thinking that. (*Pause.*) Why don't you come out for a drink with me. (*Beat.*) Take you somewhere a bit classy. Wine bar. Cocktail bar. You'd like that. (*Pause.*) No? (*Pause.*) You've got a fantastic body. (*Beat.*) Look at me. (*She does.*) I mean . . . You could do worse.

Ange You reckon?

Mark Much worse. See I'm not the sort of fella who fiddles about with little girls' minds.

Ange No, I know what you fiddle about with.

Mark I'm good at it, too.

Ange I'll bet.

Pause.

Mark So. Try it?

Ange Up yours.

Mark You should be so lucky. (*Pause. He gets up and goes back to the table.*) I might start exercising my tenants' rights, y'know. You're not exactly my idea of a positive addition to the household, if you know what I mean. I might have to complain.

Ange All the bloody same, ain't you?

Mark Yeah. Deep down. I suppose we are.

Will *enters in his dressing-gown.*

Will Morning.

Mark Morning.

Ange Hello, Will.

Will Ange.

Beat.

Mark Here, media joke. You'll like this one, it's about your lot. How many feminists does it take . . .

Will You've told me.

Mark It's a new one. How many feminists does it take to screw in a lightbulb?

Will I don't know.

Mark Thirty-six. One to screw in the lightbulb and thirty-five to make a documentary of it for Channel Four.

Will That's not funny.

Mark Loosen up, pal.

Ange *gets up.*

Ange D'you want some tea, Will?

Will Thanks.

Mark Do us some coffee.

Ange You know where the kitchen is.

She goes.

Mark Obviously, I don't have your charisma.

Will Obviously.

Pause.

Mark Being a bit naughty, aren't we?

Will Who is?

Beat.

Mark You given her one yet?

Will What are you talking about?

Mark Simple question.

Will From a simple mind. You've got to reduce everything, haven't you? Drag it all down to the gutter. Well, for your information, Ange has been through a pretty rotten experience, and what she needs is support. That's the only thing I've given her. Support. Human warmth. A couple of things you know nothing about.

Mark I know about quite a few things. You'd be surprised.

Will Such as?

Pause.

Mark She's using you as much as you're using her.

Beat.

Will You're a walking insult, you know that? It's not just progressive ideas you can't cope with, it's basic human relationships as well. Just because you think with your prick, you imagine we all do. (*Beat.*) It must be a pretty weird experience, seeing, feeling everything from only that high above the ground. (*He gestures at groin level.*) I'll tell you what, you should trade in that nice company Volvo you drive. You'd be happier swinging through the trees.

Mark Nice one.

Will Well, wouldn't you?

Mark Bollocks. You know your trouble? You can't change your socks without pretending you're changing the world.

Will You just don't understand, do you?

Mark Don't be so piss-arrogant.

Will Don't be so thick.

Ange *comes in with a cup of tea and gives it to* **Will**.

Ange Here y'are.

Will Thanks.

Mark *gets his jacket and case.*

Mark You'll be late for work.

Will Got the morning off.

Mark Yeah. Figures.

He laughs and goes.

Will Has he been giving you a hard time?

Ange Not really.

Will Tell me if he does.

Ange Yeah. (*Beat.*) He said I had a fantastic body.

Will I'm sorry. Look, if he does it again . . .

Ange 'S OK. I don't mind.

Will You should do. Fantastic body. Christ, that's all he can see, isn't it?

Ange Don't worry about it.

Will I can't help it. I just do. (*Pause.*) It just seems to me sometimes, that all that's required is the tiniest amount of thought. If we all, suddenly, one day said, 'Yeah, OK, I'll try it.' All at once. Then . . . And it could happen. It would happen. (*Pause.*) Not like me to be optimistic first thing in the morning. I'd better see a doctor. (*She smiles.*) That's better.

Ange You're funny.

Will I'm not quite sure how to take that.

Ange You think about everything all the time. I never know what you're gonna say next.

Will Me neither.

Ange That's not true. You got an answer for everything.

Will If only. (*Pause.*) Ange. D'you think of me as old?

Ange You what?

Will Do I seem . . . a lot older, to you?

Ange Never thought about it.

Pause.

Will I was in grammar school, fourteen, studying for O-levels the day you were born. All acne and pubertal angst.

Ange Sounds filthy.

Will It probably was.

Pause.

Ange You're only as young as you feel. That's what they say, isn't it?

Will Is it?

Ange Yeah.

Will Well, then . . .

Ange How old do you feel? (*Beat.*)

Will Eighteen . . . Eighty . . . It varies.

Ange Stick with eighteen if I was you.

Will What, never grow up?

Ange No, never.

Will I'll think about it.

Ange No, don't think about it. Just do it.

Pause.

Will You didn't answer my question.

Ange Which one?

Will D'you think I'm old?

Ange I don't think about it.

Will Very diplomatic.

Ange I don't.

Beat.

Will 'Course, the main danger in feeling old, is that you start getting boring about it. Let me know if I'm boring you.

Ange You're not.

Will And you don't have to be polite.

Ange Wouldn't know how.

Will You're not daft.

Ange Ain't got no O-levels.

Will Some of the daftest people I know are graduates. Including me.

Ange Well *you* ain't daft.

Will No?

Ange 'Course not.

Will Shows how little you know me. (*The doorbell rings.*) Who the bloody hell's that?

He goes to the door. We hear muffled voices. **Oliver** *comes in followed by* **Will**.

Oliver I rang your office. They said you wouldn't be in today. Hope you don't mind.

Will No.

Oliver Hi, Ange.

Ange Wotcher.

Will You look bloody terrible, mate.

Oliver I've been up all night.

Will Problems?

Oliver Since when did I have anything else?

Will Martin?

Oliver Oh, yes. Very much. Martin.

Ange Shall I do some tea?

Will Great idea. Ta.

Oliver Coffee for me.

She goes.

I'm sorry, Will. I just don't know who to turn to.

Will Come on, it's OK. (*Beat.*) So what's happening?

Oliver Jesus, where do I start. (*Beat.*) Basically, I haven't seen him for two days. See, I gave him a sort of ultimatum. Yeah. I know. Pretty naff, right? Standing there in my curlers, with the rolling pin. Not exactly progressive, I know. But. Like. I had to do something. I mean, we're falling apart. Our so-called relationship is just about ready for the knacker's yard.

Will It happens.

Oliver Sure, it happens. Happens all the time. All over the world. (*Pause.*) Will, *why?*

Long pause.

Will Lots of reasons, Ollie. Depends on the people.

Pause.

Oliver When my ex-wife left me, I said, right, that's it. I am never again going to get myself stung like that. Never. I don't care what it takes. I'll never again put myself in a position where one person can single-handedly dismantle my life. Y'know? (*Beat.*) You build it up, slowly . . . (*Beat.*) Like the business . . . I mean, I've put everything into that stall. Even started thinking about getting premises. A shop. Yeah. A shop. Hip capitalism. Well, I haven't made or sold a thing all week. I can't. It's just collapsing. I'm paralysed. (*Pause.*) Martin. I thought, it'll never turn out like it did with Marie, my ex-wife. I won't let it. This is different. Martin's a guy, for chrissakes. He won't do that to me. (*Pause.*) Will. We don't have sex. I know we pretend . . . I mean, it's not that we don't want to, it's just . . . It's another complication. And Martin knew that. The ad I put in Time Out, it said, 'Guy wants guy for friendship.' That's all. All. Christ, isn't it enough? Doesn't anybody want to be friends in this world any more?

Pause.

Will Ollie . . . Maybe Martin didn't like the pretence.

Oliver Maybe Martin just wanted to get his rotten little end away. Maybe Martin doesn't give a damn if he fucks our relationship up. (*Pause.*) And maybe Martin didn't like the pretence. Shit. Pretence? Let's not kid ourselves. Lies, Will. What it boils down to. Lies.

Ange *comes in with tea and coffee on a tray and puts it down.*

Ange I'll . . .

Will Yeah.

Oliver Thanks. For the coffee.

Ange 'S OK.

She goes.

Oliver I've realised it too late, haven't I?

Will Maybe.

Oliver Why do I find it so hard to admit the truth? Marie once said to me that, when I died, I'd refuse to lie down and admit it. Why do I find it so hard?

Will We all do, don't we?

Oliver Do you? Even you?

Pause.

Will Yes. (*Pause.*) Look . . . Don't despair. (*Pause.*) Sorry. That's all I can say. If Martin's gone for good, then you'll have to adjust.

Oliver Have you ever been lonely, Will?

Will Yeah . . .

Oliver I mean . . . *Lonely. Alone.* (*Beat.*) I've gone days without talking to another person. Whole days of drinking coffee, pretending to work, drinking a bottle of scotch. All in total silence. God, I hate silence. (*Beat.*) One of the things . . . About Martin: he talks a lot. I like that. I always dry his hair for him when he's had a shower. And we babble. Nothing in particular, y'know. Chat about the weather. You've got split ends, that's a nice shirt . . . (*Pause.*) Sorry. (*Pause.*) It's why I hate the country. The silence. It frightens me. (*Beat.*) Have you ever tried listening to the radio? When you're alone?

Will Sure.

Oliver I don't really mean *when* you're alone, I mean *because* you're alone. Anything to fill the gap. I always do it. And it makes it worse. Well-bred voice, sort of hanging in the middle of the room. I look at the radio, and I think, there's nobody fucking there. (*Pause.*) I remember a rainy afternoon. My mother doing the ironing. The smell of clean shirts. And the radio on.

Pause.

Will He might come back.

Oliver Don't know if I want him back. (*Beat.*) Of course I bloody want him back. He's all I've got.

Will Have you tried to find him?

Oliver Where? I don't know any of his friends. I wouldn't know where to start. I just have to sit and wait.

Will I'd offer to let you stay here, but . . .

Oliver No, no. I want to be there if he comes back.

Will And if he doesn't?

Oliver I suppose I'll just . . . be there.

Pause.

Will You're still coming round tonight, aren't you?

Oliver Yeah. He might turn up.

Will That's what I was thinking. Look on the bright side.

Oliver Yeah. (*Beat.*) Will. You're a good man. Thanks.

Will Any time.

Oliver Say goodbye to Ange for me.

Will Will do.

Oliver See myself out.

He goes. **Ange** *comes in.*

Ange Funny little bloke, inne?

Beat.

Will Yeah. Funny little bloke. (*Beat.*) I don't know what it is, but something about him . . . makes me very angry.

Ange Why?

Will I wish I knew.

Pause.

Ange Have you had some breakfast?

Will Angela. Stop doing things for me.

Ange Have you?

Will Had some muesli when I got up.

Ange Rabbit food. You'll turn into a rabbit. He's like a rabbit. Or a mouse. (*Pause.*) Lenny always has a cooked breakfast. Bacon, sausage, fried slice. And he covers it in HP sauce. Then he goes out. And all day there's this smell . . . Grease . . . all round the flat. I open the windows, keep washing my face, but it just stays there. All day. (*Pause.*) Why ain't you at work then?

Will Basically, I'm skiving.

Ange You'll get the sack.

Will But I'm pretending I'm working. Nobody knows.

Pause.

Ange What you gonna do all day then?

Will Lounge around. Read a book. I dunno. Have a think.

Beat.

Ange You and Ronee . . .

Will What?

Beat.

Ange You having a barney?

Will We don't have barneys. We have orgies of socio-political truth-telling.

Ange Maybe you should have a barney.

Will Maybe you're right.

Pause.

Ange She must be mad . . .

Will Why?

Ange Bloke like you. One in a million. (**Will** *laughs*.) What's funny?

Will I'm not very different.

Ange I think you are.

Will Well, thank you very much.

Ange Don't muck about. I do.

Beat.

Will If only you knew.

Ange What?

Will What a . . . mucky sort of person I am. You'd find I'm the same as anyone else. Worse.

Ange No.

Will *sits and plays with the backgammon set open on the table.*

D'you want a game?

Will Didn't know you played.

Ange Ronee showed me. Not very good though.

Will OK. I'll give you a thrashing.

Ange You good at this, are you?

Will Pretty good. Used to be the strip backgammon king of Sussex University. That's the smutty version. If one of your counters gets taken off, you take off an article of clothing.

Ange Like strip poker.

Will Yeah. Anyway throw for start. (*They throw.*) You go first. (*She throws and moves. He throws and moves. She throws again.*) Oh dear.

She moves two counters, both uncovered. He throws and smiles.

Sorry about that.

He takes one of her counters off. Pause.

Ange We playing the smutty version?

Will If you like.

Blackout.

Scene Two

Monday evening, 6.30 p.m.

Ange *is polishing the table, singing to herself.* **Ronee** *enters, sees her and smiles.*

Ronee Well.

Ange (*very cheery*) Hi.

Ronee What are *you* on?

Ange Come again?

Ronee You been at the gin?

Ange Don't drink. You know that.

Ronee First time I've seen you smile in days.

Ange Not against the law, is it?

Ronee No. Definitely not.

Pause.

Ange I've cleaned upstairs and the kitchen.

Ronee Thanks. You don't have to, y'know.

Ange I wanted to.

Ronee Fine by me. (*Beat.*) God, I think I'll have a drink. (*She pours a sherry.*) Had a finance committee meeting this afternoon. Council want to cut our grant. Not a lot. Just enough. Enough to make running the place an even bigger headache. I've got to try and decide which is more important: amplifier for the music workshop, or a new ping pong table. And they call this creative administration. Pretty soon, y'know, the only activities we'll be putting on will be benefits. Save the Centre. Rock for a new ping pong table. That kind of thing.

Ange Councils are stupid. Trouble we had getting our flat. Like the football league, Lenny said. We never had enough points. When the bloke came round, Lenny asked him if we was gonna get relegated to the second division. The bloke laughed and said, far as the council's concerned, we're division four. Yeah. What a pig.

Ronee It's not their fault. Well, not all of them. The orders came from on high. I vos only oabyink orders, jawohl. (**Ange** *laughs.*) Shall we have that talk now?

Pause.

Ange If you like.

Ronee Come and sit down. (**Ange** *sits next to her on the sofa.*) Right.

Ange 'S like being back at school.

Ronee Hey, do me a favour.

Ange Sorry.

Beat.

Ronee First, what are you going to do about Lenny?

Ange Dunno. Shoot him?

Ronee An attractive, if impractical, suggestion. No. Are you intending to go back to him?

Ange You gotta be joking.

Ronee OK. So that's out. It's separation, then. Where are you going to live? (*Pause.*) Ange?

Ange What?

Ronee Where are you going to live?

Ange Dunno.

Ronee Your mum's?

Ange Could do.

Ronee You've got to think about it.

Ange Well, I thought that . . .

The phone rings.

Ronee Shit. Hang on a minute. (*She picks up the phone.*) Hello? (*Beat.*) Oh, hi. (*Pause.*) Ja. Nach zwei Stunde. (*Beat.*) Oh. (*She laughs.*) But my pronunciation's improving. (*Beat. She laughs again.*) Rat. Schwein. (*Beat.*) Ja. Ich werde dich dahin gesehen. (*Beat.*) What? (*Beat.*) I'm trying to say I'll see you there in a couple of hours. (*Beat.*) Well I think it'd be easier if you learned English, so there. (*Beat.*) Ja. OK. Ich liebe dich. Wiedersehen. (*She puts down the phone.*) That woman is totally crazy.

Ange Andrea?

Ronee Well, I don't talk to my mother in German, do I? (**Ange** *shrugs.*) Right, where were we?

Ange Ronee? Can I ask you something?

Ronee Trying to get off the subject?

Ange I want to ask you something.

Ronee Go on then.

Beat.

Ange You and Andrea . . . When you . . .

Ronee And stop it right there. If you were going to ask what I think you were going to ask, the answer is: none of your bloody business.

Ange I was just . . .

Ronee Curious. Well, use your imagination.

Ange I mean, I can't imagine . . .

Ronee So don't. (*Pause.*) Sorry, love. It's just that my relationship with Andrea is private and personal, y'know? I don't like it being . . . spied on.

Ange I wasn't spying . . .

Ronee I know. Just curious. (*Pause.*) I don't think I could describe it, anyway.

Ange But . . . It's different, innit?

Ronee Yes. It's very different.

Ange Better?

Ronee For me, yeah.

Beat.

Ange What about Will? (*Beat.*) Don't you like him?

Ronee We're married.

Ange So am I, and I don't like Lenny.

Ronee They're very similar, Will and Lenny.

Ange Get off.

Ronee Oh, I know, one's a TV researcher, the other's a mechanic; one went to University, the other left school at sixteen. But they're both men. And very similar ones at that.

Ange I think that's horrible. Will's nice.

Pause.

Ronee Will is evil. (*Beat.*) And that's it. No more. There's nothing he'd like more than to think that we were sitting here talking about him. Bit of an egomaniac, is our Will.

Will *enters with* **Bruce**. *They've been mending the car and are both covered in oil. They each have a can of beer and two more unopened.*

Will You called?

Ronee Done it?

Will Not quite. Got to bleed the brakes. Thought we'd have a quick beer. So. Talking about me?

Ronee Pick it up on your radar, did you? Someone, somewhere, says 'Will' and a little bleep appears on the screen?

Will Something like that.

Ronee I was just disabusing Ange of a rather peculiar notion she had. She seems to have been labouring under the misapprehension that you are nice.

Will But you put her straight.

Ronee Of course, dear heart.

Will You're a treasure.

Will *crushes his empty can.*

Ronee I know. (*Beat.*) God, this is all too macho for me. I've got to get changed, anyway. Come on, Ange, we can carry on talking. I intend to get you sorted out. (*She stands.*)

Will Come along, Angela. Walkies.

Ronee Let's leave the boys to their beer and motor cars.

She and **Ange** *go.*

Will Ain't she sweet? (*Beat.*) Never get married, Bruce.

Bruce I . . . won't.

Pause.

Will Hey, listen, mate, thanks for your help. That car's been a pain in the arse since I bought it. I'd never have got it straight if you hadn't come over.

Bruce No problem. I . . . enjoy it.

Beat. **Will**, *as always, is uncomfortable with* **Bruce**.

Will You can take a shower later, if you want.

Bruce 'S OK. You've got some . . . uh . . . Swarfega . . .

Will Yeah. I'll get it . . .

Bruce No, I'll . . . finish this . . . (*He holds up his beer.*)

Will Sure. (*Pause.*) So.

Beat.

Bruce You don't have to . . . talk. If you don't want to.

Will Bit pre-occupied, that's all.

Bruce Ah.

Will Ronee and me. Well, you can probably see . . . We're not . . . I dunno . . .

Bruce Maybe you should split.

Beat.

Will Does it look that bad?

Bruce Doesn't . . . look good.

Will No. (*Pause.*) Rationally . . . you're probably right. But who thinks rationally at times like this? (*Pause.*) Ten years we've been together. Married for six. Very unfashionable, marriage, when we did it. Which is probably why we did it. (*Beat.*) Ten years. (*Beat.*) That . . . is a bloody long time.

Pause.

Bruce I've got a flat.

Will Good news. Where?

Bruce Earl's Court. Sharing.

Will Who with?

Bruce Couple of . . . blokes I know . . .

Will That's you sorted out, then.

Bruce Yeah.

The doorbell rings.

Will I'll get it.

He goes to the door. There are muffled voices. **Martin** *comes in, followed by* **Will**.

Drink?

Martin Yeah. Gin. On its own. (*He glowers at* **Bruce**. **Bruce** *ignores him and sips his beer.*)

Will There you go. (*He hands him his drink.*) Cheers. (**Martin** *drinks most of it down in one go.*) So. You're early.

Beat.

Martin Yeah.

Beat.

Will To what do we owe the pleasure? (*Pause.*) Well, it's OK. Since you're here. Know anything about cars?

Martin No.

Will Oh, well. (*Pause.*) Ollie was round this morning.

Martin Oh, Christ . . .

Will He was . . . in a bit of a bad way.

Martin What else is fucking new?

Will He was worried about you. (*Pause.*) Have you seen him?

Martin No.

Will Not to worry. He'll be here soon. He's usually early. (*Pause.*) Look, Martin . . .

Martin (*to* **Bruce**) What the fuck are you playing at? (*Pause.* **Will** *is baffled.*) Come on. It's only a speech defect. You're not dumb.

Bruce, *very calmly, goes over to* **Martin** *and suddenly grabs the hair on the back of his neck. It is very painful.*

Bruce (*speaking carefully so as not to stammer*) Don't ever speak to me like that. OK? (*He lets go.*)

Will Er . . . I get the feeling there's something I'm missing here. (*Pause.*) But . . . Maybe the penny's dropping.

Pause.

Bruce Can I have another . . . beer?

Will Oh, help yourself.

Bruce *does as* **Martin** *takes a piece of paper out of his pocket.*

Martin I mean, what is this?

Beat.

Will Looks like a piece of paper to me . . .

Martin (*reading*) 'Dear Martin, I've moved. Don't try to find me. Don't come round. Goodbye. Thanks. Bruce.' (*Pause.*) I mean, y'know . . .

Will Sounds like the brush-off to me.

Pause.

Martin Bruce?

Beat.

Bruce Sounds like . . . the brush-off to me, too.

Martin But why?

Bruce I got bored.

Martin You what?!

Will He got bored.

Pause.

Martin Jesus Christ, what have I done?

Will Tell you one thing: you've made a little man very unhappy, for a start.

Martin Please, Will, I think this is between me and Bruce.

Will So go to your place to discuss it. (*Beat.*) Look, Ollie was here in what I can only describe as a mess, this morning. A mess on your account. You appear to be in a mess on Bruce's account. Why don't you and Ollie get your respective messes together and live happily ever after?

Martin Don't patronise me, you sod.

Will I wish there was a way not to. I wish it wasn't inevitable. (*Beat.*) You, and Ollie, what is it you're always on the verge of? Huh? You're always teetering on the brink. The brink of what?

Beat.

Martin The same as you.

Will Cryptic.

Martin You know what I mean.

Will Enlighten me.

Martin What are you going to do when Ronee leaves you?

Beat.

Will Oh, oh, oh, I see what you're driving at.

Martin Not going to teeter on the brink? Huh?

Will (*arch*) I'll burn that bridge when I come to it. Until then, let's remember that it's my private affair.

Martin Oh, so cool.

Will If by that you mean that I don't wank my private life all over other people's boots, then you're dead right. (*Pause.*) It's just occurred to me. We shouldn't be having this discussion. We're not quorate and we haven't got a chairperson.

Bruce *laughs*.

Martin Bruce?

Bruce It was fun. That's . . . all.

Beat.

Martin OK. (*He gets up and starts to pour a drink.*)

Will I'm really going to have to think about setting up a drinks kitty.

Martin *pulls a pound note out of his pocket and throws it in* **Will**'s *direction.*

All I meant was – ask.

Martin (*having poured*) May I?

Will Be my guest.

Martin *goes to* **Bruce** *and theatrically throws the drink in his face. Beat.* **Bruce** *starts to laugh, as does* **Will**. *As they laugh* **Bruce** *indicates that he's going to the bathroom. He goes, still laughing.*

You definitely get tonight's Joan Crawford award.

Martin *is nearly in tears.*

Think about it. He's only doing what you did to Ollie.

Martin I know. (*Pause.*) Except, Bruce and me . . .

Will Yeah. (*Beat. He goes to the window.*) Beautiful day. (*Beat.*) I've got an idea. Let's have a barbeque.

Martin What, now?

Will I'll have to go and get some mince . . . (*He goes to the door.*) Ronee?

Ronee (*off*) Yeah?

Will What time are you back tonight?

Ronee (*off*) Not late.

Will I've got an idea.

Ronee (*off*) Golly.

Will What about a barbeque in the garden? (*Beat.*) Eh?

Ronee (*off*) Yeah. Great.

Will You back by half nine?

Beat.

Ronee (*off*) I suppose so.

Will OK. Bring Andrea, if you like. (*Beat. He comes back into the room.*) It'll be beautiful out there tonight. Just right.

Ange *appears.*

Ange Need any help?

Will Uh . . . Not really. I've got to get to the shop . . .

Ange I'll go.

Will 'S OK. I want to get out. (*Beat.*) Come with me, if you like.

Ange Yeah.

Will Know anything about barbeques?

Ange What, hot dogs and stuff?

Will I was thinking more in terms of burgers and kebabs.

Ange You can show me.

Will OK. (*Beat.*) See you later.

Martin Yeah.

They start to go as **Bruce** *comes in.*

Will Just going to the shop, Bruce.

Bruce I'll finish the car.

Martin Bruce.

Will *and* **Ange** *go.*

Sorry. I made a fool of myself. (*Beat.*) I'm apologising. Say something.

Bruce What?

Martin I don't know.

Pause.

Bruce The only . . . creatures on this earth worth pitying . . . are animals. 'Cause, like . . . people . . . y'know? People are so stupid. They're . . . happy with all their crap . . . Like . . . They don't want to get any better. (*Beat.*) Politics is a joke. People don't want to be . . . liberated. I think people . . . like being chained up. Not real chains . . . Y'know. Keep those for the animals.

Pause.

Martin (*sings gently*) Chains, my baby's got me locked up in chains. And they ain't the kind . . . that you can see . . .

Pause. The doorbell rings. **Bruce** *goes.* **Oliver** *enters.* **Martin** *sees him and carries on singing.*

Whoah-oh these chains of love, gotta hold on me.

Beat.

Oliver Are you pissed? (**Martin** *shakes his head.*) What's Bruce doing?

Martin Mending Will's car.

Pause.

Oliver (*sitting*) Martin . . . (*Beat.*) Where have you been?

Ronee *comes in.*

Ronee Boy scout night again already?

Oliver Hi, Ronee.

Ronee Hi. Look, if you bump into my husband, tell him I'll do my best to be back in time, will you?

Oliver Sure.

Ronee But, I can't promise.

Oliver OK.

She goes.

In time for what?

Martin It'll be beautiful out there tonight.

Oliver Eh?

Martin We're having a barbeque in the garden. Songs round the old campfire.

Oliver What for?

Martin Because it's nice.

Pause.

Oliver Where were you?

Martin The truth?

Oliver Please, yeah. The truth. (*Beat.*) I know I haven't been too good at the truth but I need it now. I really do.

Martin I needed time to think. (*Beat.*) About us. (*Beat.*) About me. (*Beat.*) I went and stayed with an old friend. From way back?

Oliver Did you sleep with her?

Martin Did I sleep with her? (*Pause.*) Sorry. Yeah. But it didn't mean anything. Just a way of paying the rent. (*Pause.*) You wanted the truth.

Oliver It's all I ever wanted. (*Pause.*) And . . . Did you think?

Martin Yeah.

Oliver And?

Beat.

Martin What would you like me to say?

Oliver I don't know.

Martin I mean . . .

Beat.

Oliver Are you going to need to go away and think any more?

Martin I might.

Oliver Often?

Pause.

Martin No. I don't think so.

Oliver Honest?

Martin Honest.

Oliver Good. (*Pause.*) Martin. Come back. If you want to. I've changed. No more fussing. No more stupid ultimatums. Just us. Friends. Or more, if you want. (*Beat.*) What I'm saying is: I'll do anything to have you back. (*Beat.*) If you want sex . . .

Martin Ollie . . . Let's just see what happens.

Oliver OK. (*Beat.*) What, you mean you're coming back?

Martin Why not?

Beat.

Oliver It'll be different. I promise.

Martin I believe you. (*They hug.* **Martin** *sings.*) 'Whoa-oh, these chains of love . . . (**Bruce** *appears, wiping his hands on a cloth.*) . . . got a hold on me. Yeah.'

Blackout.

Scene Three

Monday evening, 9.30 p.m.

Lenny *is sitting nervously at the table.* **Ange** *enters from the kitchen.*

Ange I'm busy. What d'you want?

Beat.

Lenny What you doing?

Ange A barbeque. (*He looks away.*) Y'know, kebabs and things.

Lenny I know what a barbeque is.

Pause.

Ange Well?

Beat.

Lenny Y'know Tony? Landlord down the Duke? Yeah? (*She nods.*) I had a long chat with him the other night. (*Pause.*) I tried me dad, but . . . (*Pause.*) Tony says it ain't all my fault. Not all of it. We been stuck in that flat. Bloody rathole. So it ain't all my fault. But . . . (*Pause.*) He was telling me about his first wife. Apparently, she done a bunk when he hit her. (*Beat.*) Eight years ago. Still loves her, he says. (*Pause.*) Well, I was telling him about us and everything and he started having a right go at me. Yeah. (*Long pause.*) See, it's a question of respect. Gotta respect each other, ain't we? That's where we was going wrong. I didn't have no respect for you. (*Pause.*) And the thing is . . . I'd never thought about it.

Ange Lenny, don't go on. I'm not coming back.

Long pause.

Lenny See, I got it all wrong. (*Pause.*) Tony says what we oughta do is: you get a job, if you can, start saving, and try and get a mortgage on a decent place. He reckons this is a good time to be buying your own house. Interest rates and that.

Ange What you talking about? Since when did you know anything about bloody interest rates?

Lenny Since I talked to Tony.

Ange You have half an hour's chat with a bloody alcoholic and suddenly you know all about everything?

Lenny He ain't alcoholic.

Ange Drinks like a fish.

Lenny He helped me out. Advice and that.

Ange So go and live with *him*.

Lenny I don't wanna live with him, I wanna live with you.

Ange Well, that's tough Lenny. I'm staying here. (*Pause.*) 'Cause, d'you know what? You're just an animal, Lenny. 'S all you are. I never knew till I came here. 'Cause you and your family and your mates, the lot of you, you're all just a pack of animals.

Lenny That ain't fair.

Ange Bloody well is. And I'll tell you something else. I'd rather slit me wrists than come anywhere near you again.

Pause.

Lenny Gimme another chance . . .

Ange I won't give you nothing. (**Will** *is listening from the kitchen.*) Why should I? I'm starting again. New place. New people. (*Beat.*) Nice people. (*Beat.*) So go away, Lenny.

Lenny It ain't fair.

Ange My heart bleeds.

Lenny It ain't. I've tried to understand things. And you won't give me a bloody chance.

Will *enters with a tray of cups.*

Will Sorry to break things up, but I'm just about to start cooking. So, if you're . . .

Lenny Please, Ange . . .

Will Time to go, Lenny.

Lenny I wasn't talking to you, cunt.

Will Careful. Or I might have to set my wife on you.

Beat.

Ange Time to go, Lenny.

Beat.

Lenny You know what my dad said? He said you wouldn't have gone if I'd hit you where it didn't show. Said it was just 'cause it was your face got marked. (*Pause.*) Look, you know where I am, if you . . . (*Beat.*) Fuck it. Fuck the lot of you.

He goes.

Will OK?

Ange Good riddance. (*Beat.*) I'll do those.

He kisses her. She pours wine into the cups. **Will** *runs his hand down her back. She turns.*

Don't muck about.

Will This is serious.

She picks up the tray.

Ange I don't wanna spill this.

He runs his hands over her body. She can't move in case she spills the drinks.

Will . . .

Will You've got a . . . fantastic . . . body . . . (*He dissolves into laughter.*)

Ange Daft sod, you're drunk. (*He just laughs.*) Don't laugh at me.

Will I'm not . . .

Ange You are. Don't. I don't like it. (*He composes himself.*) 'S better.

He stares at her.

Will Hey, listen, don't forget . . .

Ange I dunno . . .

Will You promised.

Ange But, she might not . . .

Will Make her. You could make anybody do anything.

Ange Sure. And what about Andrea?

Will She rang. She's coming home alone.

Beat.

Ange I don't know if I can.

Will You can. (*He lifts a cup to her lips.*)

Ange I don't drink.

Will You do tonight.

Beat. She takes a swig. He makes her take a drag of the joint he's smoking.
OK?

Ange OK.

She starts to go as **Oliver**, *already fairly pissed, comes in. He takes a cup from the tray and she goes.*

Oliver Give that woman a medal. (*Beat.*) Do you know, Will? Do you know what women are? What they really are? (*Beat.*) Apart from our sisters in the struggle, of course. Hmm?

Will You're either going to say something dreadfully silly or misogynist.

Oliver What? (*Beat.*) Me? I love women. Love them. The problem is, the problem is, Will . . . They don't love me.

Will Ah. Something dreadfully silly. That's a relief.

Oliver No, no, no, you don't understand. Non comprendo, old sausage. I mean, not *me*. I mean, all of us. Men. You. Me. All of us. (*Pause.*) Is that controversial, or what?

Beat.

Will Vague.

Oliver Oh, granted. You want chapter and verse?

Will No.

Oliver Why not?

Will You're pissed.

Oliver What the hell difference does that make? I'm being honest. I'm going to empty my soul.

Will You're going to bore me rigid, if you're not careful.

Oliver You can't take emotion, that's the trouble. Here I am, speaking from the heart, and all you want to do is shut me up. Well I won't be shut up. (*His voice rises to near tantrum level.*) This anal social life, this English, tight-arsed, clenched-buttock politeness. It should be . . . blown away. I won't shut up. I am a Russian. I am a Papua, New Guinea headhunter. I am alive.

Martin *has entered.*

Martin Oh, shut up, Ollie.

Beat.

Oliver That's all they can say, isn't it. Oh, shut up. (*Beat.*) Shall I compare thee – oh, shut up. Tyger, Tyger, burning bright – put a sock in it, will you? We're British. Stiff upper lip. Arsehole like a vice. Emotion? The occasional fart. Love? One big shit. (*Pause*). There's no poetry in life. No beauty.

The front door opens and **Mark** *enters.*

Mark Yo.

Oliver This man looks like a fascist. Doesn't he? Tell me, are you a fascist? (**Mark** *is bemused.*) Come on, you're English, aren't you? You must be a fascist.

Beat.

Mark What's this? Alternative cabaret?

Oliver Ha. A sense of humour. I like him. What's your name? I don't care if you are a fascist.

Mark Go boil your bum.

Will His name's Mark.

Oliver Mark. Mark. I don't know if I like that. We might have to change it. (*Beat.*) I know. Vladimir. I'll call you Vladimir. OK, Vladimir? Or may I call you Vlad?

Mark Don't be formal. Call me 'sir'.

Oliver Beneath his sarcasm is a soul of pure poetry. I can tell.

Mark *pats him on the face.*

Mark When did they let *him* out?

Will Wait till the valium wears off.

Martin Ollie. Let's grab some food.

Oliver Grab. Grab, grab, grab. Crab. Blab. Stab. Let's stab some food.

Martin Whatever you say.

Ronee *enters*.

Oliver (*to* **Ronee**) Why don't you love me?

He and **Martin** *go*.

Ronee Oh, dear.

Mark Where do you get your friends? Joke shop?

Will (*aware of the joke*). Local Labour Party.

Mark That's what I said.

Will For once, you might have a point.

Ronee If tonight is going to consist of the poison dwarf embarrassing everyone in sight, I might just pass.

Will I think he's got it out of his system.

Bruce *enters*.

Come and get some food.

Ronee OK.

They go.

Mark Hi. I'm Mark. I live here.

Bruce I'm Bruce. (*They shake*.)

Mark You're not crackers like that other bloke, are you?

Bruce Who?

Mark Short-arsed fella with the big mouth.

Bruce No.

Pause. **Bruce** *pours himself a drink*.

Mark Here, d'you hear the one about the two Irish queers? Patrick Fitzmaurice and Maurice Fitzpatrick?

Beat.

Bruce No . . . I didn't.

Beat.

Mark I see.

Bruce What's a queer?

Mark Eh?

Bruce What's a . . . queer?

Beat.

Mark Well, you *have* led a sheltered life. A queer is a poof is a woofter.

Bruce Oh. Like . . . Pakis.

Beat.

Mark Sort of.

Bruce And nig nogs.

Pause.

Mark Except woofters are white.

Ange *comes in with the tray and cups.*

Ange That stupid little git just knocked all the cups over, then collapsed on the rockery. Squashed all the flowers. Bloody nerd. (*She puts the cups out and starts pouring more wine.*)

Mark Shouldn't you be wearing a pinny? And a mob cap?

Ange Tie a knot in it.

Mark Could tie a sheep shank in mine. (*Beat.*) Here, seeing as you won't come upstairs to me, how about I come below stairs to you?

Oliver *appears carrying a couple of squashed flowers.*

Here comes laughing boy again.

Oliver What have I done? Look. Murder. I've killed something of beauty.

Mark Well, you know what they say. A thing of beauty is a boy forever.

Oliver *goes over to him and puts his arm round his neck.*

Oliver Vlad. Oh, Vlad. Is this all that's left to us? Cruelty? Arbitrary killing and cruelty?

Mark Yup.

Oliver It can't be. Where's hope?

Mark In the bath with Faith and Charity.

Ange (*enjoying it*). Don't.

Oliver Look what a precious jewel I've cast away . . .

Mark Terrible.

Oliver *absent-mindedly puts the flowers in his mouth and starts chewing them.*

Ange Oh, he's horrible.

She starts to go. As she passes **Oliver** *he takes a cup. She goes.*

Oliver A toast. To flowers. Everywhere. May they forgive me? (*He drinks.*) Hey, listen . . . (*He starts to laugh.*) . . . Where have . . . Where have all the flowers gone? Eh? (*Beat.*) Squashed them all, haven't I? (*He laughs.*)

Mark Yeah, nice one.

Oliver I like you, Vlad. Let's be friends. Hmm?

Mark You smooth talking man.

Ronee *enters.*

Oliver I mean it. Let's be blood brothers. Cut our arms. Let the blood intermingle. What do you say?

Mark Tell you what, I'll cut my arm if you cut your throat.

Ronee If it's blood you're after, Will's just done some burgers.

Mark Right. (*To* **Oliver**.) Come on, smiler, let's find you some flowers to press.

Oliver They haunt me. Hollyhocks, geraniums, nasturtiums . . .

Mark Pansies?

They leave.

Ronee And hello, Bruce.

Bruce Hi.

Ronee You know what this reminds me of?

Bruce What?

Ronee The bad trips tent at the Isle of Wight festival. (*Beat.*) Actually, life sometimes reminds me . . . (*She waves her hand in the air and smiles.*) Found a flat, I hear.

Bruce That's right.

Ronee Sharing it with a couple of leather queens . . . (**Bruce** *looks worried.*) Come on, just a joke.

Pause.

Bruce One . . . is. The other isn't.

Ronee Ah. (*Beat.*) And you've been a bit naughty, I also hear. (*He shrugs.*) Listen, can I ask you something?

Bruce Sure.

Ronee This might sound odd . . . (*Beat.*) You're not married, or anything?

Bruce Not now.

Beat.

Ronee Do you miss the security? Of a permanent relationship?

Beat.

Bruce I'm . . . not sure. Maybe. I'm not very . . . good with people. They don't stay very long. Sometimes . . . I want them to.

Ronee Martin?

Beat.

Bruce Martin was just a fuck.

Ronee Uh-huh. (*Beat.*) I might leave Will and live with Andrea. She wants me to. (*Beat.*) She's getting understandably pissed off. Having to share me, you see.

Bruce So's Will.

Beat.

Ronee Poor old Will. When we first met, y'know, I was a real wallflower. And he was something of a celebrity. Well, a big fish in a little pool.

Beat.

See, in the last nine, ten years, whatever it is, he hasn't changed.
He's just sort of . . . got worse. (*Beat.*) He's like someone
drowning. If you try to help, you just get dragged down. (*Beat.*)
He tries. The men's group and what have you. But it's such an
effort. I mean, you can see it. He's actually going against his
nature.

Bruce But he's doing it for you.

Beat.

Ronee Perhaps.

Pause.

Bruce His nature can change.

Ronee I don't know about that.

Bruce He's changed in the time I've known him.

Ronee How?

Bruce He . . . listens now. I mean . . . without offence . . . he's got
things into perspective. Like . . .

Ronee He's not such a big-headed bastard.

Bruce Yeah. No offence. (*Pause.*) You mean a lot. I think.

Ronee Is that good or bad?

Bruce It's security. (*Beat.*) Yes, I do . . . miss it.

Ronee So might I.

Pause.

Bruce I think you owe him a chance. (*Pause.*) Really.

Will *enters.*

Will Hey, party poopers. (*He gets a drink.*) What's this? Illicit
joint-smoking? The passing-out room? It's not that kind of party.
I admit the paper cups may be somewhat reminiscent of a late
sixties bring a bottle bash, but I like to think we've progressed.

Beat.

Ronee I think you're enjoying yourself.

Will Darling, I'm having a ball.

Ronee Good. (*She kisses him.*)

Will I'm now over the moon. Official. (**Ange** *comes in.*) Hey, Bruce. Give us a hand with the fire, will you? It's a bugger to get re-started if it goes out.

Bruce I don't know . . . much about it . . .

Will Then learn, baby, learn.

They go. **Will** *winks at* **Ange** *as he goes.* **Ronee** *stretches out on the sofa.*

Ronee (*expansive*) Angela. Peel me a grape.

Ange (*uptight*) Eh?

Ronee Get me a glass of wine, angel. A glass. This is nineteen eighty-three and we're grown-ups now. (**Ange** *pours a glass of wine, hands it to her and sits on the edge of the sofa.*) Ta. You know, I think I might have a cigarette. I think I dare. There's some on the table. (**Ange** *gets them and sits.* **Ronee** *takes one out.* **Ange** *lights it for her.*) Thanks love. (*She runs her hand down* **Ange***'s face and rests it on her shoulder.*) Well. Having a good time?

Ange Yeah.

Ronee Good. Against all the odds, so am I. And I intend to have a better time.

Ange, *misunderstanding, visibly relaxes.*

Ange It's all new to me.

Ronee You'll get used to it. We're all a bit crazy. But then, who isn't?

Ange Right. (*Beat.*) Ronee. You ain't half been good to me. Letting me stay and everything. I really want to pay you back.

Ronee You're your old self, that'll do for now.

Ange But I wish there was something . . . (*She leans down and gives her a friendly kiss, her hand now resting on* **Ronee***'s shoulder.*) There.

Ronee Where? (*She laughs.* **Ange** *kisses her again.*)

Ange There. (*She laughs.*) There. (*She kisses her each time she says 'there'.*) There. There. There. (**Ange** *starts running her hands over* **Ronee***'s body.*)

Ronee Ange . . . (*She breaks away and sits up.*) Break. Cool it. OK? (*Pause.* **Ange**, *unsure what to do, slowly puts her arm round* **Ronee***'s neck* *and tries to kiss her again.* **Ronee** *stands up.*) I don't know what you think you're doing, but whatever it is, don't.

Ange I was . . . (*She is completely shattered.*)

Ronee I know what you was. Where the bloody hell'd you get the idea? . . . (*Beat.*) I mean, just because . . . (*Beat.*) Honestly, Ange . . .

Ange I'm sorry. I thought . . .

Ronee What?

Pause.

Look, forget it. Don't feel you have to pay me back. You don't owe me anything. And you certainly don't want to complicate your life any more than it already is.

Ange That's not it.

Ronee What?

Ange I wasn't trying to pay you back.

Ronee What, just a sudden impulse, was it?

Ange No.

Ronee Then what? (*Pause.*) Come on. (*Pause.*) What put the idea into your head . . . ? (*Beat.*) Oh no. (*Beat.*) Tell me Will had nothing to do with this. (*Beat.*) Ange. Tell me. Will. Tell me. (**Ange** *nods her head.*) Oh, my Christ. I am so stupid. What a fool. What a soft bloody fool. (*She goes to the door.*) Will. (*Beat.*) Will!

Will (*off*) What is it?

Ronee Come here.

Will (*off*) The fire'll go out.

Ronee Too bloody right. (*Shouts.*) It's important.

Will (*off*) OK.

Ronee *comes back into the room.*

Ange Ronee, I want to go home.

Ronee No. Not yet.

Will *enters.* **Ange** *is sitting looking crushed.* **Will** *is smiling. He slowly stops smiling.*

I told Ange that you and Lenny were very similar. I was wrong.

You're worse than Lenny. Much worse. (*Beat.*) What you've done to her is certainly as bad as anything he did. (*Pause.*) That's not to mention what you've done to me. Will, are you so insensitive, so feeble, that you had to do this?

Beat.

Will Er, yes?

Pause.

Ronee Look at him, Ange. Look at him. There's your 'nice' man. There's your open, honest, charming man who can't get his mind past your tits. Whose idea of maturity is to screw everything in sight. (*Beat.*) Talking of which, did you? (*Beat.*) Did you two screw?

Will Yes, this morning . . .

Ronee I don't want to know when, I don't want to see the pictures or . . . read the book or see the bloody film . . . (*Pause.*) Oh, why do I care? (*Beat.*) Will, did you seriously think that if you sent Ange in here to . . . That I would or could possibly go along with it? After everything I've told you? Did you?

Will Obviously.

Ronee How?

Will Why should I change? I've done what you expected. You can't pretend to be disappointed.

Ronee Don't you feel *anything* for anybody else?

Pause.

Will Contempt and lust. Those are my two strongest feelings.

Ronee Why?!

Beat.

Will Because . . . I can't feel anything else. I can't love anybody. I can't even bring myself to like very many people. (*Beat.*) I keep thinking back to ten years ago, when people *did* things. Nobody was expected to do the 'right' thing. We just did them, right or wrong, good or bad, nasty or nice. (*Beat.*) Thing is, I think I preferred them wrong, bad and nasty. Is that a crime?

Ronee It hurts people.

Will So what? (*Pause.*) The problem with you is, you still want love. After everything, after all the disillusion, the naked facts of life, the ugliness, the pointlessness, the kicks in the teeth, the bad scenes in bed, the downright bloody failure . . . You . . . still want love. Well, where is it? Andrea? She got it? Is Andrea a mystical receptacle of all that's good and fair in life? Is she?

Ronee No. She's another human being who wants love. Who wants me.

Will Then you deserve each other.

Ronee Yes! (*Pause.*) Nobody deserves you. Nobody who ever smiled or had a simple thought without wanting to soil somebody else deserves you. Live in the dirt. There are plenty of others there like you. But don't ever expect to find me down there again. I'm going to live knowing that I don't need to cut people to prove they're flesh and blood. Knowing that I don't need to smear their faces in shit to prove that it exists. Knowing, most of all, that I don't need to carve my name on their face to prove that *I* exist.

Beat. Enter **Oliver**.

Will Well, climb every mountain.

Ronee *goes.* **Oliver** *sings, loudly.*

Oliver Ford every stream. Follow every rainbow. *Till you find your dream!!* I have always wanted . . . to perform . . . cunnilingus . . . on Julie Andrews! I admit it.

Will And I have always had a secret desire to roger Judith Chalmers.

Oliver Anna Ford.

Will Valerie Singleton.

Oliver The Queen.

Will The world.

Mark *comes in, followed by* **Martin** *and* **Bruce**, *who leans in the doorway, watching.*

Mark here, has no secret desire whatsoever. Do you, Mark? Because little Mark's desires are always well out in front where they ought to be.

Oliver Vladimir, me old pal, is this right?

Mark I don't know what you're on about.

Oliver We're talking about desire. The turgid electricity in the loins. The dark, insatiable fire in the belly. Fucking.

Mark I dunno.

Oliver Well, that's not a very intelligent remark, is it for chrissakes? I expect better of you, Vlad.

Martin Ollie, do us a favour.

Oliver Certainly. What had you in mind?

Martin Keep it down.

Oliver Keep it down? I have trouble keeping it up. (*Liberal helpings of drink are being poured.*) The one-minute wonder, they used to call me. Oh, yes. Inoutinoutinout? In, mate. That was my lot. Thank you for coming, do call again.

Mark Here, this bloke, right. He's just got out of the nick. Been in for thirty years. And he thinks, 'Christ do I need a fuck.' So he goes off, right, and finds this scabby old whore, throws it on the bed and gives it the shagging of its life. When he's finished, he says, 'That was good. Just one thing, though.' 'What's that?' she says. 'Why was it that every time I give it some thrust, your toes turned up?' 'Next time,' she says, 'remember to take my tights off.' (**Mark**, **Ollie** and **Will** *laugh.* **Martin** *looks embarrassed.* **Bruce** *just stares.*)

Oliver Hey, you should join our group. We could do with a few laughs.

Martin Ollie, let's go home.

Oliver And rut like healthy stags.

Martin Let's just go home.

Oliver I . . . am . . . enjoying myself. I am letting it all hang out.

Martin Fab.

Pause.

Oliver (*slurring*) What is it? What's all this? . . . Killjoys . . . Why can't I have fun, for once? Just for once in my life, why can't I fart in church?

Martin Because it's stupid.

Oliver How dare you?! You dare to call me stupid?! Why, I've got more brains in my big toe than you've got in your entire body. I was a socialist when you were in nappies. I'm still a better socialist than you.

Martin What's that got to . . .

Oliver Everything. I am a socialist. I don't kowtow to the ruling class.

Martin What are you talking about?

Oliver Socialism's about truth and love and fucking. It's blood and sperm. What do Tories know about fucking? Nothing. (*In a tantrum.*) I've fucked my way around the world. There's nothing you can tell me. I've fucked socialists, fascists, pigs, my mother, myself. So I know what I'm talking about. *All right?!*

Martin If you say so.

Oliver I do say so! And don't contradict me. (*He hurls his drink in* **Martin**'s *face.*)

Martin For God's sake, Ollie . . .

Oliver God? How the fuck did he get into this? I've fucked God. (*He pours whatever he can lay his hands on over* **Martin**'s *head.*) God is a Nazi. And I don't have anything to do with Nazis. I shit on them. I fuck them. You're a Nazi. You're an anti-semite. Don't tell me you're not, because . . . (*He bawls into his face.*) *I know you bloody are!* (*Pause.*) I'm sorry, but you deserved that.

Pause.

Martin It wasn't a woman. It was Bruce.

He goes.

Oliver (*advancing on* **Bruce**) Ha. So. (*Beat. He stops.*) What?

Pause. He suddenly lunges at **Bruce**, *attempting to throw a punch.* **Bruce** *clocks it and knees him in the stomach. He falls to the ground out of breath and hurt.*

Bruce I won't be . . . coming to the group any more. I don't think I . . . need it.

He goes.

Mark Often like this, is it? (*He picks up* **Oliver** *and dumps him on the sofa.*)

Will Better, usually.

Mark Don't know what I've been missing.

Oliver (*doubled up*) Christ, what happened?

Will Martin went.

Oliver Where?

Will How the fuck should I know?

Oliver Vlad, Vlad, come and live with me.

Mark Sure thing.

Ronee *enters.*

Will Ah. Goodnight, sweet lady.

Ronee Yeah. Ange, get your case. You're coming with me.

Ange *goes upstairs.*

Will Ronee . . .

Ronee Don't, Will. You know where you're going. See it through. You might as well. It's all you've got.

Will It is now.

Beat.

Ronee I'll pick my stuff up tomorrow. And I'll see my solicitor.

Will What's it going to be? Mental cruelty?

Ronee I hadn't thought about it. But yeah, I think mental cruelty would do very nicely.

Will Y'know, deep down, deep inside somewhere . . . I hate you. I think I always have.

Ronee You poor, dried up little man. (*Beat.*) I used to love you.

Ange *reappears.*

Will Yeah. Funny, isn't it?

Ronee Bloody hilarious . . .

*She and **Ange** go.*

Mark Don't forget to leave that window open . . . (*Beat.*) You must be mad. What I wouldn't have done for a piece of your wife.

Will What *I* wouldn't have done . . .

Beat.

Mark Why don't we drop the laughing gnome off and hit the town? Maybe pick up some crumpet.

Will I dunno . . .

Mark Listen. We've never been out for a drink together, you and me. Let's go and get rat-arsed, find some dirty slags and have a bachelor night. Eh?

Beat.

Will Be just like old times. (*Pause.*) No. Not tonight, Josephine.

Oliver (*holding up a flower*) Look what I did. Why did I do that?

Mark 'Cause you're a prick.

Oliver No, no, no, I've got a prick.

Mark I call them as I see them.

He nods to **Will** *and goes.* **Will** *finishes his glass and goes to* **Oliver**, *who is asleep.* **Will** *sighs and goes to the stereo. He switches it on. The tape plays.*

Oliver I need help.

Martin Ollie, don't make it so hard on yourself.

Oliver I can't help it. (*Beat.*) I'm sorry everyone, I'm talking too much. I'm sorry. I'll give someone else a chance.

Will It's OK. It's not right to keep it bottled up, Ollie. It's not honest. (*Beat.*) No, I really think we're getting somewhere here. Let's keep going.

Hard Feelings

Hard Feelings was first seen at the Oxford Playhouse on
5 November, 1982, with the following cast:

Vivienne, *25. An unpredictable, slightly
matronly woman, prone to nervousness and
sudden changes of mood. Not conventionally
attractive, not totally unattractive either. She is
a university graduate, temporarily out of work.*   Frances Barber

Jane, *24. A law student studying for Part
Twos at a London College. She has Jewish
dark good looks. She is quite timid, but fierce
and stubborn when cornered.*   Jenifer Landor

Annie, *25. A part-time model and artist. She
is fashionably beautiful. She is acid and
devious, though easily put off.*   Diana Katis

Rusty, *24. He is 'hip' or 'cool'. Has an
exaggerated sense of style, and dresses in New
Romantic fashion. He is studiedly casual.*   Ian Reddington

Baz, *24. He is the national organiser of the
UK Frisbee Association. A Northerner, he is
short and easy going, though assertive when he
wants to be.*   Chris Jury

Tone, *27. Jane's boyfriend. He is educated
working-class, working as a freelance
contributor to political papers and magazines.
He is outspoken and aggressive.*   Stephen Tiller

Directed by Mike Bradwell
Designed by Geoff Rose
Lighting by Raymond Cross
Sound by Jan Bevis Hughes

This production was subsequently seen at the Bush Theatre,
London on 3 February 1983.

The play is set in a newly gentrified house in Brixton. The set is
the living-room and kitchen area, which is actually part of the
living-room, separated by a counter. The action begins in April
1981.

Act One

Scene One

Rusty and **Annie** are asleep on the sofa-bed, under a sleeping bag. It is 11 a.m. Sunday morning. The room is very messy; empty beer cans, wine bottles, clothes all over the place. **Tone** enters, goes to the fridge, takes out a pint of milk and swigs. He peers round the room and sees **Rusty** and **Annie**. He walks across the room, watching them, and picks up a pack of cigarettes. He opens it; it's empty.

Tone Ah.

He crushes the empty packet and starts to go, throwing the packet over his shoulder. **Baz** enters wearing a dressing-gown and a Sony Walkman, grooving to the music. He is taking a cigarette out of a packet. **Tone** takes the cigarette.

Ta.

He goes out. **Baz** takes out another cigarette and lights it. Door slams off. **Baz** walks across to the window, singing along with the tape.

Baz Goin' back to my roots . . .

He peers through the venetian blinds. **Rusty** groans. **Baz** goes out.

Rusty Whaaa . . . ?
He puts his head back down. Pause. **Jane** enters and puts the kettle on. She thinks about putting the light on, hesitates, shrugs and puts it on. She puts cornflakes in two bowls and coffee in two cups. **Rusty** groans and pulls the sleeping bag over his head.

Jane Sorry. I only live here.

She picks up the bowls and starts to go off. **Viv** enters.

Hi.

Viv Hi. (*Beat.*) How do you do it?

Jane Do what?

Viv Look so great first thing in the morning?

Jane (*slightly embarrassed*) Dunno. Clean living, I s'pose.

Viv Yeah, probably.

Jane *goes off.* **Viv** *stands for a moment, then opens the blinds and puts on the table-lamps.*

Rise and shine. (*She tousles* **Annie***'s hair.*) C'mon. (**Annie** *wakes and looks around.*)

Annie Oh.

Viv Hi.

Annie Hi.

Viv Coffee?

Annie *nods.*

Annie Whassa time?

Viv Nearly eleven?

Annie *counts on her fingers.*

Annie That's only five hours. (*She feels under her eyes.*) I'll get bags. What a life. (*She nudges* **Rusty***.*) C'mon, slob, wake up. (*He stirs.*) Wake up. (*She pushes him. He groans and puts his head in his hands.*)

Rusty Fuck. Oh . . . Fuck. (*He sits up, putting his foot in an ashtray.*) Shit!

Annie This man has an English degree.

Viv Don't we all?

Annie Hundred words a minute, darling, that's all I've got. Well, that and my sublime good looks.

Rusty Christ, this room looks like I feel.

Annie Yeah, but the room we can straighten up.

Rusty I'll have to stop enjoying myself so often. It's killing me. (*He starts to roll a joint.*)

Viv Get up, will you? I want to hoover.

Rusty Leave it. Live fast, die young, right? Bugger the mess.

Viv Bugger you. (*She brings their coffees.*)

Rusty What's the scam, then?

Annie We could go and see if Nigel's still alive.

Viv No, I want to go to Camden Lock, buy some clothes.

Annie Aren't we s'posed to be having lunch at Nigel's?

Viv We can take him to Routiers.

Annie Or he could take us.

Viv *picks up the phone and dials.*

Rusty Why don't we just meet Nigel at the Elgin?

Annie 'Cause it's full of middle-aged wogs.

Rusty Tut, tut.

Annie Still trendy to like wogs, is it?

Rusty Trendy? *De rigeur*, darling. James Brown is muh maaan.

Annie Well, it's one fad I'm not falling for.

Rusty It'll be the first.

Viv (*into the phone*) Nigel? It's me. Vivienne. D'you get home all right last night? (*Pause.*) How much? (*Pause.*) Are you up yet? (*Pause.*) OK. So it's plan B.

Rusty The Elgin.

Viv Camden Lock, lunch at Routiers.

Rusty The Elgin.

Viv And a drink at the Elgin. OK?

Annie Oh, for God's sake.

Rusty Don't pout.

Annie It's not you who gets your bum groped.

Rusty Wanna bet?

Viv (*into the phone*) OK. See you in about half an hour. (*Pause.*) Yeah. See you. (*She puts the phone down and shouts.*) Baz? You up yet? (*Pause.*) Baz? (**Baz** *enters, singing along to the tape.*)

He's up. (*She lifts his headphones.*) Camden Lock, Routiers. OK?

He nods and goes. He comes back.

Baz I thought we were having lunch at Nigel's.

Viv *shakes her head. He goes.*

Rusty Time I abluted. (*He gets up and picks up his clothes.*)

Annie Time you aborted.

Viv Knock it off, you two. You've only just woken up.

Rusty We can row in our sleep.

He goes.

Annie Too right.

Viv You gonna keep this up all day?

Annie Sorry. (*Pause.*) I think Rusty gets off on crashing on your sofa. I woke up and he was still at it. Must think you're watching through the keyhole.

Viv I've got better things to do.

Annie You'll wear the batteries out. (*Pause.*) I tell you. Viv, Rusty gets on my tits. Literally. (*She shouts.*) And don't take all the hot water, slob!

Viv None to take. It was all gone when I got up. 'Someone' had used it all.

Annie Any prizes for guessing who?

Viv *gives a mirthless smile.* **Rusty** *enters.*

Rusty Viv, how can I shave in cold water?

Viv Take the kettle.

He does.

Rusty Christ, get the tin bath out.

He goes.

Annie She does it on purpose. She must do. (*Pause.*) I couldn't put up with it.

Viv Well . . .

Pause.

Annie Is she likely to move in with her new man?

Viv Dunno.

Annie If she does, remember I'm looking for somewhere.

Viv 'Course. (*Pause.*) Don't think she will, though.

Annie But if she does . . .

Viv I won't forget. (*She kisses* **Annie** *on top of her head.*)

Jane *enters. She looks for the kettle.*

Jane What happened to the kettle?

Viv Rusty took it. He's shaving.

Annie There was no hot water.

Pause.

Jane It's just . . . I put it on for coffee.

Viv *You* put it on? Sorry, I've used your cups as well.

Jane Doesn't matter.

Viv I'll get you some more.

Jane *goes off.*

Annie Whose bloody kettle is it?

Viv Annie . . .

Annie Pain in the arse.

Viv She'll hear you.

Annie I should worry.

Jane *enters with the kettle.*

Viv Let me do it. (*She takes the kettle.*)

Annie Anybody got any aspirins?

Viv They're on the shelf.

Annie Oh. (*Pause.*) Jane, you couldn't . . . ?

Jane Sorry, yeah. (*She gets the aspirins and gives them to* **Annie**.)
They're not very good for you, y'know.

Annie Is that right?

Jane Yeah. They make your stomach bleed.

Annie Oh. I'll remember that. (*She swallows them.*)

Baz *enters.*

Baz Give us a break, girls. Not all three at once, eh?

Annie Hark at the virgin prince. (*Pause.*)

Baz (*tries again*) Sleep well, happy campers?

Annie What d'you think? (*Pause.*)

Jane What was Rusty's group like last night?

Annie Band, dear, band.

Viv They were really good.

Baz If you've never seen Kraftwerk. All style, no content, if you ask me.

Annie We didn't.

Baz I mean, they just stand there poking at their Stylaphones. They don't *do* anything.

Annie What d'you want them to do? Get on down and boogie?

Baz It beats watching rigor mortis set in.

Annie It's supposed to be conceptual, dummy.

Baz Oh, it was. Very.

Viv D'you want to go and get the papers, Baz?

Jane It's OK. Tone's gone.

Annie Ah. Tone. I get to meet him at last. What's he like?

Viv Not your type.

Annie And what, exactly, is my type?

Baz Conceptual rigor mortis.

Annie He's my affliction, not my type.

Baz Let's just say Tone doesn't wax his legs or use nail varnish.

Annie Oh, God. Don't tell me he's dirty-fingernail-and-bomber-jacket brigade. I can see it now: he drops his aitches, drinks Carlsberg Special Brew – from the can – is heavily into Bob Marley and wants to smash the Tory government.

Baz Sounds like a nice boy.

Annie If you like that kind of thing.

Jane People aren't kinds of things. They're people.

Annie Not in my experience.

Jane I'm sure.

Annie No, dear. In my experience, people play it strictly by the book. The handbook of social conditioning, and all that.

Baz Depends how you look at it.

Annie Sorry?

Baz I said . . . depends how you look at it.

Pause.

Annie Well, Baz. You really have cornered the market in stupid comments, haven't you?

Baz Bollocks.

Annie Oh, scathing.

Pause.

Viv Can I have your rent cheques today? And there's an electric bill to pay.

Jane How much?

Viv Thirty-five each.

Baz What?

Viv It's right. They checked it.

Baz Bloody hell. Rusty's gonna have to start buying his own.

Jane Can I give it to you tomorrow? I'll have to get it off my mum.

Viv I wanted to pay them tomorrow.

Jane If I give you a cheque now, it might bounce.

Viv Me, too, that's the trouble.

Baz Pay it on Tuesday.

Viv I want to do it tomorrow, OK?

Jane How about if I give you the rent today and the electric tomorrow?

Beat.

Viv Yeah, that'll be all right.

Jane I'll get my cheque book.

Viv Don't worry. Do it later.

Jane Might as well do it now.

She goes off.

Annie Like getting blood out of a stone. (*She rubs her nose.*) If you know what I mean.

Baz I should leave those sort of comments in the playground.

Annie Hmm? Sorry, don't follow.

Baz (*to* **Viv**) I'll give you mine later.

Viv No hurry. Can't pay it in till tomorrow, anyway.

Baz What's all the fuss about, then?

Viv I just want to make sure I get it, that's all.

Door slams off stage.

Baz 'Course, you'll get it.

Annie She doesn't mean yours, silly.

Baz Fucking hell.

Tone *enters with* The Observer *and* Sunday Times.

Tone Mornin' all.

Annie Well hello, Tone.

Tone Hello.

Annie I'm Annie. (*She holds out her hand.*)

Tone Yeah, I guessed. (*He shakes her hand. She stares at his fingernails.*) It's a hand.

Annie I know. With fingernails.

Tone Yeah. I got a full set. Wanna see me teeth?

Annie It's a bit early for me.

Tone Some other time.

Annie Who knows?

Jane *enters and hands* **Viv** *a cheque.*

Viv Thanks.

Jane (*to* **Tone**) Coffee?

Tone Ta.

Viv *and* **Baz** *both take bits of the papers and sit and read at the table.* **Tone**, *looking slightly annoyed, takes a bit of the paper.*

Annie Well. This is cosy. (*Pause.*) I said . . .

Baz Shut up, woman, I'm trying to read.

Annie Keep trying. You'll get the hang of it. (*Pause.*) Newspapers are so boring.

Baz Blah blah blah.

Pause. **Jane** *gives* **Tone** *his coffee.*

Annie Look at you. Bunch o' stiffs. What's so interesting about bloody papers anyway?

Tone It's called information.

Annie About what?

Tone Oh, this an' that.

Viv And 'Peanuts'.

Pause.

Annie Sorry?

Viv 'Peanuts'. In the magazine. (*She holds it up.*)

Annie Oh, 'Peanuts'. Well, that changes everything. Sling it over. Let me read and learn. (*Pause.*) 'Peanuts'. Christ.

Viv You gonna be like this all day?

Annie Who knows? I have a feeling it could be one of those days. I mean, you know how it is when you wake up in the morning and get out the wrong side of the futon.

She stands, naked, picks up her clothes and goes off.

Tone She often do that?

Viv What?

Tone Stumble around wi' nothin' on.

Viv I didn't notice.

Tone I did.

Jane It's a bit . . .

Viv What?

Jane Unnecessary.

Baz Only does it to be noticed.

Jane It worked.

Baz It's yer sheltered upbringing, lass.

Tone Naah. We've all seen Woodstock, maaan.

Pause. **Viv** *gets up and goes off.*

Baz Ah. Baz's first law. Never criticise Viv's pals. It'll only end in tears. (*Pause.*) Baz's second law. Keep *stumm* and keep your head down. (**Tone** *glowers at him.*) I think I just broke that one.

Tone (*arch*) You must let me have a copy of the rules. I'd so hate to make a gaffe.

Baz They're highly strung round here. You have to play it by ear.

Tone You know me. Only open me mouth to change feet.

Baz No good playing dumb. Can't have two of us doing that.

Tone How about if I maintain a dignified silence?

Baz That's just dumb with an English degree.

Tone Which would seem to be the prevailing human condition round here.

Jane So don't come round then.

Pause.

Tone Joke? (*Pause.*) No? (*Pause.*) For fuck's sake, darlin' . . .

Jane Oh, shut up.

Baz Time for Baz's second law.

Tone You should know.

Viv (*off*) Hurry up, you two. (*She comes on.*) And you, Baz.

Baz I'm ready.

Pause. She puts up the futon; **Jane** *helps.*

Viv Are you two staying in all day?

Jane Probably.

Viv Don't forget to double lock the door if you go out. (*Pause.*) I'll feel a lot happier when the burglar alarm's put in.

Tone Burglar alarm?

Viv Yeah. What's wrong with that?

Tone Nothin'. I s'pose.

Viv The number of break-ins you get round here's incredible.

Tone Yeah? I don't find it very hard to believe.

Viv You know what I mean.

Tone Oh, yeah. I know what you mean.

Pause.

Viv Nothing wrong with wanting to protect your own property, y'know.

Tone Never said there was.

Viv I've got every right to live here.

Tone Course, you've got a nice house, an' you wanna keep it that way, I can understand that.

Viv Thank you very much.

Tone 'S OK.

Viv I bet you'd do the same.

Tone I might.

Viv Well, then.

Tone Well, then.

Pause. **Rusty** *enters. He looks stunning, fully done up in New Romantic gear.*

Rusty I'm ready for the world. Is the world ready for me?

Baz You're never coming out like that.

Rusty And why not?

Baz Eee lad, I don't know where we went wrong. It's enough to make you throw your bollocks at the clock.

Rusty London's swinging again. I intend to swing with it.

Baz It's OK on stage, but . . .

Rusty But in the real world it's all fade to grey, right? Let's all do the conformity dance, right? No chance. This is me. If people don't like it . . .

Tone Let them eat cake.

Rusty Right. (*Pause. He is not amused.*) Ha ha. (*Pause.*) Who is this person?

Baz This is Tone.

Rusty Yes it is, isn't it.

Tone 'Ullo.

Rusty *gives a mirthless smile.*

Jane I really like your trousers.

Rusty Jodhpurs, darling. Jodhpurs.

Baz I give up.

Rusty Right. Full stop.

Annie *pops her head round the door.*

Annie Viv. Borrow a T-shirt?

Viv Yeah.

Annie Where are they?

Viv I'll show you.

She goes off.

Tone Does it really bother you that much?

Rusty Does what really bother me that much?

Tone Clothes. What people think.

Rusty It bothers people. It doesn't bother me.

Tone Proper little threat to society, aren't we?

Baz (*mock professor*) Ze vay I see it, Rusty is reacting against ze industrial drabness of contemporary Britain by making his stand as ze individual against ze crowd; by asserting his free spirit against ze dreaded collective vill. (*Beat.*) And ziz he does by going to clubs, vere two hundred uzzer free spirits stand around in identical clothes looking at each uzzer.

Rusty Piss off back to Bradford, Baz.

Baz Sheffield

Rusty Look, Baz, baby, I don't make jokes about what a wimp you are, or about the fact that your jacket's at least two sizes too big for you. So stay off my back and I'll stay off yours, OK?

Baz Touch-ee.

Rusty I just don't need the hassle, right?

Baz Whatever you say. (*He flashes a peace sign.*)

Rusty Look, I'll let you off, you do one thing for me.

Baz How much?

Rusty A fiver.

Baz You must be joking. I'm skint.

Rusty Well, so am I. Obviously.

Baz What about your dole?

Rusty In case you hadn't noticed, Baz, the bastards are on a work to rule. I haven't had a giro for two weeks. So come on.

Baz I haven't got a fiver to lend you.

Rusty Fucking hell. (*Pause.*) Jane? Till the end of the week? A measly fiver?

Jane I'll have to have it back.

Rusty What d'you think I'm gonna do? Emigrate with it?

Jane End of the week?

Rusty Yeah.

Beat.

Jane OK.

Rusty You're an angel. (*To* **Baz**.) And you're a shit.

Tone (*to* **Jane**) An' you bin done.

Jane (*giving* **Rusty** *a fiver*) Just don't forget.

Rusty Scout's honour. (*He gives her a peck on the cheek as* **Annie** *comes back in.*)

Annie Well. Can anyone join in?

Rusty Just sealing a financial transaction.

Annie Thought there must be a reason. Spontaneous demonstrations of affection not being exactly your thing.

Rusty I can be nice when I want to be.

Annie Yeah. Calculating sod.

Viv *enters.*

Viv We ready then?

Baz I've been ready for half an hour.

Viv We'll clean up when we get back.

Jane I'll do it. Don't worry.

Viv Don't be silly. It's our mess. Right. See you later.

Jane Bye.

Annie Enjoy the papers, Tone.

Tone I intend to.

They go. As the front door slams, **Jane** *and* **Tone** *both exhale loudly.*

Jesus Christ.

Jane You said it.

Tone What'd you give that creep a fiver for?

Jane Could hardly refuse, could I?

Tone Last you'll see of it.

Jane Better bloody not be.

Tone Look on the bright side. I think I'd quite enjoy wringing his neck if he don't cough up. (*Pause.*) C'mere. (*She sits on his lap. They kiss.*) 'Ow d'you get shacked up wi' this nest o' vipers, anyway?

Jane They're my friends.

Tone Unlucky, son.

Pause.

Jane Wanna go back to bed?

Tone What a good idea.

They turn to the door. The phone rings. She answers it.

Hello? (*Pause.*) Yeah. (*To* **Tone**.) It's for you. Someone called Lloyd.

Tone Ah. Do us a drink, will you? (*He takes the phone.*) Hi, Lloyd. (*Pause.*) Hang on, hang on, I can't hear you, you're talkin' too fast. (*Pause.*) 'Old it a minute. (*He gets his notebook and writes.*) Right. (*Pause.*) Who knifed him? (*Pause.*) Uh huh. How old is he? (*Pause.*) I'm just trying to get a story. (*Pause.*) How many? (*Pause.*) Any ol' bill get hurt? (*Pause. He smiles.*) I'd like to've seen that. (*Pause.*) What, SPG? (*Pause.*) So, what's the score now? (*Pause.*) You reckon? (*Pause.*) OK. Where are you?(*Pause.*) The Railway. Yeah, I know it. I'll be all right, will I? (*Pause.*) Is it worth comin' down now? (*Pause.*) I can do. (*Pause.*) OK. Say one o'clock outside the Railway. (*Beat.*) Hey listen, man, put a bleedin' film in your camera this time, will you? (*Pause. He laughs.*) Yeah, up yours an' all. One o'clock. See you. (*He puts the phone down and looks in the A to Z.*)

Jane What's happened?

He raises his hand.

Tone (*to himself*) Bingo. (*He shuts the book.*)

Jane Tone?

Tone Some black kid gets himself knifed. The ol' bill are givin' 'im first aid. Crowd gathers. Think he's gettin' roughed up. They go ape-shit. Turn the car over, the lot.

Jane My God, where?

Tone (*he points*) About four 'undred yards . . . that way.

Pause.

Jane So, are you going out?

Tone Not yet.

Jane Is it safe?

Tone Dunno. (*Pause.*)'S OK. Any trouble, I'll just flash me NUJ card. (*Pause.*) Wanna drink?

She starts tidying up.

What you doin'?

Jane Cleaning up.

Tone What for?

Jane Because it's a mess.

Tone It's their mess. Viv said so. Let them clean it up.

Jane She knows I'll do it.

Tone So don't.

Jane I've got to. There'll only be a broody silence if I don't.

Tone So? Let her brood.

Jane It's not worth it. (*She tidies up.*)

Tone You oughta give this place a name. Little plaque on the front gate. Something nice an' cosy, to go with the burglar alarm. 'The Pressure Cooker.' How about that? Very domestic. Or p'raps, 'Dunthinkin'.

Jane Stop it.

Pause.

Tone I thought we was goin' back to bed.

Jane I thought you were going out.

Tone Not yet.

Jane Don't let me stop you.

Tone I won't. (*Pause.*) Fuckin' burglar alarm . . . (*Pause.*) Look, I'm not meetin' Lloyd for an hour an' a half . . . (*He puts his arms round her.*) We could have a bath.

Jane I've had one.

Tone Have another one.

Jane If you don't think Lloyd'll mind.

Tone You got work to do, ain't you? So. I'll be outa your way.

Jane But, I don't want you out of my way.

Tone Can't spend your whole life in bed.

Jane Can try. (*They kiss.*) Water should be hot.

Tone Makes two of us. C'mon then.

Jane Wait. (*She quickly tidies the counter.*)

Tone Leave it. (*She does and starts to go. As he goes.*) This is Tony March. News at Ten. South London. (*He laughs and goes.*)

Fade.

Scene Two

Six forty-five that evening. **Tone** *is sitting very still with a look of mild horror on his face, watching 'Songs of Praise' on the TV. A hymn is playing very loud. He has a pile of papers and notes on his lap. He finishes his drink* *and stands, rather wobbly. He pours the last of the vodka and goes and looks out the window. He then turns the TV down, picks up the phone and dials.*

Tone Lloyd? Tone. How'd the pictures come out? (*Pause.*) Great. (*Pause.*) Yeah, I'm writin' it up now. I don't wanna make it too . . . sorta final, y'know. (*Pause. He laughs.*) Yeah. (*He gives a short whoop of joy.*) Look, why don't you meet me in the boozer over the road? (*Pause.*) I dunno. The Lamb an' somethin' or other. Lamb an' Goose, I dunno. (*Pause.*) 'Bout 'alf an hour. (*Pause.*) Right. Yeah, I'm 'alf outa me tree now. (*He's about to put the phone down.*) Eh? (*Pause.*) Never. (*Pause.*) Swamp as in . . . ? (*Pause.*) Boy, oh boy. (*Pause.*) OK. See you. (*He puts the phone down.*) Come on, God, strut that funky stuff. (*He turns the TV up. A door slams off stage.*) Oh, oh.

He sits. **Viv** *enters with her shopping.*

Viv Hi. (*He waves. She puts her shopping down and pours a scotch.*)

Tone (*agonised*) Enough. (*He turns the TV off. She stares at him.*) You weren't . . . ?

Viv No. Just surprised you were.

Tone Anti-torture training. Seein' 'ow long I could stand it. Bit of a failure, really. The SAS'd only 'ave to come in singing 'Abide wiv Me' an' I'd be putty in their 'ands. (*Beat.*) Hymns. Oughta be kept in their proper place. Church. Christmas. Fuck. Christmas. My ol' mum, y'know – godless ol' bugger three 'undred an' sixty four days o' the year. Then Christmas comes along an' wallop. Feudal 'ysteria. I say to 'er, 'Mum, what are you doin'?' Y'know, she's singing along wi' the goons on the box. She says, 'Sod off. Ain't doin' you no 'arm.' No 'arm in civilised people prattin' about celebratin' the invisible? 'S all a bit Freudian, you ask me. 'Ands an' buttocks clenched in the kneelin' position, 'avin' a rabbit wi' the almighty invisible one . . . Belongs in the Karma Sutra. (*Pause.*) What was I sayin'? (*Beat.*) Yeah, Christ, we all 'ave a good laugh at the Druids on Salisbury Plain every summer, don't we? An' that bloke, what's 'is name, outa Coronation Street, 'e's one. (*Beat.*) Druid. Ken Barlow. Prat. (*Beat.*) But 'ave a good look at St Paul's. What is it? I'll tell you. Stonehenge built by unionised labour. Thass what St Paul's is. (*Beat.*) No 'arm? As far as its 'arm value goes, I'd stick it on a par wi' the stock exchange, Soviet Communism and the MacDonald's hamburger. (*Pause.*) Where'd I start on this?

Viv Christmas, I think.

Tone Christmas? I 'ate Christmas. An' churches. An' Christians. I mean, they seem to think that 'cause they left their brains at the door on the way in, we gotta do the same. Gainful employment o' the ol' grey matter is takin' an unfair advantage, apparently. An' that ain't cricket. Ain't British. Ergo, rational debate is fairly an' squarely plonked back where they like to keep it. On the playing fields of Eton. Know what I mean?

Viv Not really.

Tone I shoulda thought it was crystal clear.

Beat.

Viv My mum once told me that the fact that I didn't believe in God was evidence of my own limited imagination.

Tone Yeah. There's only one thing I 'ate more than a Christian.

Viv What's that?

Tone A glib Christian.

Beat.

Viv She also told me to respect other people's beliefs.

Tone Impeccable bloody liberal, your mum. Why? Respect?

Viv I dunno. 'Cause it takes courage?

Tone So does jumpin' out of a plane without a parachute. Don't earn you a lot o' respect, though.

Viv Can't you talk about it without . . .

Tone Descending to cliché?

Viv Quite.

Tone No, I meant you were . . .

Viv Charming.

Tone Not at all. Fuckin' rude, I'd say.

Viv I was using bourgeois understatement.

Tone I know. I can smell it a mile off. (*Pause.* **Viv** *takes out dope gear and rolls a joint.*) I've tried, y'know. Prayin'. Seriously . . . When I 'ad a bit of spiritual crisis. I went down on me knees, clenched tight, and I asked God if he had any ideas on the theory of surplus value. An' did 'e? Not a sausage. So. That left me with two possible conclusions: One, God doesn't exist. Two, God exists, but 'e's never read Marx. Now, on the basis that two is correct, I can only draw one conclusion: 'Arold Wilson is God. (*Beat.*) Frightenin' innit? (*He finishes his drink and pours a small scotch.*) I went to Sunday School once. Sat there an' cried me eyes out. Never went again. From that moment on, I was a born-again pagan.

Beat.

Viv Aren't you frightened of dying?

Tone No. (*Long pause.*) D'you know what I'm frightened of? I'm frightened of Sir Geoffrey Howe. And his new Jerusalem. His Property Owning Democracy. That's what I call death. (*Pause.*) They love it, don't they, our rulers? They love their Christianity. Gives us something to blame. Kids got rickets? Bugger. Ol' God again, up to 'is tricks. Lost your job? Believe in God an' die 'appy. 'Alf the world starves while the other 'alf over-consumes? Funny ol' world innit? Still, blame God. An' don't try 'avin' a go at 'im about all this death an' destruction, 'cause 'e ain't fuckin' there! Well, 'e is, but 'e ain't. Get it? Good, now toddle along an' don't ask no more stupid questions. An' we do! We all toddle along. A conspiracy of ignorance. An' 'cause *we're* all past 'elp anyway, all our bright-eyed missionaries an' would-be martyrs trot off an' take it, like rabies, to another lot of unsuspectin', thick, punters. 'The West suckin' *your* country dry? Not got enough to eat? Never mind. Read this bible. Tells you all about 'ow it's got to 'appen 'cause God made the world an' business believes in God. An' you'll love the miracles, you bein' a bit primitive an' all.' I tell you, when I see all those smug vicars an' smilin' nuns an' serene fuckin' monks I feel sick. They're so proud. Proud they got the answer. Proud we 'respect their courage.' Proud they're immune. (*Beat.*) Honest, sometimes I could murder Cliff Richard. (*Pause.*) I'm an extremist, y'see.

Viv Oh.

Tone Yeah. Oh. No compromise. No accommodation. I don't suffer fools gladly. Loony left. I won't drown in the waters of the middle ground. (*Beat.*) My other hobbies include mixing metaphors and getting drunk.

Pause.

Viv Where's Jane?

Tone Upstairs, workin'.

Viv When do her exams start?

Tone Six, seven weeks, I dunno.

Viv And what are your feelings on that?

Tone On what?

Viv A girlfriend who's training to be a solicitor?

Tone Up to 'er. There's law an' there's law. (*He takes out a couple of pills, blue, and swallows them.*)

Viv What's that?

Tone Speed.

Viv Wouldn't have thought you needed it.

Tone I'm a very shy, retiring boy, really. (*Beat.*) Better'n that stuff. Last thing I need's slowin' down.

Viv Helps me relax.

Tone So, who wants to relax? 'Specially today.

Viv What's so special about today?

Tone Today, with any luck, is the day we tell 'Operation Swamp' to stuff it.

Viv Operation what?

Tone Swamp, darlin'. Swamp. Ring any bells? Remember the phrase, 'swamped by an alien culture?' Remember who said that?

Viv No.

Tone The copper's friend. Margaret Thatcher. Accordin' to 'er penetratin' analysis, we are in danger of bein' swamped by an alien culture. Viz: nasty darkies in Brixton. Hence: 'Operation Swamp.' Christ. Where you bin?

Viv Camden.

Pause.

Tone You, er, notice anythin' outside?

Viv Like what?

Tone Like, more coppers 'n a Freemason's ball?

Viv Oh. The police.

Tone Yeah. The police.

Viv I did notice one or two.

Tone One or two? Thass an army of occupation. An' armies start wars.

Viv I find it hard to think of a few policemen as an army of occupation.

Tone You ain't black.

Viv Neither are you.

Tone 'S not the point. You own a house. A nice house. Unfortunately, you're gonna be right slap bang in the middle when it all goes up. You'll be lookin' to the police for 'elp.

Viv That *is* what they're there for.

Tone Nah. Christ, I thought you went to University. The police force was created to protect the property an' persons o' the middle an' upper classes from the poor people o' the slums. Dixon o' Dock Green didn't just sort of evolve outa the primeval slime. He was made. For a reason. A bloody great patch on the rotten social fabric. (*Beat.*) An' 'e's carryin' on 'is 'istoric mission out there now. Tonight. Liftin' anyone wiv a black face for whatever reason he cares to make up. It's known as positive policing. An' it's a mistake. There's gonna be 'ell to pay. (*Pause.*) Anyway. I feel like a jolly-up. (*He goes to the door and shouts.*) Jane.

Jane (*off*) Coming.

Tone I'm off.

Viv I don't think you'll get your war.

Tone I'll huff an' I'll puff an' I'll . . .

Jane *enters.*

Jane What are you doing?

Tone Goin' over the boozer.

Jane What for?

Tone A drink? Make sense?

Jane I thought we were going to have a meal.

Tone 'Nother time. I gotta meet Lloyd.

Jane Bloody Lloyd. Why don't you go *out* with Lloyd? He sees more of you than I do.

Tone Nah. I've 'ad 'im. 'E's rubbish. (*Beat.*) C'mon, doll. This is important.

Jane So you keep telling me.

Pause.

Tone I'll catch you later. (*He kisses her.*)

Jane I might be out.

He stops and smiles at her, then goes.

Viv Men. (*Pause.*) Drink?

Jane Yeah. Why not.

Viv *pours two scotches and hands one to* **Jane.** *She clinks the glasses.*

Viv Cheers.

Jane Cheers.

Pause.

Viv How's work going?

Jane Boring. Company law. Who needs it?

Viv Companies? (*They smile.*) Lovely earrings.

Jane Oh, I made them.

Viv They really go with your eyes.

Jane Thanks. I could make you a pair if you want.

Viv Have to be a different colour. To go with my eyes. Something small and pinky.

Jane Your eyes are a lovely colour.

Viv And what colour, exactly, would you say that was? I've never been able to make my mind up about that.

Jane (*looking into her eyes*) Sort of . . .

Viv See? Nondescript.

Jane No. Sort of . . . browny grey.

Viv Sludge.

Jane No.

Viv Mud.

Jane Browny grey. What's wrong with that?

Viv It's not a colour, that's what's wrong with it.

Pause.

Jane Been shopping?

Viv Yeah. Camden Lock. I went mad. Spent fifty quid.

Jane No.

Viv Yeah.

Jane How can you afford it?

Viv I can't. But I got some lovely things. Look. (*She takes out a jacket.*) I just bought whatever I fancied. Trousers. (*She takes the things out.*) Jumper for work. If I ever get any. Some T-shirts.

Jane I like the trousers.

Viv Annie's got a pair almost the same.

Jane They're nice. I've seen them.

Viv Nice on Annie. Probably make me look like a horse.

Jane 'Course they won't.

Viv If I try them on, will you give me an honest opinion? 'Cause I can take them back if I don't like them.

Jane They'll be fine.

Viv I may need your help, Jane. (*Pause.* **Viv** *puts the trousers on. They won't do up.*) I *do* need your help. (*She takes a deep breath as* **Jane** *yanks the zip up.*)

Jane There.

Viv (*breathing out*) Oh . . . God . . . (*She laughs.*) Is it worth it?

Jane They'll stretch. (**Viv** *undoes the button, takes a deep breath and does it up again.*) OK?

Viv Mmm. What do they look like?

Jane Fine.

Viv Be a bit more positive.

Jane They look great.

Viv Am I the most beautiful woman you've ever seen?

Jane You are, without doubt, the most beautiful woman in the world.

Viv You're saying this of your own free will?

Jane Would I lie to you?

Viv End the conversation there, I think. (*She laughs.*) Oh. Look, I bought this. (*She holds up a T-shirt.*) I know it doesn't suit me. D'you want it?

Jane It's yours. Put it on.

Viv (*holding it up against herself*) Look. (*The T-shirt is very flashy.*) If that's me, I must be someone else.

Jane Try it on.

Viv So you can have a good laugh? (*She takes her top off and puts the T-shirt on.*) Oh, repulsive. Here. (*She takes it off and throws it to* **Jane**.)

Jane You sure?

Viv Sure, I'm sure.

Jane *takes off her top.* **Viv** *stares.* **Jane** *puts the T-shirt on.*

Jane Well?

Viv *walks around* **Jane** *arranging the shirt.*

Viv It's yours.

Jane How much was it?

Viv Only a couple of quid.

Jane Let me give it to you.

Viv Don't worry.

Jane No. I insist. (*She gets the money from her purse and hands it to* **Viv**.)

Viv It was supposed to be a present. (*Pause.*) Another drink?

Jane No, I've got to work.

Viv One more won't hurt. (*She pours.*) Cheers.

Jane Cheers. You'll catch cold.

Viv Mmm? Oh no. Not only do I look like a horse, but I've got the constitution of an ox.

Jane You shouldn't be so negative.

Viv *gets up and walks to the door.*

Viv I'll try to think beautiful thoughts.

Viv *goes out.* **Jane** *puts the scotch bottle away, thinks, and takes off the T-shirt. She examines the price label.* **Viv** *comes back in.*

Jane A couple of quid? Five seventy-five.

Viv Was it? Oh well.

Jane Viv . . .

Viv Sssh. (*She puts her finger to* **Jane**'s *lips and smiles.*) Please? (**Jane** *puts the T-shirt back on.* **Viv** *gives her a gentle hug.*) It's nice. Very you. (*She looks around, puzzled, then looks all round the room.*)

Jane What've you lost?

Viv Have you hidden it or something?

Jane What?

Viv The scotch.

Jane I put it back in the cupboard.

Viv Why?

Jane I dunno.

Viv I want some more.

Jane It's only in the cupboard.

Viv I didn't put it there.

Pause.

Jane Sorry.

She gets the bottle and holds it out to **Viv**. **Viv** *holds out her glass. Pause.* **Jane** *takes the top off the bottle and pours. They look at each other.* **Viv** *takes a swig.*

Viv Have one yourself.

Jane I . . . might go over the pub.

Viv Chasing after Tone? Bad move. I'm meeting the others at 'Rumours' in Covent Garden. Why don't you come?

Jane No thanks.

Pause.

Viv You should come out with us sometimes.

Jane I've got too much work. Anyway, I don't like trooping around in a gang.

Viv A gang. Is that what we are?

Jane I don't mean . . . Well, you know what I mean.

Viv I think I do. A gang of what? (*Beat.*) A gang of kids?

Jane No . . .

Viv Just a gang. (*Beat.*) I don't want to go to this bloody cocktail bar.

Jane Don't then.

Pause. Then **Viv** *laughs.*

Viv That's right. I don't have to, do I? (*Pause.*) I might as well, though. They're expecting me. The gang. (*Pause.*) 'S a funny thought, isn't it? That this is all mine. The chairs . . . carpet . . . table . . . saucepans . . . wallpaper . . . Even the dirt in the corners is mine. The ring round the bath is mine. I own it. 'S a funny thought. I mean, what are you supposed to do with it? When you own it? Look. Here it all is . . . And what?

Pause.

Jane Just live in it.

Viv Just live in it. What a drag. (*Pause.*) I know. I'll have a party. Haven't had a party for ages. A weekend bash. We'll go on for days. Maybe never stop. Tell your friends. (*Pause.*) What I'd really like is a house with a garden. Chelsea or somewhere. That's what I should aim for.

Jane Chelsea? Cost the earth.

Viv My parents . . . My parents look on it as an investment. I'm sort of sitting on their money watching it grow. (*Pause.*) I'd rather watch it grow in Chelsea, frankly. With a garden.

Pause. **Viv** *stands and starts getting dressed.*

Jane I'd better get back to work.

Viv Not going lusting after Tone?

Jane Not right now, no.

Viv Good for you. Not worth it, men I mean, look at Rusty . . .

Jane Rusty?

Viv I lusted after Rusty. God, did I lust.

Jane You didn't . . . ?

Viv Screw him? Did I ever. (*Pause.*) I tend to go off people after I've had sex with them, though. Odd, isn't it?

Jane Yes. I don't.

Viv No. You're the deeply faithful type.

Pause.

Jane I'll probably see you later. If I'm still up.

Viv Yes.

Pause.

Jane Thanks for the T-shirt.

Viv 'S OK.

Jane *goes.* **Viv** *is now dressed.*

Drinky-poo.

She pours a scotch and drinks. She picks up **Jane**'s *discarded top and gently smells it. Pause. She takes out her new jacket and puts it on. She poses, then flops down in the chair. She looks around.*

Hello room. You're all mine.

Beat.

Fade.

Scene Three

Midnight that night. **Baz** *is connecting wires between two reel-to-reel tape recorders.* **Viv** *and* **Annie** *are making cocktails from a recipe book. They are all very drunk and the women are laughing.*

Viv You haven't got enough ice.

Annie Bollocks, Viv. There's masses of ice in there.

Viv Bollocks, Annie. It needs more. (*She goes to the fridge.*)

Annie We're making cocktails, not sinking the Titanic.

Viv *puts more ice in the shaker.*

Viv There.

Annie You're s'posed to crush it first. Oh Christ. Now we'll have to put more everything in.

Viv Uh-huh. (*They giggle.* **Viv** *reads from the book. As she calls them out,* **Annie** *pours them in.*) OK. Dark rum.

Annie Dark rum.

Viv Light rum.

Annie Light rum.

Viv Squeeze of lime.

Annie Squeeze of lime.

Viv Squeeze of lemon.

Annie Squeeze of lemon.

Viv Bitters.

Annie Bitters.

Viv Cointreau.

Annie Cointreau.

Viv Vodka.

Annie Vodka. Eh ?

Viv (*pouring them in as she says them*) Vodka. Gin. Brandy. Martini.

Annie Jesus Christ, Viv. What are you doing?

Viv This cocktail is my very own invention. The Neutron Bomb. Destroys human flesh, but leaves the house intact.

Annie Don't spill it on the carpet. It'll burn a bloody hole.

Viv Now . . . We shake (*She shakes it.*) And stand well back and pour. (*She pours four drinks.*) Bit of a funny colour.

Annie You're telling me.

Viv Ah. Cherries. Where are the cherries? Can't have a cocktail without cherries. Very bad form.

Annie They're here somewhere. (*She turns out the kitchen cupboard. They both laugh.*) Anchovies. Olives (*She holds up a jar.*) Er . . . cockles?

Viv Cockles? (*Pause.*) Tone!

Annie (*holding her nose*): Ugh. (*She puts them back in the cupboard.*)

Viv Wonder if he's got any winkles?

They laugh. **Baz** *looks round and shakes his head.*

Baz Where's me bloody drink?

Annie We're just looking for the cherries, dummy.

Baz Well, hurry up. Oh, sod the cherries. (*He goes to take his glass.*)

Viv (*holding them up*) Cherries!

Annie Wait wait wait. Cocktail sticks.

Viv Cocktail sticks . . .

Baz Bugger the cocktail sticks. (*He takes a cherry and drops it in his glass.*)

Annie Ooh, you're so couth.

Baz I'm in need of a drink, woman. (*He sips.*) Bloody hell fire. (*They laugh.*) What you put in there?

Annie Oh . . . Rum . . .

Viv Vodka . . .

Annie Vinegar . . .

Viv Meths . . .

Annie Harpic . . .

Baz Bloody tastes like it an' all. I can't drink that.

Viv 'Course you can. Look. (*She picks up a glass and downs it in one.*) See?

Baz You'll kill yourself.

Annie Don't be such a wimp, Baz. (*She downs a glass. Pause.*) Oh . . . My . . . God. (**Viv** *laughs.*) He's right. I'm gonna die. (*They both laugh.*)

Baz You're both round the twist.

Rusty *enters.*

Rusty Baz, haven't you got it fucking set up yet?

Baz No, I fucking haven't.

Rusty How long does it take, for Christ's sake?

Baz Do it your bloody self.

Rusty Darling, you're the one with the magic screwdriver, right? (*Viv and* **Annie** *giggle.*) Oh, for crying out loud.

Annie Have a drink.

Rusty If you insist.

Viv We do.

Rusty (*takes a sip*) Oh yeah. Very funny. What is it?

Annie It's a bloody cocktail, isn't it?

Rusty Yeah? Well maybe it needs a little more eye of newt.

Viv Of course!

Baz *goes back to the tape recorders as they start making more cocktails.*

Rusty See if you can do a proper one. See if you can manage a 'Between the Sheets.'

Annie Be more than you can. (*They laugh.*)

Rusty Pathetic.

Annie Oh, poor old Rusty. Did we hurt his feelings?

Viv Shall we make it better? (*They both go over to him.*) Where's it hurt, then?

Annie Is it very bad?

Viv You poor old thing. (*They're both pawing him.*)

Annie Mmm. Poor old thing.

Rusty (*ignoring them*) How's it going, Baz?

Baz Won't be long.

Rusty Good. (*He takes a piece of paper out of his pocket and reads.*)

Annie For God's sake.

Viv Rotten bastard.

Rusty Sorry? D'you say something?

Annie Conceited little rat.

Rusty Look, darlings, I'm just going to put some words over a backing track, right? It won't take very long. And when I've finished, you'll have my undivided attention, OK?

Annie (*to* **Viv**) Don't hold your breath.

Viv I'm gonna make another cocktail.

She goes back to the drinks.

Annie (*to* **Rusty**) Why d'you have to do that now?

Rusty I promised Phil I'd give it to him tomorrow.

Annie Can't he wait?

Rusty No.

Annie It's only a piddling song.

Rusty It's not only a piddling song! (**Annie** *blows a raspberry*.) Baz!

Baz All right!

Rusty Christ!

Jane *enters.*

Jane Hi. Sounds like you're having fun.

Viv *and* **Annie** *are immediately more subdued.*

Viv We're doing some cocktails. Have a taste.

Jane Is it very strong?

Annie Wouldn't be a cocktail if it wasn't, would it?

Jane S'pose not. Well. (*She sips.*) Crumbs. Not for me.

Viv Chicken.

Jane You actually drinking that?

Viv Drinking it? We're awash with it. (*She finishes off the glass and pours some more.*)

Rusty They're being really heroic. Dead impressive.

Annie I'd tell you to drop dead if you didn't give the impression that you already have.

Viv (*serious*) Rusty, we're s'posed to be having a party. It's s'posed to be fun. This is my house, and when I say everybody have fun, then everybody has fun.

Rusty Fun. Right. (*He suddenly picks up the glasses and drains them,* *drinks from the shaker and bottles as*) Hey! This is great! I'm having a great time! Whoopee! Fun fun fun!! (*Pause. Out of breath.*) How's that? (*Pause.* **Viv** *suddenly slaps him on the shoulder.*) Hey, that hurts.

Viv Good.

She slaps again and again, pushing him onto the sofa. He starts hitting her back. They struggle. He tickles her. She giggles and suddenly kisses him. He kisses her back.

Annie Someone give Ken Russell a ring, he'd love this.

She grabs **Rusty** *and joins in.* **Baz**, *headphones on, is still busy with the tapes.* **Jane** *stands, faintly embarrassed, uncertain what to do. Then she goes over to them.*

Jane If Tone comes in, can you tell him . . . ?

Rusty *grabs her and pulls her over. She becomes part of the melee, but pulls herself away and stands up.*

Yeah. Great fun.

She goes. Pause. They all burst out laughing.

Annie Got rid of her.

Rusty Can't we get her back?

Viv No.

Annie Uptight bitch.

Viv I need a drink.

Rusty I know what I need.

Annie Tough titty.

Rusty Oh, come on.

Annie Gotta do your backing track, haven't you?

Rusty I'm putting my voice over the backing track, stupid.

Annie Same difference.

Rusty It can wait.

Annie (*going over to* **Viv**) Right. What shall we put in this one?

Viv Arsenic. We'll all commit ritual suicide on poisoned cocktails.

Annie What a lovely way to go.

Viv We could get in the car and just drive, knowing we only had ten minutes to live. Leave now, in the dark, never see the sun again. Hit the motorway, never see the end. Ever.

Annie Let's not get morbid, dear.

Viv It's the booze.

Annie No, it's not. It's you. (*Pause.*) C'mon. We're s'posed to be having fun.

Viv Yeah. (*She downs a drink in one.*) Come on.

Annie *does the same.*

Annie We need a top up.

Viv How right you are.

Rusty Look girls, you're gonna make yourselves ill.

Annie So who gives a flying one?

Rusty I do. I'm the one who's gotta sleep with it, right?

Annie No one's forcing you. You're not exactly gonna be dragged screaming into bed.

Rusty Oh. I was rather hoping . . .

Annie Ha ha. Look, if you don't like it . . .

Rusty I know what I can do.

Annie Yeah. Don't forget.

Viv She can always sleep in my bed.

Annie *puts her arm round* **Viv**.

Annie (*to* **Rusty**) I don't need you.

Rusty Stop playing games.

Viv Who's playing games?

Rusty You're gonna feel very silly in the morning.

Annie How do you know?

Pause.

Viv You should be nicer to us. Treat us with a little more respect. We're a little bit fed up with being used, y'know. A little bit miffed that you seem to think we're only here for your benefit. (*Pause.*) You like to break the rules, Rusty. So do we. Don't we?

Annie Yeah.

Pause. They kiss.

Viv See?

Rusty (*dry*) Revolutionary. Real fifth form stuff. (*Pause.*) Honestly, girls, I'm not impressed.

Baz (*taking off the headphones and turning round*) All set to go.

Pause.

Rusty About time.

Baz All set to go? Thanks, Baz. That's all right, Rusty. Anything for a pal. (*Pause.*) Just don't ask again.

Rusty What is this? Open season? I mean, what did I do?

Annie You breathed.

Pause.

Rusty OK. Whatever it is I've done to offend everyone . . . I'm sorry. Right? Now, please, just get off my back.

Pause.

Annie Well . . . He did say sorry.

Viv Only just.

Annie Well, it *was* his first time.

Viv Frighten you, did we?

Pause.

Baz Look, I'll play this . . . (*He switches on the tape recorder. Music comes out: electro-synthesizer pop style.*) . . . OK? Now, you wear the headphones and you sing into this mike, which then records your voice over the voice and backing track that's already there. Got it?

Rusty What d'you think I am? An idiot?

Annie Don't answer that.

Baz Have you got it?

Rusty 'Course I've got it.

Baz Right. I'll just wind back to the beginning, then you're ready.

Rusty OK.

Viv What's the song called?

Rusty (*self-conscious*) 'The Shock of the New.'

Viv Catchy.

Rusty Look, don't put me off while I'm doing it, will you?

Annie Wouldn't dream of it.

Viv D'you want us to stand out of the way?

Rusty Yeah, that's cool.

Viv Must do what the man says, Annie.

They stand by the window, every now and then breaking into laughter.

Rusty And don't make any noise. It'll come out on the tape.

Annie Ssssh

Rusty *puts the headphones on. The girls giggle.*

Rusty I heard that.

They stand, trying not to laugh. **Baz** *switches on the tape.* **Rusty** *clicks his fingers in time with the music. He looks unsure where to begin. He starts.*

There's a – fuck it. (*They laugh.*) Sorry, Baz. I wasn't sure where it started. Back to the beginning?

Baz You know where to come in?

Rusty Yeah. I got it now. (**Baz** *starts the tape again.* **Rusty** *clicks his fingers and starts to sing.*) 'There's a –'

The door flies open and **Tone** *rushes in. He's wearing gloves and a bandana round his neck.*

For fuck's sake!

Baz, **Annie** *and* **Viv** *are in hysterics.*

Tone What 'appened to the milk bottles?

Rusty Milk bottles?!

Tone Yeah. There was a load 'ere.

Rusty How should we know where they are?!

Tone *looks and finds them in a plastic bag*

Viv What d'you want the milk bottles for?

Tone Cocktails.

He goes.

Rusty Stupid prick. OK, Baz. Try again.

Viv *and* **Annie** *peer through the blinds.* **Rusty** *puts the headphones on.*
Viv *gets* **Annie** *and herself a drink. The tape starts.* **Rusty** *clicks his*
fingers and sings.

There's a finger on my pulse / And the pulse is getting weak /
Hold your head back / Look around / People dying / What's that
sound / It's heading for you / It's the shock of the new / Can you
feel it too / It's the shock of the new. Lights are going out / Walls
falling down / You ask yourself / What did I do / Your eyes are
shut / They're stuck like glue / To the shock of the new / And it's
heading for you / Can you feel it too / It's the shock of the new.

During the last verse and chorus we hear police sirens outside. **Annie**, **Viv**
and **Baz** *stare out.* **Rusty** *is oblivious.*

You can't resist / So don't fight back / You can't resist / So don't
fight back / That's their game / They'll suck you in / They'll chain
you in / Eernal sin

Jane *enters.* **Rusty** *continues.*

But it's heading for you / It's the shock of the new / Can you feel it
too / It's the shock of the new.

Rusty *keeps clicking his fingers till the song ends, then he hears the sirens.*
He pulls off the headphones. They turn and look at him, frightened.

Jane It's a riot.

Pause.

Rusty THEY RUINED MY SONG!

Blackout.

Scene Four

4 a.m. next morning. The room is dark, dawn just coming in through the
window. **Viv** *is sitting in the chair. The front door slams off stage. The door*
opens. **Tone** *enters. He goes to the fridge, takes out a can of beer and opens*
it. He turns on the light. There is a small trickle of blood on his forehead. He
sees **Viv**. *Pause.*

Tone Still up?

Pause. She holds up a large kitchen knife.

Doin' yer nails? (*Pause.*) Whassat in aid of, then? (*Pause.*) Ah. This must be what Jane calls your broody silence. (*Pause.*)

Viv Does she talk about me a lot?

Tone Not 'specially.

Viv What does she say about me?

Tone Nothin'.

Pause.

Viv I feel threatened.

Tone I 'ad gathered that. (*Pause.*) 'S no need. No one's gonna break in 'ere.

Viv How do I know?

Tone 'S all dyin' down now. Everyone's knackered. (*Pause.*) You bin out?

Viv No.

Tone Should 'ave. Quite an experience.

Viv D'you enjoy yourself?

Tone A wonderful time was had by all.

Viv You should be shot. (*Pause.*) You've cut your head.

Tone Yeah. Pretty rotten trick, as it 'appens. There we are, lobbin' rocks at the ol' bill, an' they start lobbin' 'em back. Crack. I catch one on the bonce.

Viv Good. (**Tone** *smiles.*) What's funny?

Pause.

Tone Want some beer?

Viv No. (*Pause.*) I could arrest you. Citizen's arrest. Hand you over.

Tone What for?

Viv You're dangerous. Might be about to rob the house. I could stab you. Self defence. You could be a rapist. Who knows? (*Pause.*) Pour me a scotch.

Tone Nope. (*Pause.*) If I pour you a scotch, will you put the knife away?

Viv Nope! (*Pause.*) You know my parents live in California?

Tone Yeah?

Viv They have a gun. Two. One each.

Tone 'S only fair.

Viv Yes. (*Pause.*) Please will you pour me a scotch?

Tone I think you've already 'ad a few.

Viv I've been drinking all day. I've drunk myself sober. Please.

He gets up and pours a scotch. As he hands it to her, she slowly cuts the back of his hand with the knife. He holds the glass out to her. Pause. She takes it.

Thank you.

He takes the scarf from his neck and wraps it round his hand.

Tone You can put it away now. (**Viv** *smiles.*)

Viv Are you frightened?

Tone Of you?

Viv Yes.

Tone Leave it out.

Viv What if I stabbed you?

Tone I'd put it down to experience.

Viv You'd bleed.

Tone That too.

Viv You deserve to bleed.

Tone I ain't doin' too badly so far. (*Pause.*) Not gettin' on very well, are we?

Viv No. I think it's because we despise each other.

Tone I'll go along wi' that.

Pause.

Viv It's a bit of a nerve, isn't it? Coming into my house, spreading your trail of disgust around. Like a slug. Everywhere you look, a little silver trail. I'd say it's a bit of a nerve.

Tone Would you?

Viv Yes. (*Pause.*) You make me think of creepy crawlies. Things that make your skin creep. Slugs. Leeches. Spiders. Things that live in your house whether you want them there or not. Things you leave little traps for. Chemicals. If I pour salt on you, will you shrivel up?

Tone Maybe.

Viv That'd be nice. To watch your skin bubble and melt. Slowly pouring on more until you were dead. It takes a long time. Oh, the pain.

Tone Like that, would you?

Viv Very much.

Pause.

Tone Pretty little mind you got there.

Viv I like it. (*Pause.*) I wouldn't think things like that if you weren't here. It's really your own fault. I mean, I've not been inhospitable. I've let Jane have you here. And all you've done is shit on us.

Tone What I do outside these four walls, what I am, is none o' your business. None at all.

Viv But, you're not outside these four walls, are you? I mean . . . Here you are. And what you are is my business. You squat there like you own the place. Looking down your nose at us. Sneering. Superior.

Tone An' we can't 'ave two of us lookin' like we own the place, can we?

Viv I do own it.

Tone Here endeth the lesson.

Viv Talk to me! Don't sit there making statements, sneering.

Tone I don't wanna talk to you. What's the point? All I get is abuse.

Viv Abuse is all you know. A steady trickle, hidden away, very subtle. But all the time, you're trying to dig away, scratching holes in my life.

Tone You can't scratch holes in a string vest.

Viv You can tell Jane I don't want you here any more.

Tone Tell 'er yourself. It's 'er decision.

Viv It's my decision.

Tone Look, just because mummy an' daddy own the bricks an' mortar, don't mean you got any say in 'ow Jane runs 'er life.

Viv We've all got to live here.

Tone Oh, finally noticed, 'ave yer? I was beginnin' to think this was your own private party. No gatecrashers allowed. That's 'ow you think o' me, innit? Wasn't invited, didn't bring a bottle, doesn't join in. Well, honestly, darlin', I don't wanna join in wi' the crummy little scene you got 'ere. I'm 'ere 'cause Jane asked me to come. As is 'er right. Now, if you don't like it, I suggest you learn to live wiv it, or stick it. (*Pause.*) Can't understand it, can yer? Everyone else treats you like yer the belle o' the ball. They respect you, don't they? That's what you'd like to think. Dead popular, you are. An' I can tell 'ow much you want that. Not surprisin', really. I mean, if I was like you, I'd wanna be loved. I'd pretend, like you. I s'pose I'd 'ate me as well, 'cause . . . see . . . I respect people, not the things they own. An' you 'ave to earn respect, which is prob'ly where you fall down. I mean, when 'ave you ever 'ad to earn anything? (*Pause.*) Least I can stop pretendin', now. I don't 'ave to be polite any more, pretend I can actually stand bein' in the same fuckin' room as you. (*Pause.*) Message ends.

Pause.

Viv You don't know the first thing about me.

Tone Got 'idden depths, 'ave you?

Pause.

Viv Get out.

Tone In me own good time.

Viv Get out. Or I'll call the police.

Tone I wouldn't do that. I reckon they'd be quite interested in some o' the substances in common use round 'ere.

Pause.

Viv I don't think I like people very much.

Tone Awkward, ain't they? Minds o' their own. Bit of a bugger, eh?

Viv You've got no right to say any of this.

Tone Talk to me, you said. So, I'm talkin'. Sorry you don't like what you 'ear.

Viv You really think I don't know? What I am? You really think I don't hate myself?

Tone Shows good judgement.

Viv Don't. Please.

Tone Don't expect me to go all soft 'cause you finally own up to the truth. You'll be your ol' self again tomorrow. 'Ave to be. Otherwise, 'ow could you go on? (*Pause.* **Viv** *looks at him, then puts the knife to her wrist.*) Let's not get silly. (*Pause.*) You ever seen a corpse? (*She shakes her head.*) No. Me, neither. Don't reckon I missed much.

He stands and calmly takes the knife from her. She takes his hand and holds it gently.

Viv Sorry I cut you. (*He pulls his hand away.*)

Tone Piss off. (*He looks through the blind.*)

Pause.

Viv You'd probably have to leave anyway. I'm thinking about moving to Chelsea. A smaller place. I'm thinking quite seriously about it.

Tone Good for you.

Viv Yeah. This place is a bit of a handful, y'know . . .

Tone Actually, let you into a little secret – Chelsea's next on the list. 'Ad it planned for ages, we 'ave. So maybe it's not such a good idea, Chelsea. (*Pause.*) Ever thought of emigratin'?

Viv Leave me alone!

Tone Just bein' practical.

Viv I'll go wherever I have to to get away from all this.

Tone All this? What about all that? (*He points to the window.*) Look. Look outside. There's people there. People 'oo actually live 'ere. Not playin'. Not practisin' for the suburbs. Livin'. (*Pause.*) You've 'ad a nice break. P'raps now you oughta go back where you feel safe.

Viv This is my country. I'll live where I like.

Tone I s'pose it's mummy an' daddy's country too, is it? Livin' in America, earnin' a packet, buyin' up 'ouses for you to 'ide yerself in.

Viv This is also a free country. People can do what they like with their money.

Tone If they 'appen to 'ave any.

Pause.

Viv What am I supposed to say? Sorry? Or what? (*Pause.*) I'm sorry I don't do anything? I don't contribute? Sorry my way's been smooth for me since the start? That I'm perfect? I've turned out just the way I'm supposed to. I don't think much. I'm ideal. (*Pause.*) What have I got? A degree? I can understand French movies and read the quality papers? Sorry I want to end up at the BBC with all my friends? Custom bred, with our minds perfectly trained to jump fences and stay the course? Because what else is there? Sorry I'm nothing? Our precious freedom's made me a zombie? (*Beat.*) Freedom to rot, that's all this country's given me. (*Pause.*) Is that what you want me to say?

Tone You fuckin' said it.

Viv But did I mean it?

Baz *enters in his dressing-gown and Sony Walkman. He sees them and takes the headphones off.*

Baz Still up then? Christ. I need an Alka-Seltzer. Where are they?

Viv On the shelf. (**Baz** *gets the Alka-Seltzer.*) What are you doing up?

Baz Phone call. San Francisco. Frisbee is big business. (*He notices* **Tone** *holding the knife.*) Uh . . . Don't tell me . . . Jack the Ripper.

Tone Spot on.

Pause. **Baz** *looks at his watch.*

Baz I've gotta be at Crystal Palace in three hours' time.

Tone What for?

Baz First day of the UK Frisbee Championship. I'm in charge. I can think of better ways of spending a Monday morning.

Tone So can I.

Baz Like, in bed.

Tone So chuck it.

Baz It happens to be my job. If I don't turn up, I get the sack. And if I get the sack, I lose the car and my expenses-paid holiday in sunny California in August.

Tone Middle-management of the world unite. You've nothin' to lose but your perks.

Baz I like that. I think I'll write that up in the office. (**Viv** *gets up*.) You going to bed?

Viv No.

She goes off.

Baz Is this an argument or something?

Tone Compulsory re-education.

Baz Eh?

Tone Nothin'.

Pause.

Baz Doesn't do to argue with Viv.

Tone D'you spend your 'ole life duckin' for cover?

Baz More or less.

Tone You oughta toughen up, mate.

Baz What for? I'm very comfortable. I can't think of a single reason why I should upset the routine.

Tone Because it's a routine, maybe?

Baz No. I find routine very . . .

Tone Comfortable.

Baz Yeah. (*Pause.*) It's not really your place to say anything, y'know. It's not as if you live here. (*Pause.*) Well is it?

Pause.

Tone This belonging thing, it's a bloody obsession. You block the 'ole world off wiv it. Middle class barricade, thass all this 'ouse is.

Baz I don't think it's unreasonable to ask people to be considerate when they're in your house.

Tone 'Course you don't. You're a fuckin' lapdog.

Baz Well. That's how you see it.

Tone 'S 'ow you see it an' all.

Baz (*sarcastic*) We can't all be as aware as you, Tone.

Pause.

Tone No, you can't, can you?

Pause. He gets up. **Viv** *comes back in. He hands her the knife.*

'Ere. Do us all a favour. Use it.

He goes. She looks at **Baz** *then at the knife and makes a gesture of puzzlement. Then she calmly puts the knife in a drawer and sits down.*

Baz Off then, is he?

Viv Yeah, for good.

Baz Oh.

Viv What else could I do? He suddenly went into this great rant. Really chewed my head off. And he frightens me. He as good as said we'd be attacked if I threw him out.

Baz Attacked?

Viv The riots.

Baz Bloody hell.

Viv But I won't be threatened. Not in my own house.

Baz What brought it all on?

Viv Search me. One minute I'm sitting here having a quiet drink, the next . . .

Baz Where'd the knife come from?

Viv Must have taken it out with him. The man's a lunatic. Luckily, I calmed him down a bit. Otherwise, God knows what might have happened.

Baz You should have called me.

Viv I nearly did. I knew you were there if I needed you.

Baz I'm always here.

Viv Thanks, Baz. (*Pause.*) I've never met anyone that resentful, that jealous of other people.

Baz Are you OK?

Viv Yeah, just about.

Baz Sure?

Viv Yeah. Don't worry about me. (*Pause.*) Look, Baz . . . What shall I do about Jane?

Baz How d'you mean?

Viv Well . . . Some of the things he said . . . It was like he was speaking for both of them.

Baz What things?

Viv They despise us, we've got a crummy little scene, we're just a gang of kids.

Baz Well, what d'you want to do about her?

Viv I don't know. It'll just be very heavy living with her here, don't you think?

Baz She's pretty easy going.

Viv But I couldn't stand it. Looking at her, knowing what she's thinking, knowing she despises us . . .

Baz I'm sure she doesn't.

Viv You didn't hear the things he said.

Baz No.

Pause.

Viv If I ask her to move out, will you support me?

Pause.

Baz Do what you want. It's your house.

Viv Yeah. It is, isn't it? (*Pause.*) It's time I was firmer, don't you think?

Baz Up to you, Viv.

Viv Yes, definitely. I won't be abused in my own house. (*Pause.*) So long as you think I'm doing the right thing.

The phone rings. **Baz** *picks it up.*

Baz Baz here. Hi, Max. (**Viv** *starts tidying up.*) Eh? (*Pause.*) What d'you mean, they're not coming? (*Pause.*) Oh, Jesus. (*Pause.*)

There's more important things in the world than money. Didn't you tell them that? (*Pause.*) Well that's something, I s'pose. When do they get here? (*Pause.*) Tuesday. Is this definite now? (*Pause.*) Well no, but I'll see what I can salvage. (*Pause.*) Yeah. OK. Bye. (*He puts the phone down.*) Bastards.

Viv What's the matter?

Baz The star attractions won't be turning up till the day after tomorrow. They've been offered more money to do an exhibition in Chicago.

Viv Are they important?

Baz They're only the world pairs champions. Nothing special. (*Pause.*) They'll all be doing it now. I'm slinging this job. (*Pause.*) Anyway, we'll have to sort all this out tomorrow. (*Beat.*) Fuck it.

He goes to the door.

Viv Baz! You're a friend.

Baz Eh? (*Beat.*) Oh. Don't be soft.

He goes. She smiles. She picks up **Tone**'s *beer can, holds it gingerly at arm's length and takes it to the waste bin.*

Viv Goodbye. (*She drops the can in the bin.*)

Beat.

Act Two

Scene One

One week later. Midday. **Baz** *is alone in the room, on the phone.*

Baz Listen, if it was up to me . . . (*Pause.*) I just run the bloody company. It's not my decision. (*Pause.*) So what do I tell the organisers tomorrow? (*Pause.*) Ha ha. (*Pause.*) For Christ's sake, Ron, see sense.

Pause. The door opens and **Annie**, *carrying a wrapped picture, comes in.* **Baz** *waves to her. She nods and puts the picture down, then goes to the kitchen area. He puts his hand over the mouthpiece.*

There's coffee on the stove. (*Back into the phone.*) Look, let me speak to Joey, will you? (*Pause.*) Why not? (*Pause.*) Meditating? (*Pause.*) Levitating? (*Pause.*) You mean to tell me that I can't speak to one of my employees because at this moment in time he's in the bedroom floating two feet above the ground? (*Pause.*) OK. I'll get on to Lawrence and see what I can do. (*Pause.*) Well maybe he'll listen to me. (*Pause.*) Yeah. I'll ring you straight back. OK. See you. (*He puts the phone down.*) Fucking hippies! Frisbee-playing bolshie Yank pricks!

Beat.

Annie Trouble?

Baz They're on strike. The stupid bastards are refusing to do the exhibition tomorrow. Honestly, they're s'posed to be Buddhists. Buddhists don't go on strike.

Annie What do they want? Meditation allowance?

Baz They reckon they're being ripped off. They reckon we pay 'em a pittance for doing the shows, then we make a killing flogging frisbees afterwards.

Annie And do you?

Baz 'Course we do. That's not the point. The point is, they're lucky we pay 'em at all. They get expenses. We feed them. Just for chucking lumps of plastic round a bloody field. Honest, I don't know why I'm in this game. I'd have joined British Leyland if I'd wanted this hassle. (*Beat.*) Let's see what I can screw out of Lawrence. (*He dials.*) Make yourself at home. (*She sits.*) Bill? Baz. Look, we've got another problem. Ron and the others won't do tomorrow's show unless we promise them more money. (*Pause.*) Yeah. (*Pause.*) Fifty each. (*Pause.*) That's what I said. (*Pause.*) How can I do that? (*Pause.*) And will you? (*Pause.*) It's a bit underhand. (*Pause.*) Yeah, I know. That's business. (*Pause.*) Yeah. I think you're right. Hey, and can we cover next week's show? (*Pause.*) Fine. I'll tell him. OK. Call you back if there's any problem. See you. (*He puts the phone down.*)

Annie Well?

Baz We promise to pay them.

Annie But . . .

Baz We promise. They do the show, we sack Ron, and everything's back to normal. Simple.

Annie Won't that leave you without any players?

Baz No. Cool Hand Ron's the shop steward. The others are out of their heads most of the time. They won't care.

Annie Not very nice, your business.

Baz Not my fault. I just do like the man says, and collect the cheque each month. Beats working for a living.

Annie Aren't you going to let Cool Hand Ron know?

Baz Later. Let him sweat for a bit. Serve him right. (*Pause.*) What are you doing here, anyway?

Annie Thanks. It's nice to feel welcome.

Baz I wasn't expecting you.

Annie I brought this picture round for Viv. I thought she'd be here.

Baz No . . . she's gone out.

Pause.

Annie Don't be coy. You mean *they've* gone out.

Baz Do I?

Annie I assume you do. Unless Rusty's hiding in the cupboard. Which wouldn't surprise me.

Baz Yeah. They've gone out.

Annie Oh. Where?

Baz Dunno. Raif's?

Annie No. I've just come from there.

Baz I see.

Annie Get it where you can, darling, that's my motto. (*Pause.*) I don't mind, y'know. There's no need to look so worried.

Baz It's like musical bloody chairs with you lot.

Annie More like postman's knock.

Baz How come I never get a go?

Annie You're too nice.

Baz I'm a seething animal under this nice exterior.

Annie Probably. That's the trouble. Let's stick with the nice exterior, shall we? Don't spoil a good thing. (*Pause.*) What a schmuck.

Baz Rusty?

Annie You guessed.

Baz I can see you don't mind.

Annie I don't. It's just he swore blind he wasn't having a thing with Viv. According to Rusty, she's the most boring thing on two legs. Then I get chucked out of the flat, he hasn't got a regular place to doss, and hey, presto, it's true love. God, I don't know how he has the nerve. And Viv. How could she fall for it? (*Pause.*) Anyway, I don't give a damn. Honest. It was hell while it lasted. I wish her well. And I hope he breaks his bloody neck.

Baz What about me? I've got him here permanent now. And when Rusty moves in, Rusty moves in.

Annie I know. (*Pause.*) Jane still here, is she?

Baz Yeah. Why?

Annie No reason.

Pause.

Baz What's everyone got against her?

Annie Who said we've got anything against her?

Baz Oh, come on . . .

Annie She's a boring little hausfrau.

Baz You *don't* like her, do you?

Annie Whatever gave you that idea?

The phone rings. **Baz** *picks it up.*

Baz Hello. (*Pause.*) Ronnie, hi, I was just about to ring you.
(*Pause.*) Yeah, I spoke to him. He says OK. (*Pause.*) Yeah. (*Pause.*)
What d'you think he's gonna do? Go back on his word? (*Pause.*)
Yeah, fifty each. (*Pause.*) Don't thank me. I'm just doing my job.
(*Pause.*) Well, I'm glad you're glad. Fine. I'll see you tomorrow.
See if you can be there on time, huh? (*Pause.*) And wish Joey a
happy landing for me. (*Pause.*) Right. Bye (*Pause. He hangs up.*)
You are screwed, you lousy, long-haired little git.

Annie Baz, you are *not* very nice.

Baz I told you.

Annie I could almost find you attractive.

Baz Now you're talking.

Annie Almost, I said. (*Pause.*) You don't know when they're
coming back, by any chance?

Baz Couldn't tell you.

Annie Shit. I want the money for the picture.

Baz How much?

Annie Normally, I'd charge about fifty. But seeing as it's Viv, I'm
letting her have it for seventy-five.

Baz For one picture?

Annie Took me a long time. Seventy-five's actually very
reasonable.

Baz Let's have a look, then.

Annie OK.

*She takes it out. It is a glamorous print combining a black and white picture
of Hitler's face with heroic swastika flags and the slogan 'Nur Hitler'. She
holds it up.*

Tell me what you think? (*Beat.*) Well?

Baz Really . . . striking.

Annie See, it's two pictures in one, really. The face is taken from a photo and the rest's from a wartime poster I found.

Baz Why Hitler?

Annie Forties, dummy. Next big thing. Anyway, I'm fed up with Blondie and Iggy Pop.

Baz Where d'you want to put it? (*They look round the room.*) There's a nail there.

Annie OK, let's try it. (*He hangs it. They stare at it.*) What d'you think?

Baz Great.

Annie Worth seventy-five pounds of anyone's money, I'd say.

Baz 'Specially Viv's. (*Pause.*) You doing anything special today? .

Annie No.

Pause.

Baz Fancy going out?

Annie No.

Pause.

Baz Purely social.

Annie Of course.

Baz No, honest.

Annie Look, Baz . . .

Baz Don't say it.

Pause.

Annie We wouldn't look right together. You're not my type.

Baz Thanks.

Annie No, really, Baz. You have to think about these things. I don't wear clothes that clash, do I? Everything blends. It has to, otherwise you look silly.

Baz You talk like people are watching you all the time.

Annie Well, Christ, they are.

Pause.

Baz Don't you like me?

Annie I like you a lot.

Baz I'm only asking you to come out with me on a Sunday afternoon. For a drive or something.

Annie You're asking me to go to bed with you, and you know it.

Pause.

Baz We're not all like Rusty, you know.

Annie Oh, yes you are.

Pause.

Baz Forget I asked.

Annie OK.

A door slams offstage.

Baz That's probably them. Or noisy burglars.

Annie Yes.

The door opens, **Viv** *and* **Rusty** *come in. No trace of embarrassment.*

Viv Annie! (*They hug.*) What are you doing here? (**Annie** *points at the picture.*) Oh, great. Wow. Hey, it looks terrific.

Annie Glad you like it.

Viv Really forties. Rusty reckons the forties are gonna be the next big thing.

Annie Well he should know.

Rusty *is pouring two scotch and Americans.*

Rusty Drink? Or have you got to rush?

Annie No thanks. And I haven't got to rush.

Rusty Oh, good. (*He hands* **Viv** *her drink.*)

Baz I'll get my own. (*He does.*)

Annie Hate to say this, Viv, but . . .

Viv Oh right. (*Getting out her cheque book.*) What did we say? Eighty, was it?

Annie Er . . . yeah.

Viv Right.

She writes out the cheque and gives it to **Annie**. **Rusty** *turns on the video and sorts through some film cassettes.*

Rusty Anybody fancy *Casablanca*?

Viv Not just now. (*He carries on.*) When are you off to Italy?

Annie Day after tomorrow.

Viv Lucky thing.

Annie I know. Hey, Nigel says you've got some job or other.

Viv Sort of. It's just temping. Switchboard on the phone-ins at LBC.

Annie It's something.

Viv Just. (*The TV comes up very loud.*) Rusty. (*She turns the sound off.*) You can watch it later.

Rusty I only wanna look at the clothes. The words are boring.

Annie You know Dennis? He says if this Italian thing goes off all right, he should be able to keep me in work for a while. Said there's even a chance of a job for Cosmo.

Viv Fantastic.

Annie I know. 'Course, it all depends . . .

Viv Yeah. (*Pause.*) Why didn't you come round in the week?

Annie I had some things to do. Packing, phone calls, interviews, you know . . .

Viv We're going to see some band tonight. Coming?

Annie I don't know . . .

Viv Go on.

Annie Actually, I said I'd go out with Baz. Didn't I, Baz.

Baz Eh?

Viv Where you going?

Annie Oh, that new place . . . The one with the piranha.

Viv The what?

Annie They've got this glass dance floor; it's bullet proof or something. And underneath, in the water, there's a piranha fish.

Viv A live one?

Annie Well a dead one wouldn't be much fun, would it?

Viv I s'pose not.

Annie And, anyway, while you're dancing . . . Under your feet
. . . There's this piranha.

Slight pause.

Rusty Riots.

Viv What?

Rusty It's called Riots. It's a dump.

Annie We just thought we'd give it a go.

Rusty It's all fat Arabs. And the piranha's a goldfish with
dentures.

Annie No-one's asking you to come.

Rusty Bit deal.

Pause.

Baz I can't go anyway. I'm having an early night tonight. Sorry.

Pause.

Viv Come with us.

Annie Don't want to go where I'm not wanted.

Viv Don't be silly.

Pause.

Annie I'll have to see how I feel.

Pause.

Viv We've just been and looked at the most fabulous place in
Chelsea. Two bedrooms, garden, patio. Great. I've just got to
convince the folks they want it.

Annie I don't see what's wrong with this place.

Viv If things carry on the way they are, this house'll be worth
about two pounds fifty in a year's time. I've had the aerial on the
car broken twice. It's just so heavy. The riots and everything. I
don't feel safe.

Rusty What's for lunch?

Viv Chicken.

Rusty When's it gonna be ready?

Viv I haven't put it in the oven yet.

Rusty I'm starving.

Viv Have a sandwich.

Rusty I don't want a sandwich, I want lunch.

Viv It'll be at least an hour. Why don't you go over the pub?

Rusty Yeah, why don't I? (*Pause. She gives him a fiver. He gives her a peck on the cheek.*)

Viv And I want some change.

Rusty Baz? Fancy a drink?

Baz You buying? Bloody hell . . .

Viv About an hour.

Rusty Yeah.

Rusty *and* **Baz** *go.*

Annie Well. Who's under whose thumb?

Viv Nobody.

Annie Come on. It's fatal giving Rusty money. You only give it if you don't expect it back.

Viv I don't expect it back.

Annie Christ. True love.

Viv Not at all.

Pause

Annie I really don't mind, you know. I don't see why we should let a little thing like Rusty come between us. (*They both smile.*)

Viv Good.

Annie Watch him, though.

Viv I am.

Pause.

Annie When he first moved in with me, it was twice a night, regular. Then once a night, then once a week, then only months with a 'z' in.

Viv We're on three times a night at the moment.

Annie Off to a flying start.

Viv Novelty value, I expect.

Annie Yeah. What'll you do when he slows down?

Viv Kick him out.

Annie Just don't kick him in my direction.

Viv No fear.

Pause.

Annie Are you happy?

Pause.

Viv No. (*Pause.*) Happier. (*Pause.*) It's just not how I want it yet.

Annie Did Che Guevara ever come back?

Viv I've been keeping out of the way. But, I'm sure he's been here. And she's been really hostile.

Annie Have you spoken to her about it?

Viv Why should I?

Annie I dunno. Clear the air?

Viv It's my house. It's my decision. If she doesn't like it she can move out.

Annie Is she in?

Viv She's probably upstairs, revising. (*Pause.*) God, I hated it when he was here. The perfect bloody couple. Like 'mummy and daddy'.

Annie I did warn you.

Viv Yeah. (*Pause.*) I mean, what right does she think she has?

Annie Forget it.

Viv Am I going on?

Annie A bit.

Viv Sorry. (*The phone rings.* **Viv** *picks it up.*) Hello. (*Pause.*) I could. Hang on. (*She goes to the door and shouts.*) Jane? Phone.

Jane (*off*) I'll take it up here.

Viv *picks up the phone, listens, then hangs up.*

Viv Talk of the devil.

Annie Is it him?

Viv Yeah. Rude sod. I'm not his errand girl. If he thinks he's coming round here . . . (*Pause.*) I better put the chicken in. Are you staying?

Annie I can do.

Viv *takes out a chicken from the fridge, puts it in a baking tin and into the oven.*

Viv I tried being friends with her. She just doesn't want to know. I don't think she's capable of being friends. She doesn't give anything.

Annie Viv, for God's sake.

Viv I'll throw a party when you get back from Italy.

Annie Celebrate my suntan.

Viv Yeah.

Jane *enters with an empty coffee cup and goes to the kitchen.*

Jane Viv . . . (*She notices* **Annie**.) Hi. Viv, Tone says he's rung a couple of times and you've said I was out.

Viv Yeah?

Jane Could you *check* that I'm not in when he rings?

Viv I do.

Jane But . . .

Viv If I say you're out, you're out. I wouldn't say it otherwise, would I?

Jane I don't know.

Viv Don't be ridiculous.

Jane I'm not being ridiculous. I'd just like you to check whether I'm in or not. (**Viv** *ignores her.*) Viv?

Annie No need to go on.

Pause. **Jane** *goes round to* **Viv**, *and notices the picture on the wall.*

Jane Is that supposed to be a joke?

Annie I don't see anybody laughing.

Jane What's it doing there?

Annie Hanging.

Jane I can see that. Is it one of yours?

Annie I created it, if that's what you mean.

Jane Well what's it doing on the fucking wall?

Viv I PUT IT THERE! I BOUGHT IT! IT'S MY PICTURE, HANGING ON MY WALL! OK?!

Pause.

Jane Is it deliberate? Because if it is, it worked. (*Pause.*) Please, you can't leave it there. (*Pause.*) Please. (*They ignore her.*) Don't you understand? What it means? (*Beat*) Look, why don't you just call me Yid. (*Beat.*) I'll wear a yellow star. (*Pause.*) Annie. Doesn't that face mean anything to you? (*Beat.*)

Annie Yeah. About eighty quid.

Pause.

Jane Is that what you do with everything? Glamorise it? Turn it into another fashion? Millions of deaths? A glamour print? What next? The Auschwitz coffee table book? (*Pause.*) Don't you know what the Nazis did?

Annie Of course I do.

Jane What?

Annie They killed Jews, I s'pose.

Pause.

Jane And is that it?

Annie What d'you want me to do? Cry about it?

Pause.

Jane I feel sorry for you.

Annie Don't bother.

Pause.

Jane Understand, please. Jewish jokes, swastikas on walls, National Front marches. We've learned to live with all that. But this . . . I don't have to live with this. Not here. (*Pause.*) I'm just asking for a little humanity. (*Long pause.*) Imbeciles. It's hopeless.

Jane *goes.* **Viv** *pours herself a drink.*

Annie I wouldn't mind one of those.

Viv Why don't you go over the pub?

Annie Why?

Viv I've got some talking to do. (*Pause.*) How dare she? (*Pause.*) Go over the pub.

Annie Will you be OK? I mean, I'll back you up . . .

Viv I'll be fine.

Annie I'll wait for you over there.

Viv I won't be long. (**Annie** *gets up. They look at one another.* **Annie** *goes.* **Viv** *goes to the door and shouts.*) Jane. (*Pause.*) Jane. I want to speak to you.

She sits. Pause. **Jane** *comes back in. Pause.*

If this is a taste of things to come, I think you'd better move out.

Pause.

Jane If what is a taste of things to come?

Viv This hostility.

Pause.

Jane I'm sorry. I don't believe I'm hearing this. (*Pause.*) You're saying you want *me* to move out because *I'm* being hostile?

Viv Yes.

Jane That's absurd.

Viv First of all, you bring your boyfriend here when you know that one of the house rules is no couples. Then you behave very hostile towards me, and then . . . This.

Jane House rules? What the bloody hell are you talking about?

Viv I don't want to live with a couple.

Jane What were Rusty and Annie? What are you and Rusty now? And what's all this 'hostile' stuff?

Viv I don't want to rationalise it.

Jane You've got to. You can't just tell me to go.

Viv I can and I am. (*Pause.*) Cleanliness.

Jane What?

Viv Cleanliness in the house. You don't do your bit.

Jane I'm sorry, I do more than anybody else. I don't think you know what you're talking about.

Viv You never clean the windows.

Jane I what?!

Viv That's right. You never clean the windows.

Pause.

Jane You're mad. (*Pause.*) I mean it. You're insane. (*Pause.* **Viv** *just sips her drink.*) Come on, I want to discuss this.

Viv Nothing to discuss.

Jane There's everything to discuss.

Viv I told you, I don't want to rationalise it.

Jane But we're supposed to be rational people. Come on. Why do you want me to move out? (*Silence.*) Vivienne. (*Silence.*) Aren't you going to say anything?

Viv *gets up and goes to the window and looks out. Then she goes to the oven and checks on the chicken. She washes out her glass and looks at the TV section in the paper. She makes this last a long time. Then she gets her things and goes to the door.*

Viv Goodbye. (*Pause. Then as if* **Jane** *is being unreasonable.*) Goodbye, Jane.

Silence. She goes. Pause. **Jane** *sits on the sofa, close to tears.*

Beat.

Fade.

Scene Two

Two and a half weeks later. It is about 7 p.m. **Tone** *is sitting on the sofa.*
Jane *is staring out the window. As the lights come up,* **Tone** *crushes an
empty beer can, drops it in the bin and takes another from the fridge.*

Tone I'm gonna start thinkin' you've gone off me. (*Pause.*) If you
don't fancy me any more, just say. (**Jane** *turns and looks at him then
looks out the window again.*) You gonna stand at the window all
night?

Jane They're still in the pub.

Pause.

Tone Marvellous. Thass made my night, that 'as. Fer fuck's
sake . . .

Jane I had to do without you when you were out playing cowboys
and Indians.

Tone That was different.

Jane No, it wasn't. (*Pause.*) You've got plenty of sympathy for the
people out there, but none for me. The only thing bothering you is
you're not getting screwed as often as you'd like. Well I'm sorry. I
don't feel like it. All right?

Pause.

Tone Maybe we oughta . . .

Jane What?

Tone Knock it on the 'ead.

Pause.

Jane You're just a bloody coward.

Pause.

Tone Right. I'll go over the pub an' break their fuckin' arms, shall
I? 'S that what you want? Or get 'em when they come through the
door.

Jane Is that all you know?

Beat.

Tone Yeah! Thass all I know. Sorry.

Jane Tone, I can't do it like that. I've got to know why. (*Pause.*)

For over two weeks she hasn't spoken to me. None of them have. She avoids me. These people. My friends.

Tone Middle class mind games.

Jane The working class don't have a monopoly on misery, Tone!

Tone Thass not what I meant! (*Pause.*) Look, this is fuckin' us up. It's fuckin' you up. Why don't you move out?

Jane Where?

Tone I dunno. (*Beat.*) My place? (*Long pause.*) Point taken.

Jane We've only known each other six weeks.

Tone Wouldn't 'ave to be permanent. (*Pause.*) Think about it.

Jane I will. (*She walks around the room.*) She has that picture in her bedroom.

Tone She don't know any better. She's not a fascist. She's just stupid.

Jane *picks up an LP record and takes it out of its sleeve.*

Jane This is her favourite record. I want to scratch it.

Pause.

Tone What is it?

Jane Lou Reed.

Tone Christ, scratch it. Call it a mercy killing.

Jane Why don't I? (*Pause.*) Descending to her level.

Tone Something like that. (*Pause.*) Oh, I'm very interested in that Rusty geezer. Considerin' 'oo 'is dad is. Very interested.

Jane What d'you mean?

Tone Thass all I'm sayin'.

Pause. **Jane** *goes back to the window.*

Jane I just want to know why. It's not a lot to ask. Oh, God, they're coming back. Look at me. I dread it. I'm a wreck every time they come in. (**Tone** *goes to the door.*) Are you going upstairs?

Tone Yeah. I'll just leave it a minute. (*He kisses her.*) Just act natural.

Jane Some hope.

He goes. She looks around, momentary terror on her face, then picks up a book and starts to read. The door slams off. We hear talking and laughing. The door opens. **Viv**, **Baz**, **Annie** *and* **Rusty** *come in. They're eating doner kebabs.*

Annie For the last time, I will not get anorexic just because I don't eat a rotten greasy kebab.

Viv But you haven't eaten all day.

Annie Because I don't want to.

Rusty (*mock Jewish*) Eat, eat, you should eat. Your mama she say so.

Baz *gets out a bottle of Demestica.*

Baz Here we are, then . . . a cheeky little vintage to remind you of that glorious Greek holiday. The chalky soil, the pungent grape, the gippy tum.

Rusty (*reading the label*) Oh Baz, you have such style. A Nana Mouskouri evening. How quaint.

Viv (*to* **Annie**) Here, have some taramasalata at least.

Annie OK. Makes a change from bloody pasta anyway.

Rusty Italy stories? Again? (*Pause.*) Anything on the box?

Viv Have a look in the paper.

Rusty Where is it?

Jane *is half sitting on it. He sees it and gently tugs it from under her. She looks at him. He ignores her.*

Viv Sure you don't want a bite?

Annie I have to think of my figure.

Rusty (*reading*) World in Action. Boring. News at Ten. Very boring. Ah. There's a film on later.

Viv What is it?

Rusty Some American cop rubbish.

Viv I got a job interview, by the way.

Annie Terrific.

Viv If I get it.

Annie What's it for?

Viv Nationwide. Researcher.

Annie Christ. That's a bit high-powered.

Viv No, not really. But it's an opening.

Baz Who knows, you might work your way up to Play School.

Viv I wouldn't mind.

Annie Any more news about Chelsea?

Viv My folks won't budge. Anyway, I don't mind this place so much now. I think I've got used to it.

Annie So . . .

Viv Hmm. Yeah.

The door opens and **Tone** *comes in. Shocked silence at the table.*

Tone Evenin' all. (*He sits.*)

Silence.

Annie I heard a pleasant rumour that the band's kicked you out.

Rusty Oh yeah?

Annie Yeah.

Rusty Shouldn't listen to rumours, darling. We're just not working at the moment.

Annie Consideration for the audience?

Rusty Musical differences.

Annie Ah. Like, they're musical, you're not.

Rusty Not at all. We're going in different directions, that's all. They want to stick with the synthesiser thing and I want to get into soul-funk. I want to use the Beggar and Co horn section, stuff like that. The others are just stuck in a rut, y'know? But, like, every band you hear today sounds the same, right? I just think we oughta move on. Anyway, I prefer the clothes.

Annie I thought there must be a deeper reason.

Tone Well, 'ello there.

Pause.

Viv Can I have some more wine?

Baz Yeah. (*He pours them all some more.*)

Annie Anyone see 'Holocaust' the other night?

Rusty Yeah.

Annie What'd you think?

Rusty Bit one-sided.

Baz *is embarrassed.*

Tone (*to* **Jane**) I see what you mean. (*Pause.*) Pathetic. Shall we go out? (**Tone** *and* **Jane** *get up.* **Tone** *turning to them at the door.*) We're over the pub if nobody wants to see us.

They go.

Rusty Bastard.

Pause.

Annie Poor Viv. Isn't there anything you can do?

Viv I've told her to go. She just hasn't moved.

Baz Well where d'you expect her to go? You can't just chuck her out on the streets. Give her time, for God's sake.

Beat.

Viv Traitor.

Pause.

Baz Viv, in the five years I've known Jane, we've always got along fine. It's not easy treating someone you've known that well as if they're public enemy number one. Whatever happened, surely it's between the two of you. Why should I have to get involved?

Viv You know I had a terrible row with her. You know what she thinks of me. What she said. (*Pause.*) She's hanging on here because she knows it makes me miserable. Doesn't that bother you?

Annie Bloody well should.

Viv She makes everything heavy, just being here. Just seeing her things in the bathroom makes me want to scream. I can't sleep at night with her on the other side of the wall. I hear her breathing. She doesn't sleep. She sits there knowing I'm awake. Knowing I'm awake because of her. And she's smiling. Thinks she's winning. And if I do sleep, I have a nightmare that she never goes away. Only she's not *in* the house any more, she *is* the house. She's everything, everywhere I look, I can't get away from her.

The door suddenly opens and **Tone** *comes in.*

Tone Right . . .

Rusty What the fuck d'you want?!

Beat.

Tone You'll do.

Rusty (*very angry*) Well here I am. (*He gets up and advances on* **Tone**.) What's it to be, bully boy? Out on the pavement, or what? (*He starts jabbing* **Tone** *backwards.*) That what you're after? A good punch-up to satisfy your blood lust? Eh? You neanderthal ape. You fucking thick shithead. Come on, then. Or aren't you brave enough?

He's pushed **Tone** *against the wall. Suddenly* **Tone** *gives him a hard shove in the chest.*

Tone Actually, pal, since you ask (*He shoves him again.*) – the reason I came back over 'ere (*He shoves him again;* **Rusty** *falls into the chair.*) – is that I 'appen to be skint, an' you owe my bird a fiver. (*Pause.*) Now, if that money ain't forthcomin' pretty sharpish, bein' the neanderthal ape that I am, I'm gonna start pullin' your teeth out. Through the top o' your 'ead. Understand?

Pause.

Rusty I haven't got it.

Tone Wrong.

Rusty I haven't.

Pause.

Tone Then I 'ope your BUPA contributions are fully paid up.

Baz *gets up and takes out his wallet and hands* **Tone** *a five pound note.*

You're a scholar an' a gentleman.

Baz Just fuck off, Tone.

Tone My pleasure. (*Pause.*) 'Ave you seen what you done? 'Ave you looked at yourselves? 'Ave you? No. Can't be a lotta fun, lookin' at a room full o' shit. In fact, it ain't a lotta fun. So.

He goes.

Baz You silly bugger.

Rusty Get stuffed.

Pause.

Viv Let's go out.

Baz Viv, you can't keep . . .

Viv I can't keep what, Baz?!

Baz Nothing!

Pause.

Annie Where d'you want to go?

Viv Anywhere. Out.

Annie Let's just drive. See where we end up.

Viv Yeah.

Rusty I don't want to go driving.

Annie So don't.

Rusty I *do* want to go out.

Annie Oh, for Christ's sake, Rusty. Where d'you want to go?

Rusty I don't care! (*Pause. He gets up.*) I'm going. I'll see you later.

Viv (*as he gets to the door*) Rusty.

Rusty What? (*Pause.*) Look, Viv, I've just been pushed around on your account, and I don't like being pushed around. OK? I don't see why I should always take the stick. Always be the whipping boy.

Annie Maybe if you kept your big mouth shut . . .

Rusty I'm talking to Viv. (*Pause.*) OK, V?

Viv Is what OK?

Rusty I'm going out. Now.

Viv But you haven't got any money.

Rusty I'll borrow some. Go home or something.

Viv OK. (*Pause.*) That's OK.

Pause.

Rusty What's the catch?

Viv Sorry?

Rusty How come you're letting me go?

Viv I don't intend to run after you, if that's what you mean. Do whatever you like.

Pause.

Rusty And . . .

Viv And nothing. (*Pause.*) Nobody loses any sleep over what you do. Don't flatter yourself. (*Pause.*) If you want to wait until we're ready, you can come with us. If you don't, off you go.

Rusty And don't come back.

Viv Really, Rusty. What do you think I am? Vindictive? (*Pause.*) You're free to do what you want. Free as a bird. (*Pause.*)

Rusty I'll wait.

Pause.

Viv Baz, you don't mind if Annie moves in when she goes, do you?

Baz Why should I mind? What's it got to do with me?

Viv I want everybody to be happy.

Baz I'm happy. I'm ecstatic. Over the moon.

Viv What's got into you?

Baz I just feel . . .

Viv Cheer up. There's nothing to be miserable about.

Baz Two minutes ago . . .

Viv Two minutes ago is two minutes ago. Forget it. Let's go out and enjoy ourselves.

Baz I can't.

Viv Why not?

Baz I just can't.

Pause.

Viv OK, let's go then.

Rusty Where?

Viv Your house. Pick up some money. I'm broke.

Baz And you can get my fiver while you're there.

Viv Right, well, let's go.

Rusty My father might be out . . .

Annie Then we'll nick the family silver, OK?

Viv See you, Baz.

Baz See you.

They go. Pause. **Baz** *pours some more wine, puts on the TV and sits picking at the food.*

Fade.

Scene Three

Eleven-thirty that night. The TV set is flickering silently. **Baz** *is seemingly asleep at the table, a half-empty bottle of scotch beside him. As the lights come up, 'Alison' by Elvis Costello is just finishing on the record deck. Pause. The door opens and* **Jane** *comes in. She takes the record off and switches off the TV.* **Baz** *raises his head.*

Baz I was watching that. (*Pause.*) Only joking. (*Pause.*) I must have nodded off. (*He looks at the scotch bottle.*) Or put meself to sleep. Drink? (*She shakes her head. He takes a swig.*) I don't think this bodes well for adult life. First sign of trouble and we all dive head first into a bottle. Still. Something to do, isn't it? Somewhere to go. (*She goes to the kitchen and pours coffee from the jug.*) Couldn't do me one of those, could you? (*She brings her cup and sits down.*) Ah. You couldn't. I see. (*Pause.*) I was having a dream there. I think. I mean, unless there was a six-foot naked Amazon in the room I can only assume I was dreaming. (*Pause.*) Spoke to my mum the other day. She wanted to know why I haven't settled down with a nice lass and got meself a proper job. And, indeed, why haven't I? All that fancy education, she said. Maybe education stunted my growth. It's a theory. (*Pause.*) Most of my old friends are married, y'know. They send me pictures. Those little instant polaroids that make people look like inflatable dolls. All my old friends seem to have married inflatable dolls, in fact. If the pictures are anything to go by. Handy for the kids, eh? Last thing at night, you just pull out their little belly buttons and the air comes out. Then fold them up for the night. Very handy. (*Pause. He takes a swig.*) Whoosh. Say g'night, kids. (*Pause.*) Actually, what have I got to complain about? Nothing if you think about it. Good job, nice car. Nice house. (*Beat.*) Nice fucking house. Did you hear that, eh? I sound like me mother. (*Pause.*) Will you shut up and let me get a word in edgeways. (*Pause.*) Most of my old mates think I'm gay, I reckon. When I go home for Christmas, I can hear them thinking: yellow trousers? Only poofs wear yellow trousers. (*Pause.*) I think I'm too nice. I think I'm far too amenable. Whatever that means. Sounds right. Sort of me. Amenable. Sounds like a government minister. We are amenable to talks with the unions, but insist we cannot budge an inch from our original offer. Maybe I should have been a politician. 'S easy enough. (*Pause.*) I'm probably too nice to be a politician. (*Pause.*) Too nice, too nice. Where does it get you? (*Pause.*) You're nice. Not too nice. Just nice. Which is nice. (*Pause.*) Let me take you away from all this. I'll let you take me away from all this if you like. Never let it be said I'm not a feminist. (*Pause.*) I think I'm the original little man. How's that for self-awareness? (*He takes a swig.*) Maybe I'm just going through the male menopause thirty years too early. (*Pause.*) I do enjoy these little chats, y'know. A free and frank exchange of views.

Jane Why should I bother to talk to you?

Baz A question I've asked meself.

Jane Well? Why should I?

Baz Dunno. (*Pause.*) Had a nice night?

Jane Stop it, Baz.

Baz I've had a nice night. I've sat here all on me own. Paradise.

Jane You can't sit on your own forever.

Baz Aye. 'Appen. (*Pause.*) I've been reading Henry James. Haven't read old Henry since Oxford. (*Pause.*) Remember when we were looking for a place? Before Viv's folks bailed us out? It was gonna be great, wasn't it? I had visions of sitting in a book-lined room . . . dinner parties . . . really civilized. (*Beat.*) Somewhere, up there (*He points.*) – was a malicious sod pushing us around. Park Lane? Mayfair? No chance. Go straight to jail. Do not pass Go. Do not collect two hundred pounds. And here we bloody are.

Jane We did it ourselves.

Baz No, I can't believe that. I mean, surely we couldn't do this ourselves, not even if we meant to. (*Pause.*) I'm sorry. It's got out of hand. You're hurt. I'm sorry about that.

Jane Doesn't do me much good. I want to know why.

Baz Ah.

Jane Well?

Pause.

Baz You had a row with Viv.

Jane I what? (*Pause.*) No.

Pause.

Baz Search me, then. That's what she says. Over and over. In case you didn't know, London is dotted with people who for no apparent reason see you as the new Antichrist. Word has spread. (*Beat.*) And what can I do? It's embarrassing if I don't speak to you, and it's dangerous if I do. Least I've got a roof over my head, even if it does feel like it's caving in on me. (*Pause.*) And I've been a spineless jerk, haven't I?

Beat.

Jane Yeah. You sat on the fence when you could have taken my side.

Baz Side?! (*Beat.*) It's mad. Taking sides. What *is* this?

Jane I don't know, Baz, I didn't start it.

Baz Nobody did.

Jane Viv did.

Baz All right, Viv did. (*Beat.*) OK? So. Any the wiser, are we?

Beat.

Jane I thought you were my friend.

Baz Viv thinks I'm her friend.

Jane You are.

Baz Fuck it. I'm nobody's friend. (*Pause.*) Least you've got Tone.

Jane I don't know if I have any more. (*Beat.*) Wants me to go and live in his council flat in Battersea.

Baz Ethnic. (**Jane** *smiles*.) I like Tone.

Jane So do I.

Baz Well . . . you saw him first.

They smile.

Jane Baz, why does she hate me so much?

Baz I dunno. Honest. (*Beat.*) Property's not theft. It's something much worse. That much I do know.

Rusty *enters. He takes a swig of Scotch.*

Rusty D'you know what they've done? D'you know what some bastard's gone and done? They've only gone and shopped me to the papers, haven't they? Paul bleeding Foot in the *Daily* bleeding *Mirror*. Bloody great article about *me*!

Baz Who has?

Rusty That's what I want to find out.

Baz What's it say?

Rusty Oh, nothing much. Just says how the son of the editor of the *Mirror*'s biggest rival lives off the dole at home with mummy and daddy, smoking dope and snorting coke.

Baz Well . . . It's true, you do . . .

Rusty I know it's true, Baz. What's that got to do with it? What I want to know is, why me? Eh? Who's idea of a joke *is* this?

Baz What's it matter?

Rusty Matters plenty, lamebrain. The publicity: great. I'll be famous. But I've just had two hours with my old man being roasted. And I mean burned. He's already famous y' see. He doesn't need it. He's talking life-support switch-off, man. No more money. I'm gonna be cut off without a penny. Savvy?

Baz You don't mean you'll have to get a job?

Rusty The sarcasm, Baz. Cut it. I've got big problems.

Baz You always got big problems.

Beat.

Rusty You, was it?

Baz What?

Rusty Been whispering in Comrade Foot's ear?

Baz Oh, go take a run. What d'you think I am?

Rusty A right little joker, that's what you are. Just your kind of stunt, this is. Drop Rusty in the shit. Give him a bad time. Well, joker, it's not funny. I'm not laughing.

Baz I don't know anything about it, prick.

Rusty Well, someone does.

Pause.

Jane Why d'you think it was one of us? Bit obvious, isn't it?

Rusty Somewhere out there, there's a person with a grudge. A slimy little man who wants to get even. Christ, it's enough to make you paranoid. What next? Someone gonna take a shot at me or what? What?

Baz You're not John Lennon yet.

Rusty Fuck off, I mean it. I don't feel safe.

Baz Get a bodyguard.

Rusty Yeah. I might do that. (*The phone rings.*) I'm not here.

Baz If only. (*He picks up the phone.*) Yeah? (*Pause.*) Yeah. It's for me. Sorry. (*Back into the phone.*) Joey. If you're going to give me a hard time . . . (*Pause.*) Don't do this to me, Joey. (*Pause.*) Listen . . . (*Pause. Joey's hung up.*) . . . You bastard. I don't believe it. Not again.

Rusty Do they know I'm here?

Baz Who?

Rusty Them.

Baz Fuck off, Rusty. Don't be a prat all your life, have a day off. (*He dials.*) Off the hook. (*Pause.*) Right.

He takes out his car keys and goes to the door.

Jane Where you going?

Baz I'm gonna murder me a hippy.

He goes. **Jane** *stands, uncertain.*

Rusty Where are *you* going?

Jane Bed.

Rusty What?

Jane I'm tired.

Rusty I need someone to talk to.

Jane Not me, surely.

Rusty You're the only person here.

Jane I'm so sorry.

Rusty No, I mean . . .

Jane I think it's rotten what's happened, but I still can't face the thought of having to talk to you. I'm sorry.

Rusty That's pretty sensitive of you.

Jane No one ever thinks about *me*.

Rusty Please. I don't want to sit here on my own.

Jane Neither did I. But I wasn't given any choice.

Rusty Please.

Pause. She sits.

Jane I'm not very good at comforting the wounded.

Rusty 'S OK. (*Pause.*) I'm really freaked. I feel like a target.

Jane You're not in any danger.

Rusty How do you know?

Jane I'm using my head. (*Pause.*) Lots of people have stories printed about them. It's how your dad makes his living isn't it?

Rusty He's a journalist, not a bastard.

Jane You've obviously never read his paper.

Rusty Leave off my old man. He's just doing a job.

Jane Where have I heard that before? (*Pause.*) Look, this is hopeless. I've got nothing to say to you. (*Pause.*) I don't feel very charitable. Things being the way they are.

Rusty What things?

Jane You mean you hadn't noticed?

Rusty Oh, all that. It's nothing.

Jane (*standing*) Honestly, Rusty, if you're going to stand there and shrug off my problems as if they don't exist and expect me to take yours seriously, I might as well go to bed.

Rusty *We* might as well go to bed.

Beat.

Jane I'm going to pretend I didn't hear that.

Rusty Why? Sex is a good therapy.

Jane God, you're offensive.

Rusty You're very attractive. I fancy you, right? What's offensive about that? It's a compliment.

Jane Go to hell.

Rusty You really are hung up, aren't you? Just where'd you get this idea that you're so bloody important?

Beat.

Jane I hope there is a man out there with a gun, waiting to shoot you. You deserve it.

Pause.

Rusty Viv's right, isn't she? You are a nasty piece of work. Very sweet on the outside, but it's a real snake pit inside there, isn't it? (*Pause.*) Pity we couldn't make it. I bet you're really good. Really rough.

Jane Curl up and die.

She starts to go.

Rusty You should lose some of those hang-ups, y'know. There's nothing worse than a tight-assed chick. (*She turns and stares at him.*) What you gonna do? Set your gorilla on me? Wheel out the working class hero to do his macho bit? (*Pause.*) You should ditch him, y'know. So fucking straight. Thinks Victoria's still on the throne, right? God, how boring. We're classless now. Someone should tell him. Put him out of his misery. And you. Get into some personal liberation. Get into your own head. Might loosen you up a bit.

Pause.

Jane That's why you never make any sense. You got 'into your own head'. And it's so empty in there, you probably got lost. Round and round in circles. Looking at yourself. A pointless exercise for a pointless person. (*Beat.*) You're not classless. You're dead.

She goes.

Rusty I bet you're frigid, anyway!

Pause. He sits and thinks then goes to the window and looks out. He turns out most of the lights then looks out the window again. He thinks, goes to the phone and dials.

Hi. Carolyn? It's Rusty. (*Pause.*) Terrible. I've had a bit of a shock. (*Pause.*) I was wondering if I could come round. (*Pause.*) I know it's late, but I really need someone to talk to. (*Pause.*) I'll tell you about it when I come round. I'm really freaked. (*Pause.*) I'll get a cab. (*Pause.*) You're an angel. I'll be there in about twenty minutes. (*Pause.*) You got any booze? (*Pause.*) OK. I'll see you. Bye.

He puts the phone down, looks round the room, picks up the scotch from the table and goes, turning the lights out.

Scene Four

About two weeks later. Late afternoon. **Baz** *is in the kitchen cleaning the oven and worktops.* **Rusty** *comes on. He's bare-chested, listening to* **Baz**'s *Walkman and has been snorting cocaine. He stands centre stage.*

Baz That's ninety-nine quid's worth of advanced Nip technology you've got on there. Mind how you go.

Rusty *just stares at him, singing 'Goes on, and the beat goes on . . .'* **Baz** *goes over to him and talks at him while he sings.*

Gonna be difficult, are you? Gonna fuck it all up? Poke your tongue out at teacher? Fag behind the bike sheds? That the game, is it?

Rusty I see your lips moving. I don't hear any words.

Baz What are Viv's folks supposed to make of you, eh? Man of mystery? (**Rusty** *takes the headphones off.*) Why don't you do something to help?

Rusty I don't *dig* graves, man, I dance on them.

He puts the headphones back on and sings along. **Baz** *shrugs as* **Viv** *comes in carrying a pile of papers.* **Baz** *sits.*

Viv Rusty . . . (**Rusty** *turns and goes. She stares at* **Baz**.) What are you doing?

Baz I'm having a breather.

Viv Don't take all day. There's still the floor to do. (*Pause.*) And don't sulk.

Pause. **Jane** *enters, goes to the records and takes out two or three.* **Viv** *stares.* **Jane** *goes with her records. Pause.* **Viv** *looks through the records.*

Baz They were hers.

Viv How do you know? (*She goes on checking, then sits again.*)

Baz Well?

Viv If it's not screwed down, she'll try to take it. (*Pause.*) My shampoo was gone this morning. (*Pause.*) You'll never get finished at this rate. And I want this place looking spotless. (**Baz** *gets up and goes back to the kitchen.*) Make sure you're changed before they arrive.

Baz I've washed behind my ears.

Viv For a change. (*She looks out the window.*) She'd better be gone when they get here.

Baz I don't s'pose she's exactly dying to meet your folks.

Viv She'll do anything to start a scene. (*Pause.*) And where the hell is Annie? She should have been back ages ago. (*Pause.*) Shit. I'll never get these bills sorted out in time.

Baz Stop fussing.

Viv Everything's got to be right. Dad wants to see all the bills. And he wants to see this place looking good. If anything's not right, he'll go through the roof.

Baz I'm sure he can afford a new one. (*Pause.*) Just a joke.

Viv Save the jokes for later.

Baz Oh, I will be allowed a joke then, will I?

Viv When they've had a look round.

Baz But not before.

Viv Just hurry up, will you? (**Baz** *starts mopping the kitchen floor. A door slams offstage.*) About time. (**Annie** *comes in carrying Sainsbury's* *carrier bags.*) D'you get everything? (**Rusty** *enters with coke and a mirror.*)

Annie Just about. Took hours getting through the checkout. Bloody supermarkets are hell. Grubby housewives shoving you all over the place.

Rusty *goes to the kitchen.*

Baz Don't get on my wet floor!

Rusty (*looking at the floor*) Walking on water again. Aren't I a one?

Baz You're a fucking idiot.

Viv Rusty, get out of the way, and don't make a mess anywhere. And, Baz, don't keep swearing when they get here.

Rusty (*laughing*) Fucking hell . . .

Viv The next time you say that I'll brain you, I mean it. (*To* **Baz**.) You'll have to do the floor again in a minute.

Viv *and* **Annie** *sort the shopping out, putting it in the fridge and cupboards.*

Baz Great. (*He sits down.*)

Viv Don't waste time. You might as well get changed.

He gets up and goes. **Jane** *enters and looks round the room to see if she's forgotten anything. She notices a book, picks it up and goes.*

If she's not gone . . .

Annie How long have we got?

Viv Not long. They'll have left Tim and Sheila's by now.

Annie Everything OK?

Viv I think so. D'you get the cassette?

Annie Yeah. Had to go over to Clapham for it. You ever tried buying Vivaldi in Brixton?

Rusty Vivaldi. (*He snorts.*)

Viv My mum happens to like it. Nothing wrong with that.

Rusty Beats Valium, I s'pose.

Pause.

Annie Can we have a drink?

Viv If you like. You can be in charge of the drinks, Rusty. Keep them topped up. Sherry for mum, scotch for dad, with lots of ice.

Rusty In the sherry?

Viv In the scotch.

Annie Come on then, Rusty. Chop chop.

Rusty Feel like a bloody butler.

Viv No. You feel like a butler. No bloody. Got it.

Rusty Feel . . . like . . . a butler. Got it.

Viv Good. So act like one. Get me a scotch.

Annie And me.

He does. He's gradually becoming more and more annoyed and tense.

What about you?

Rusty I think I'll give it a miss.

Annie What's the matter? Got the clap again?

He gives a sheepish grin and sits down.

Viv (*going back to the bills*) What d'you know about sport, Rusty?

He laughs.

Baz'll have to cover that. Dad's crazy about football. Has videos of all the big games sent out to him.

Rusty I'll be arts correspondent, shall I?

Viv They're not interested in the arts.

Rusty Then I'll just keep my big mouth shut.

Annie Where are we going to eat?

Viv I booked a table at San Lorenzo's.

Annie That'll cost.

Viv Dad's paying.

Annie I like him already.

Viv You can show off your Italian.

Annie God I only know a few words.

Rusty Like 'yes, please.'

Pause.

Annie (*to* **Viv**) Isn't it funny how people can be so jealous. I mean to say, I only got myself a fabulous job in Italy, terrific money, sun, and my weight in coke. Nothing special, really.

Baz *comes back in wearing a different shirt and tying a tie.*

Get you.

Baz I thought if I made a good impression they might adopt me. (*He pours a drink.*) Rusty?

Rusty No.

Baz You ill or something?

Viv Floor's free if you want to mop it.

Baz Bloody hell.

Rusty (*sharp intake of breath*) Hell. No bloody.

Baz Eh?

Rusty No swearing. By order.

Viv That's right. By order. My order.

Rusty Just telling him.

Viv You were getting at me. Don't.

Rusty What are we supposed to do? Suspend all normal behaviour?

Viv Precisely.

Rusty You frightened of them, or what?

Viv No. They happen to be my parents and they happen to own the house. And that entitles them to a little consideration. Besides, I think that's pretty rich coming from someone who cringed and crawled not to be thrown out of home. Don't you?

Pause.

Rusty Shit. I'm off. (*He stands.*)

Viv When you go through that door, you don't come back. Ever. (*He sits.*) Good boy.

Baz What do we call them?

Viv What?

Baz Your folks. Can't very well call them Mum and Dad, can we?

Viv 'Course not. (*Beat.*) Call them by their first names. That'll be OK.

Baz Right. (*Beat.*) What are their first names?

Viv Oh. Bill and Doreen. (**Rusty** *suppresses a hysterical laugh.*) What?

Rusty (*barely able to get the words out*) Nothing . . .

Viv What's so funny, Rusty?

Rusty I don't know . . .

She goes over to him.

Viv What the bloody hell are you laughing at?!

Rusty (*exploding with laughter*) BILL AND DOREEN! SOUNDS LIKE THEY RUN A WHELK STALL!

Viv *takes his coke and flushes it down the sink.*

Viv Now, get out.

Rusty Why?

Viv I won't have you sitting here making cheap comments. I've had enough of people sniping at me. And I don't have to take it from a parasite like you.

Baz Who'd like another drink?

Rusty Parasite?

Viv Yeah. Sponging little parasite.

Rusty Takes one to know one, lovey. Least I own up to it.

Viv Could hardly do anything else, could you?

Rusty Why should I want to? I'm proud of it. Best looking maggot in the heap, me.

Annie Maggot's about right.

Rusty Ah. Talking of parasites. (*Beat.*) Little Miss glam jet-set here. The globe-trotting model. Well . . . from what Dennis tells me, and he tells me plenty, your oh-so-fabulous Italian job was no more than a series of beaver shots, darling. And some very steamy group shots, darling. In short, porn-og-raphy, darling.

Pause.

Annie Liar.

Rusty (*picks up the phone*) Shall we ring him? Ask him? (*Pause.*) No? (*He puts the phone down.*) We had quite a laugh about it. Me and Dennis . . . and Alison and Raif and Carolyn . . .

Viv Leave her alone!

Rusty Stop giving me fucking orders!

Baz Someone tell me why this is going on now.

Rusty No time like the present. Right? (*He sits back.*) Where are they, then, Viv? I'm positively wetting myself with anticipation at the thought of meeting Bill and Noreen. Noreen, was it? Or Doreen? Remind me.

Baz Pretty cheap, making fun of peoples' names, isn't it?

Rusty Don't try to be sincere, Baz. It turns my stomach. (*He takes out more coke and makes up a line on the mirror.*)

Viv My Dad'll throw you out when he gets here.

Rusty I can't wait. Fancy a line? (*Pause.*) I should have thought it was very much your style. Everything in lines. Dead straight. Shoulders back. Arms folded. (*He goes to* **Baz**.) Come on, Baz. This is worth a team point. This is important. Sit up straight. Come on. (**Baz** *slouches*.) Viv won't like it, Baz. Viv likes things her way. Row after row of adoring fans all saying 'Yes, Viv. No, Viv. Lick your arse, Viv'. Come on, Baz, Annie. Viv wants you to lick her arse. This is important. Come on. (*He goes down on his knees and grabs at* **Viv**.) I thought Jane was the only one who wouldn't do it. It's OK, Viv, I'll do it. I'll lick your arse, Viv. (*She pulls away.*) Come on. THIS IS IMPORTANT!

Pause.

Viv You're a mess, Rusty.

Rusty (*worn out*) So hoover me up into your little dirt bag. I'm a stain. Rub me out.

Annie You're a bastard.

Rusty YES! We all are. So let's admit it and have a good time. Don't stand there peeping through your net curtains at me. Say something, anything. (*Pause.*) Nothing? Not even a little twitch?

Viv *hands him a piece of paper.*

What's this?

Viv Your share of the bills since you've been living here.

Rusty (*laughing*) I'll send you a cheque.

Viv Now run along.

Rusty What, playtime over already?

Viv That's right. (*He goes over to her, close.*)

Rusty You're getting grey hairs. They suit you. (*Pause.*) It's OK. I've found someone else to move in with. (*Pause.*) I *was* going to tell you. Honest.

Viv You have.

Rusty Yeah.

Viv What's she like?

Rusty A bastard. Claws bared. The real thing. I'm sure we'll be very happy together.

Viv I'm sure.

Pause.

Baz Time's getting on.

Pause.

Rusty I thought it was important.

He smiles. Pause. He starts to go.

Oh . . . about the drink . . . why I'm not . . . You were right first time, Annie. I've got the clap. (*Beat.*) Which means that you've got the clap, and Viv's got the clap. (*Beat.*) Lucky ol' Baz does it again.

Baz Oh no, he doesn't. (*He and* **Annie** *look at each other.*)

Rusty Well, really. There's hope for you all yet. (*Pause.*) OK. I'll see you guys around. No hard feelings, right? Ciao.

He goes.

Annie That's not true about Italy . . . I did a couple of shots . . . semi-nude . . . but . . .

Viv I didn't know you two had . . . (*Pause.*) You should have told me.

Baz Maybe we should have asked permission.

Viv I just like to know.

Pause.

Annie Sod Rusty. I hate that clinic. Sordid bloody place.

Baz You're obviously old hands at this.

Annie Could say that.

Baz Yeah. Well, it's my first time.

Annie It's nothing to worry about, probably NSU. Rusty's got it more or less permanent. You take anti-biotics for a week then it's gone. Think of it as being promoted to the first division. You're a big boy now.

Pause.

Viv You didn't finish the floor, Baz.

Baz Oh, Christ . . .

Viv It's not the end of the world. Forget it. Act as if nothing's happened.

Baz How can I? We're gonna be sat here, being nice to your folks, knowing we've all got bloody VD.

Viv Just don't think about it.

Baz I'm gonna feel a bloody fool.

Viv That's all right.

Pause.

Baz (*stops and thinks*) The bastard's got my Walkman.

Long pause.

Viv The floor.

Pause. He starts mopping. **Jane** *and* **Tone** *enter.*

Jane All my stuff's out. I'm going.

Viv *hands her a piece of paper.*

Viv Here.

Jane *and* **Tone** *read it. He laughs.*

Tone You must be joking.

Jane I've no intention of paying you a penny.

Annie Pound of flesh?

Jane I think I'm entitled to hurt you back, don't you?

Tone (*screwing the paper into a ball and throwing it into the bin*) What she's saying is: you can whistle for it. You know how to whistle, don't you? Just put your lips together an' blow.

Pause.

Jane Goodbye. (*She starts to go.*)

Tone *goes to the kitchen and points at the floor.*

You missed a bit.

Tone *and* **Jane** *go.*

Annie Sue her. Take her to court.

Baz Don't be daft.

Annie Can't let her get away with that.

Baz She's gone. That's all there is to it.

Viv *puts the bills into neat piles and looks around the room.*

Viv Right. I think everything's ready. Put the mop away, Baz. (*He does.*) You can move in whenever you want.

Annie Yeah.

Viv You'll probably want to decorate, won't you?

Annie Could do.

Viv Me and Baz'll help, won't we, Baz? We could maybe do the whole house. Be good fun. Doing it together. (*Pause. She straightens* **Baz***'s tie.*) Now we can all just settle down, thank God. No more hassles. We're free. (*She gives* **Baz** *the Vivaldi tape,* The Four Seasons, *and he puts it on. The doorbell rings.*) That's them. (*Pause.*) OK. Big smiles, everyone.

The music starts.

Doing the Business

Doing the Business was first presented at the Royal Court Theatre, London as part of the May Days Dialogues season on 2 July 1990, with the following cast:

Peter	Nicholas Woodeson
Mike	Nick Dunning

Directed by Mike Bradwell

Lights up. An office in central London, tasteful but spartan. **Peter** *sits at his desk, smiling.* **Mike** *has just entered the office.*

Peter Mike!

Mike Peter.

Peter *gets up and goes to him, hand outstretched.*

Peter (*laughing*) Well. How the heck are you? (*They shake hands.*)

Mike Very well.

Peter Good, good. Yes, you look splendid.

Mike Thanks. You too.

Peter Me? Yes, well, I try to look after myself. Here, have a seat.

Mike Thanks.

They sit.

Peter Dear oh dear. Is this great, or what? (*Beat.*) So good to see you again, I mean, it's been years, absolute yonks.

Mike Yeah. Too long.

Peter Little bit of grey, do I detect, there? Me too. Still, time marches on. Why fight it?

Mike *smiles.*

Peter 'Behind my back I always hear time's wingéd chariot hurrying near', eh? (*Beat.*)

Mike I think it's '*at* my back I always hear . . .'

Peter Is it? Oh well, you're the literary one. The sentiment still pertains, anyoldhow.

Mike Quite.

Peter So. So. The years have been pretty kind to us, eh? I think you could say we've both achieved a fair modicum of success.

Mike I suppose so.

Peter Suppose so? No doubt about it. Look at you. Running your very own theatre at long last. That constitutes success in my book, and it's a very slim volume my book, I can tell you. No. You definitely qualify.

Mike Thank you.

Peter Well, it's true.

Mike *has taken out a packet of cigarettes. He puts one in his mouth and goes to light it.* **Peter** *jumps up.*

Peter Ah. Right. Let me see if I can find you an ashtray. (*He clearly disapproves of smoking, but gets a small saucer from the shelf. Throughout the scene, every time* **Mike** *finishes a cigarette,* **Peter** *immediately empties the saucer into the rubbish bin.*) There.

Mike Thank you.

Peter Have you tried? (*Beat.*) Giving up?

Mike Once or twice.

Peter Stick at it. Believe me, wisest move I ever made. Looked at the kids one night, thought 'yes, I want to see them grow up', and stopped on the spot. Ran the marathon last year.

Mike Yeah?

Peter Yes. The London bloody marathon! Me! And I beat Jimmy Saville. Not bad, eh?

Mike Terrific.

Peter Learn a lot about yourself, running. Just yourself to beat.

Mike And Jimmy Saville.

Peter (*laughing*) And Jimmy Saville! Yes. Good.

Mike I didn't know you had kids.

Peter Yes, two. (*He shows* **Mike** *a picture facing him on the desk.*) Emily, she's five, and Miranda, she's three. Changed my life around, I can tell you. Bless 'em. (*Beat.*) What about you?

Mike No.

Peter Ah. Nothing medical, I hope. I mean . . . Sandy's well, is she?

Mike Very well.

Peter Good, that's good. And she's still at the Maudsley?

Mike Yes. Head of Clinical Psychology now.

Peter That's right. I saw her name on a letter in the *Telegraph* a few months back, I think. What was all that about?

Mike The usual. Funding. (*Pause.*)

Peter (*intense*) You may not believe this, Mike, I know a lot of people in your profession wouldn't, but there's a heck of a lot of us who think it's a crying bloody shame what they're doing to the health service. (*Beat.*) There. Didn't expect to hear that from me, I'll bet. But there's more than a few of us here at the sharp end of finance and funding who feel the policy's gone off the rails. (*Beat.*) Trim, by all means. Fitness counts, of course it does. But . . . listen,

I don't expect you to approve, Rosemary and I have gone private. Had to, if only for the kids. Yes, I know, shame be upon me.

Mike It's a free country.

Peter You pays your money and you takes your choice.

Mike Quite. And I'm here for money, so . . .

Peter Sponsorship, Mike, sponsorship. It's a package, not a handout. Creative funding for creative initiatives. We're about partnership, not charity.

Mike Phew.

Peter (*laughing*) OK, OK, you old bugger. No hard sell. OK, you got me. No preaching. (*Beat.*) And listen, congratulations, by the way. First chance I've had.

Mike Thanks.

Peter I didn't know you'd put in for it.

Mike I certainly didn't think I'd get it. Not against Roland.

Peter Roland? No. He was up for it?

Mike He was the hot tip.

Peter Good God. Small world. Roland. I thought he was happily installed on the South Bank.

Mike He is. But there's always room for a change.

Peter *notes something down on a pad.*

Peter Greedy. Still, between you, me and the rubber plant, he was always in your shadow as far as I was concerned. Even at Cambridge. But then, who wasn't?

Mike I can't remember that far back. University's all a bit of a blur.

Peter God, I remember it like it was yesterday. Great days. Great days. Never has accounting been so creative. Remember Roland's *Spanish Tragedy*? Everyone accused the poor devil of stealing ideas from your *Romeo and Juliet*. The corrugated iron, remember?

Mike How could I forget?

Peter Well, that was down to me. I was business manager on both shows. So . . . I sold myself your set, saved on Roland's budget and recouped some of your loss.

Mike Did we make a loss?

Peter Didn't we always?

Mike I never took much notice.

Peter Somebody had to. (*Beat*.) And listen, talking of *Romeo and Juliet*, guess who I bumped into last week.

Mike *looks blank*.

Peter Your Romeo. Mal.

Mike Good grief.

Peter Yes. With Cliff, of course. Star guests at a building society junket at the Savoy. They've been spearheading their ad campaign on the box. Very funny. Have you seen it?

Mike No. I did hear them plugging pension schemes on the radio . . .

Peter That's it. Same campaign. You wouldn't believe me if I told you their fee.

Mike I might.

Peter Well, I mustn't. Suffice to say, you could mount half a dozen new plays with it. (*Beat*.) Bloody unfair, isn't it?

Mike That's the logic of the market-place.

Peter Mal was in quite a few of yours at Cambridge, wasn't he? (*Beat*.)

Mike Three. He was a good director, too.

Peter Oh, top flight. He drives an XJS, you know. Yes. Ostentatious, moi? (*Beat*.) Still, mustn't knock. They more than pay it back with all that Red Nose Day stuff, don't you think? Anyway, they're working on a new series for the Beeb. And there's talk of another movie.

Mike Mal and Cliff. Just what the world needs. Another two Ronnies.

Peter Ooh, wicked. Like I say, Mike, mustn't knock. (*Beat*.) D'you see many of the old crowd these days?

Mike Not many. Paths occasionally cross. Like now.

Peter Yes. I suppose we ought to feel guilty, didn't we? The old boy network, and all that. But . . . I really believe this, Mike: it's the way things are, so let's accept it and bloody well get on with it. No point in agonising over the unfairness of it all. We tried that, and where did it get us? Nowhere. We've been given talents and privileges and that's all there is to it. So let's exploit them, for the good of all. It's our duty to do what we can for those who lose out, but it's our even greater duty to be successful.

Mike Our duty to whom?

Peter To ourselves. (*Beat.*) OK, I know what you're thinking.
Sure, I could work for peanuts, run a worthy little touring
company, something like that, all fine stuff, play the out of the way
venues, arts centres, you name it, or I can do what I do: help to
ensure the livelihood of the theatre in general by getting business
involved. I love the theatre. I love the arts. Full stop. I show that
love by doing what I do. And I'm proud of it. No ambiguity,
Mike, no wringing of the hands, no lost sleep. Thanks to me, there
are theatres and galleries and dance companies all over the
country who are doing very nicely. There are jobs secured,
reputations enhanced, customers served, all because I have been
able to convince hard-nosed, middle of the road businessmen that
sponsorship is a good deal for all concerned. Not an easy job, by any
means, but I get in there, roll up my sleeves and talk their language.

Mike Do you still talk mine?

Peter Fluently, Mike.

Mike I was beginning to wonder. (*Beat.*)

Peter Let me tell you something. When I first started in this job, I
did a round table. I got a dozen top businessmen and arts people
together. I felt that it was important that they saw each other close
up, get to know the whiff of each others' cologne, if you know what
I mean. Well, I was disappointed. One man, a merchant banker,
tough, no-nonsense kind of guy, he came up to me afterwards, and
I promise you, he had tears in his eyes, and he said: 'Peter, I
wanted to help, I felt pleased and proud to help, but' – and I'll
never forget this – he said: 'they despise us. They hate us. Why?'
(*Beat.*) And I couldn't tell him. (*Beat.*) There was a guy who works
all the hours God sends being told by an Oxbridge twit, no names
no pack drill, who's never once got his hands dirty, that he was a
morally bankrupt, senseless philistine. (*Beat.*) I decided that day
that I was going to do my darnedest to change all that. And I can
say I've done my best to root out all that snide stuff. (*Beat.*) But
it's not just attitudes that have to change, Mike, it's the work as
well. People have said to me: 'what right do these people, these
businessmen, have to dictate to us? What the heck do they know
about the arts?' And I reply: 'what do *you* know about *them*? You
think you know enough to attack them on the stage whenever the
fancy takes you. You think you know enough to lampoon their
morality, their motives, as a matter of course. When the plain,
unpalatable truth is that these are, in reality, just normal,
everyday people with impeccably bourgeois lifestyles and habits.
There are no sinister secrets lurking in the background, unless it's

in the fevered imaginings of some ! npen-Marxist, poly-educated scribbler who's probably never ever seen the inside of a factory.' (*Beat*.) What I most despise about those people is their sheer . . . laziness. D'you understand me?

Mike Coming through loud and clear. (*Beat*.) And am I included in this?

Peter Mike . . . look, I've been a fan of yours, as you know, from way back. I especially loved the way you used to handle the classics. I mean, I expected you to be running one of the flagships one day. But then, when you started doing the touring stuff, and writing your own plays, I don't know, it just seemed to have blown off course. I like to think I understood. God knows there were, still are, things wrong with the world. I just don't believe things were as bad as, or quite the way, you showed them. I saw the one you did at the Riverside, the one about the Falklands, and believe me, I was gutted afterwards. Mike, it wasn't just horribly naive, it was hopelessly wrong! I couldn't believe one word of it. It was just one long sneer. (*Pause*.)

Mike Everyone's a critic.

Peter Sorry. I hope you don't mind . . .

Mike No. I think it's important that we know where we stand. So thanks. You've made it very clear.

Peter No I haven't. I've done what I promised myself I wouldn't do. Because now, you'll be sitting there thinking I want you to do *Charley's Aunt* and *South Pacific* in the next season.

Mike I think I'd have to give you more credit than that.

Peter Good, thank you. I'm glad to hear you say that, because if there's one lesson I've learned over the years, it's that we mustn't have closed minds. And you'd be surprised how resistant some people are, Mike. I've sat down with people who seriously seem to regard me as the Antichrist. (*Beat*.) Think I'm joking?

Mike I can think of a few who might not like what you stand for.

Peter Plenty, Mike. But do you know what they've all got in common? All those companies who couldn't or wouldn't look to sponsorship to make up the shortfall? I'll tell you. They all went out of business. We offered them a life saver and they all happily went under, shouting and screaming. They were happier to make a racket than they were to stay afloat. And in my book, Mike, that's suicide. No other word for it. (*Beat*.)

Mike You don't think Government policy could have had something to do with it?

Peter It's just one of many factors. But the fact remains, those companies were dinosaurs, badmouthing the state on taxpayers' money. Their crime, for me, was that they never put anything back in. Not one positive message. Precious little entertainment. No *honesty*. (*Beat.*) I had a director in here a few years ago who told me he couldn't even consider taking sponsorship from any of the firms I was suggesting because they were all capitalist! Well, I ask you, what bloody country does he think we're living in? I mean, I sat here, and it was as if he was floating there on a cloud, you know: hello, can you hear me? Anybody there? You can come down if you like. But no. He stayed there, all smug and serene, and very noisily watched his company disappear. (*Beat.*) Simple message I'm trying to impart here, Mike: *he didn't have to*.

Mike Far be it from me, but it could be argued that he simply had principles and was prepared to stick to them.

Peter Oh please, please, please. What kind of principle is it to be a revolutionary socialist theatre director? It's an indulgence. Nowhere else in the country would a freak like that be taken seriously. They've laughed them out of industry, even out of the unions.

Mike Maybe that's why it's important to accommodate them in the theatre.

Peter Why?! (*Beat.*)

Mike I would have thought it was self-evident. (*Beat.*)

Peter No. Not to this theatre-loving, ordinary punter it's not. Not to this average working guy who forks out his hard-earned dosh to be entertained for a couple of hours. I don't go to the theatre to have my intelligence and my way of life roundly insulted. Jesus, this is not the Weimar Republic. Although, having seen some of the stuff I've had to endure, you could be forgiven for thinking that we had three thousand per cent inflation, fascists in Parliament, and even as we speak they're out there now, rounding up Jews and commies and chucking them into concentration camps on Epsom Downs. (*Beat.*) I have been bombarded with material purporting to tell me about the world I live in, and I'll tell you, there's more reality in a Bugs Bunny cartoon. (*Beat.*) And more laughs. (*Pause.*) Time out, Mike. OK. Sorry.

Mike *looks slightly confused.* **Peter** *looks at his watch.*

Well. It's that time. Fancy a little lubrication? (*Beat.*)

Mike Uh, why not?

Peter *stands and goes to the drinks.*

Peter Scotch? You used to be a malt man if memory serves.

Mike Fine.

Peter You'll like this. (*He pours drinks.*) The king of whiskies, in my humble opinion. (*He hands* **Mike** *his drink.*) Here.

Mike Thanks.

Peter Here's to partnership.

Mike Cheers.

They drink.

Peter Now, is that very, very good or what?

Mike Very nice.

Peter You'll probably remember, Mike, I wasn't the world's greatest boozer in the old days. But I've certainly come to appreciate the value of a good bottle. Bit of a wine buff on the quiet. I've got a cellar, try to lay down a few. Very . . . exciting. A quiet sort of enjoyment, like watching the girls growing up. I've really come to appreciate those little changes as time passes. Seems to bring it all together, helps life make sense. Don't you think?

Mike I don't really know. Does life make sense?

Peter (*laughing*) You always were a tricky bugger.

Mike No. I mean it. (*Beat.*) I sometimes find it impossible to explain anything. (*Beat.*)

Peter Deep. Too deep for me, I'm afraid. (*He lifts his glass.*) Is this a glass of malt I see before me? Yes, it bloody well is. There. End of question. A reality. A very nice reality, too. Another one?

Mike Thanks.

Peter *brings the bottle to the desk and pours another one.*

Peter Before I forget, Rosemary told me to insist you come over to us one night. I'm under strict instructions to diarise you.

Mike I'll have to check with Sandy and get back to you. She works a lot of evenings.

Peter Not good enough for you, eh? (*Very slight frisson.*)

Mike Christ, the idea of a whole evening with you two, heaven help us. (*Beat.*) No, we'd love to.

Peter Meet the girls.

Mike Lovely.

Peter And I'll bore you with a tour of the wine cellar.

Mike So long as it includes a tasting.

Peter You're on. I've got a Margaux '78 I've been saving. You can be the first.

Mike Great. I'll ring you tomorrow.

Peter Good good good. (*Beat.*) You know, it's been a secret ambition of mine for a long time now to get a reunion together. The '71 Edinburgh company. Oh, I know, sentimental crap and all that, but they do it all the time in the States. Class of '71, that sort of thing. I'd love to see just how everybody made out. I'll maybe check with you for some addresses and phone numbers.

Mike Sandy's got quite a few, but like I said, I don't really keep up.

Peter Why not?

Mike Probably because I'm a misanthropic bastard. No, I don't know. I prefer to leave memories where they are, I suppose. (*Beat.*) I had an old school friend of mine turn up to a show once. I hadn't seen him for fifteen years, and he strolled up and picked up the conversation where it had ended when we were seventeen. I just felt . . . a bit sad.

Peter Christ, cheer up. I was thinking of a party, not a wake. Anyway, it's just a back burner thing, you know.

Mike Yes.

Peter Let's step into 1990.

Mike Why not? (*Beat.*)

Peter You've had a chance to have a good look at the prospectus I sent you?

Mike Yes.

Peter And I've had a good look through the details you sent me. (*Beat.*) One hundred and ten thousand pounds. That is one hell of a deficit.

Mike You're telling me.

Peter Bloody brave of you to take it on.

Mike I like a challenge.

Peter Good. (*Beat.*) And you think your strategy can work? I mean . . . there's still quite an emphasis on new writing.

Mike That's what our reputation's built on. Anyway, like it says there, over the last three years audiences for new plays averaged out at just over sixty per cent. That's pretty good.

Peter It's excellent. (*Beat.*) Bit of a minefield though, new work. Leap in the dark, sometimes.

Mike Hmm. (*Beat.*)

Peter OK. (*Beat.*) Yes. Very exciting.

Mike There's a couple of scripts there I was lucky to get my hands on.

Peter Ah. Which ones?

Mike Sean Murphy and Thelma Cranston.

Peter Uh huh . . .

Mike Got amazing potential, both of them.

Peter I'm sure. Slight problem though, I have to say.

Mike What?

Peter Well . . . not to put too fine a point on it, Murphy's work's very Irish.

Mike *laughs.*

I'm serious.

Mike So what's the problem?

Peter Mike . . . hear me out on this one. Don't bite my head off until you've heard what I have to say. (*Beat.*) OK. New plays. Great. Vital. Accepted. One problem: balance. Too much new stuff is just one-sided . . . propaganda. And that is a very big turn-off for the sponsors. Now, Ireland's a very touchy subject, I think you'll agree. It requires perhaps more balance than any other.

Mike I don't see why. Theatre isn't journalism. It's *supposed* to have a point of view.

Peter About some things, yes. Absolutely. But Ireland . . . ?

Mike Why the hell not? If we can't have opinions about the big issues, what's the point of having opinions about the small ones?

Peter But it's always the same opinion. Give me a list of playwrights and I can tell you exactly what they'll have to say on any given subject. It's predictable. Boring.

Mike That's a myth. All it amounts to is that you don't like what they have to say, because they come from left of centre. Which is, incidentally, where the majority of the British population happen to come from. Give me a good right wing new play and I'll put it on. But they're not out there.

Peter Or perhaps you don't look for them very hard. (*Beat.*)

Mike Peter, I like to think of the theatre as a big question mark. Its function, its place, is to ask questions. About the way we behave; about the way we organise ourselves; about things we're not supposed to know. Now, most people on the right don't want that belief reflected on stage. There's a whole imaginative world they refuse to inhabit. They can finance plays, but they sure as hell couldn't write one. That's why they created advertising. To compensate. (*Beat.*)

Peter Yes. Its desire to patronise has always been one of the unlovelier aspects of the British theatre. (*Beat.*)

Mike I'm sorry, you were going to say something about Sean Murphy's play.

Peter That's right. The problem of Mister Murphy.

Mike What exactly *is* this problem?

Peter Well, in a nutshell, I don't exactly have people queueing up to sponsor plays supporting the IRA.

Mike Which is just as well, seeing as the play doesn't do that.

Peter He's a Republican, Mike. Nowhere in his work, some of which I've seen, I hasten to add, does he specifically condemn the IRA. (*Beat.*) Clear enough for you?

Mike Definitely not. Sean Murphy is an Irishman from Derry, what's he supposed to write about, for Christ's sake? Mid-life crises in Tunbridge Wells? He has never romanticised the IRA in any of his work.

Peter He writes about them as if they're human beings.

Mike Well, Jesus, they are.

Peter There! You see? Can't you understand that to present them as anything other than the murdering scum they are plays right into their hands? Making excuses for them makes them heroes?

Mike The play's not making excuses for anybody. It's about the social and political trauma that drives one young man into the IRA. His brother's blinded by a plastic bullet. His family are systematically harassed and intimidated by the police and the army. He can't get a job. That's the reality of his life.

Peter A very partially presented reality . . .

Mike Murphy writes about real people involved in tragic circumstances, and he does it with wit, compassion and humanity.

Peter Can't agree with you there, Mike. (*He has taken a photocopied article out of his folder.*) Look, this is an interview Murphy did last year for *City Limits*. I've ringed the relevant parts.

He hands it to **Mike**, *who reads it out.*

Mike 'In as much as I believe the British presence in Ireland to be wrong, I cannot condemn those who take up the gun to try and end it.' Yes?

Peter Words of one syllable: he's one of them.

Mike You'll hear the same from a large percentage of Irish people in the North, the South and all over the globe. It's a perfectly respectable position. Murphy writes about the contradictions involved in holding it.

Peter Respectable? Respectable? Surely I'm not hearing this. Do you seriously expect me to go to the Nat West bank, or the TSB and ask them to sponsor an apology for political terrorism, written by a man who considers murder respectable?

Mike If it were true, I have to say it would have a certain poignancy to it. But it's not true, and you know it's not. (*Beat.*)

Peter OK. We'll put Murphy on hold for a moment – just a moment – let's look at Thelma Cranston. Quite a pleasant prospect judging from her photograph.

Mike *sighs.*

Peter However, in conjunction with this piece of paper (*He takes a sheet out of the folder.*) the prospect becomes altogether grimmer.

Mike What is it this time? She advocates vivisection on the Royal Family or what?

Peter Just read it.

Mike *does.*

Mike Where did you get this?

Peter Not important.

Mike Like hell. This is private information.

Peter I work with businessmen. Businessmen like to know who they're getting into bed with. Businessmen have people who provide them with details of prospective employees. Businessmen tend not to look too kindly on members of far-left political parties, people with convictions for criminal damage.

Mike (*looking at the paper*) That was all years ago. She was a student.

Peter Nor do businessmen like lesbians.

Mike She happens to have written a play about the virtues of the family unit.

Peter Oh? I took it to be about child abuse.

Mike It is, obliquely. But so is *Pericles*.

Peter Don't misunderstand me. *My* problem is not the woman's past history, it is that potential sponsors have seen her background and decided they don't want to be associated with her.

Mike What this amounts to then, is censorship.

Peter I wondered when you'd get around to flinging that accusation at me.

Mike Well, isn't it?

Peter In a word: bollocks. I'm not telling you what you can and can't produce. I'm telling you what my clients are prepared to give you money to produce with their name on it. It's entirely your choice. (*Pause.*) Have a top up.

Mike No thanks.

Peter Go on. (*He pours drinks.*) In all honesty, mate, it's a bloody tragedy that you have to come here and take all this, I know that. I'm fully aware of what it means to you. But the fact is unless you clear your deficit you won't receive sufficient core funding to produce good work *and* stay open. Show me a theatre that will. So some of the business community are prepared to help you make up the shortfall . . . provided you play by the rules. Their rules.

Mike Good theatre is my only rule.

Peter And I'm behind you a hundred per cent on that. Listen, these guys are out for a good deal. For their money they get goodwill, an enhanced public awareness and bucketfuls of prestige. Jesus, they get to rub shoulders with Jeremy Irons, ogle Imogen Stubbs. Their wives get to drool over Charlie Dance. And you get to produce good theatre. (*Beat.*) In my more reflective moments I see a rosy glow of contentment around our playhouses.

Mike But not around Sean Murphy or Thelma Cranston.

Peter Leave them in the upstairs rooms of pubs where they belong. They're relics. Outmoded, hysterical throwbacks to a time before reality hit.

Mike They're both good fucking writers.

Peter If they're good fucking writers, then the theatre's doomed. You'll die through lack of funds and audience indifference.

Mike Whatever happened to the right to fail? What about the fact that if our only criterion is commercial success we'll end up playing *Shirley Valentine* day in, day out, in every theatre that's left in the country, punctuated, if we're lucky, by some old ham touring his one man Winston Churchill?

Peter A tad simplistic, don't you think, Mike? Let's not confuse the right to fail with a *duty* to fail. I'm all for experiment. Matter of fact, I have a bit of a soft spot for performance art. So do some of my clients.

Mike Yeah. No content, and acres of bare flesh. It figures. (*Beat.*)

Peter Look, let me shoot some hard facts at you: your new plays average sixty per cent audience, right? On paper that looks great. Very attractive to the sponsors, you might think. However, in business, we have to be a little more rigorous than that. We have to ask: who exactly is coming to these plays? Did you know, for instance, that last year the established plays in your theatre played to an average AB social group of nearly seventy-five per cent? That means that out of every four people in that theatre for the Stoppard, three were the perfect profile, sponsorship-wise. Take a look at the figures for the new plays and you'll find it plummets to *one* in four. To a potential sponsor, especially in these days of punitive interest rates, that means minimum return. So, even if you were to pack the theatre to the rafters every night, if it's a crowd of tatty, low disposable income types, ethnics, students, concessionaries, you still won't get sponsorship. And you'll go under. And it'll be all your own fault, because you were given the freedom to choose. (*Beat.*)

Mike This is all very reminiscent of the Nicaraguan election. Vote for me or watch your children starve. (*Beat.*)

Peter Why oh why do you all still cling to this tatty seventies pinkoism? Hmm? (*Beat.*) Everywhere, people are throwing off their chains, but you walk into a British theatre, and all you hear is the sound of actors, writers and directors clamping on the leg irons, snapping the handcuffs shut. (*Beat.*) Why are you all so scared of being free? (*Pause.*)

Mike Being free involves the right to question, to contradict.

Peter But for Christ's sake, why can't you be more grown up about it?

Mike Because when you say that, what you really mean is why can't we accept all your terms, do it your way, play to your rules. And when it comes down to it, we're dealing with the world of the imagination where the rules don't always apply. And this society, this world that you've helped create . . . how grown up do you really think that looks to some of us? Tatty pinkoism? What about tatty nineties reality? What about those heroes of the culture, the businessmen? Those arrogant, thought-free copies of American and Japanese originals. Wearing their lack of imagination like a badge of courage. Men with limited horizons who want to shrink *all* our visions. Running around trying to make money, not evil in itself, but trying to make it the state religion. And if anybody dares criticise, dares to suggest they're not the great upstanding heroic infallible creatures they want to be seen as, then they howl with indignation. And their bought and paid for mouthpieces in the media slip their leashes and snarl and froth at *us* for being out of touch and, God help us, immature. They've got all the power, but where they screw up is they won't take any responsibility. And they want to suck the rest of us into their vacuum, where nobody ever owns up, nobody admits a thing. Where the official language is the lie. (*Beat.*) And before you ask, I don't despise them for being capitalists, I despise them for being such stinking lousy *bad* capitalists. (*Pause.*) We'll scrub the dinner invitation, shall we? (*Pause.*)

Peter Let me pitch you a name, Mike. Philip Seymour.

Mike *smiles*.

Yes. Mister Brecht. The man who called *you* middle of the road. For nearly ten years he was one of our leading radical directors, right?

Mike You could say that. Or you could say he was just pissing about with aesthetics.

Peter Couldn't have put it better myself. Well. Look at him now.

Mike Do I have to?

Peter C'mon. Take me on board. You know what I'm saying.

Mike Yes. Ten years ago, Seymour suddenly stopped talking Marxist dialectics, proclaimed that the personal and psychological were now political and made pots of money directing chi-chi revivals for the eighties.

Peter He also made pots of money at the box office.

Mike So Seymour should be my role model.

Peter You could do worse. I know in your terms he's probably got the moral principles of a bendy toy, but he's a huge success. He dropped the snarl and went for a smile.

Mike He also dropped every new playwright he'd been trying to brainwash for the previous ten years.

Peter There's no return in that kind of work, Mike. That's what Seymour realised. Neo-Brechtian parables about the military industrial complex, surprise surprise, failed to generate a lot of heat at the box office. They just swallowed subsidy. And subsidy was the only reason they existed. So: take away subsidy, what are you left with? Plays that have to bring in an audience, *please* an audience.

Mike Flatter an audience.

Peter And why not?

Mike Because that's not what it's for.

Peter Oh, I suppose it's really for the already converted coterie that goes to see whatever *Time Out* or *City Limits* tells it to, is it? That particular audience is never flattered, I suppose.

Mike Not in my theatre it won't be.

Peter I'll believe that when I see it. (*Beat.*) Honestly, I can't understand why so many theatre folk hate the idea of seeing their auditoria and their bars full of decent, ordinary, real people. Why this fear of being popular?

Mike Probably because the only shows that pull them in regularly are big-name revivals, thrillers and vacuous musicals. Or what we in the business call crap.

Peter It doesn't have to be. Quality is quality, no matter what the product.

Mike We are not a product.

Peter (*laughing*) Somebody's forgetting what decade we're living in. (*Beat.*) Here. (*He pours another drink.*) Look, I admire you. I always have. Even, goddammit, when you're wrong, and trust me, Mike, you're not always right. But . . . I don't want to see you go down the tubes with all the others. Not over something which, when you really examine it, boils down to a difference of emphasis.

Mike Now there's a very tasty euphemism.

Peter If you like. But euphemism's the language of compromise, and compromise is the language of progress.

Mike Not from where I'm sitting. Not if the compromise is all expected to come from one side.

Peter Is that what you think? That all I want to do is dictate? I'm sorry. I've miscommunicated here. I'm offering you partnership, and that means give and take on both sides. I want my contribution to be as creative as possible. I want to give your organisation its freedom: I ensure your financial stability, you ensure a balanced and exciting showcase for my clients. Now, at first, no doubt, the shoes might pinch a little bit, but pretty soon, you'll see, we'll be walking steadily, and who knows, even running some lovely day. (*Beat.*)

Mike Do they send you off somewhere to learn all this stuff?

Peter Meaning?

Mike Well . . . every now and again, I feel like I'm talking to a moonie here. (*Beat.*)

Peter Motivational skills, Mike. Communication, creativity, commitment. (*Beat.*) Yes, I've done a few courses. I've learned the language of business. The can-do language. (*Beat.*) I know. It seems a little strange at first, but then so does 'lovey, darling, you were wonderful', a litany I've heard reverberating around many a theatre. (*Beat.*) But it's not just language, it's a state of mind. In order to turn this country around, we had to change attitudes. In order to change attitudes we had to change the way we thought about ourselves, talked about ourselves. I think you'll agree, we did a pretty good job.

Mike Absolutely. I could really use a phrasebook. (*Beat.*)

Peter (*intense*) Things change. (*Pause.*) Do you ever think about God, Mike?

Mike Why?

Peter I don't know . . . well, the last couple of years I've looked into it a little bit. (*Beat.*) I sometimes feel, y'know, there's maybe something missing. (*He puts his hand on his chest.*) In here. (*Beat.*) I've begun to feel that Jesus may be knocking on the door.

Mike It's very fashionable, I understand.

Peter I'm talking eternal. (*Pause.*) Y'know, sometimes life's so incredibly exciting. (*Beat. He pours another drink and opens the folder.*) I love the Pinter. I think kicking off with a major revival's a great idea. What's more, your average business guy's at least heard of Harold.

Mike I was worried you might think him a bit of a dangerous radical.

Peter Man of letters, Mike. We expect a bit of crankiness in that department. Look at Shaw, John Mortimer. A grand old British tradition.

Mike Shaw was Irish.

Peter But his plays weren't! (*Beat.*) Casting. Any thoughts?

Mike Oh, I've got a very long list.

Peter Well, let me add to that list, if I may, just a couple of names.

Mike I doubt you'd come up with anybody we haven't.

Peter You never know.

Mike OK. (*Beat.*)

Peter Mal and Cliff. (*Beat.*) Brilliant, or what? And listen, for the tramp . . . what about Billy Connolly?

Mike He's a comedian.

Peter Yes!

Mike Well . . .

Peter C'mon, it's the nineties.

Mike Can he act?

Peter Of course he can. Brilliant timing. And listen, you could do worse than join the queue for Ben Elton's next play.

Mike *stares at him.*

Peter Just a suggestion. You're a free agent, don't get me wrong. Anyhow . . . Mal and Cliff. Does that get the old juices flowing?

Mike Could do. I'll have to do an availability on them.

Peter (*laughing*) Already done. I mentioned it to them at the Savoy, they seemed interested, so I followed up with a call to the agent. They're free, so I sort of . . . made them an offer. (*Beat.*) I mean, I just got so excited! I'm sorry. What can I tell you?

Mike OK. But I'm free to ignore you, right?

Peter Right. (*Pause.*) You were looking at a budget of, what, thirty-five to forty K for that show?

Mike Thirty-five's the limit.

Peter Uh huh. Well how does seventy-five sound?

Mike The answer to a maiden's prayer.

Peter *That's* what I can do for you. Plus, Mal and Cliff have got their own production company, d'you know that? So, Channel 4, video, isn't out of the question. That one show could well end up funding your whole season. And making a dent in the deficit. (*Beat.*) You see where we can get with a little flexibility? (*Beat.*) OK. Now, I see you haven't got anyone down as director. Does that mean you're going to do it?

Mike No. I want to concentrate on the new work. I haven't got anyone yet, but there's plenty of possibilities.

Peter We need someone who can handle Mal and Cliff, *and* who understands the dynamics of this sort of project. Let's see . . . Mendes is hot, but I have a feeling Mal would have him for breakfast. Ockrent's stock's a bit low after the Frayn . . . (*Beat.*) Now, promise you won't hit me. (*Beat.*) Philip Seymour. (*Beat.*)

Mike I had a feeling . . .

Peter It makes perfect sense, Mike. There's nobody better.

Mike If you like that kind of thing.

Peter I know you think I'm rubbing it in, but with Seymour in harness, we'd have a phenomenal package. What a way to kick off your first season. Probably not what you had in mind, but that's the strength of partnership. I mean, you'd probably have cast a trio of good second division actors, got a solid, worthy production, played to sixty per cent . . . but what we'll have now will be an event. Huge media interest, and a cast iron success, to boot. (*Beat.*)

Mike I'm just wondering how I explain it to my staff.

Peter Good god, man, forget the staff. Think of the board. You'll be profitable, the place'll be packed. They'll love you for it. (*Beat. He pours more drinks.*) Now. Murphy and Cranston. (*Beat.*) Let's clear the air. Get rid of any bad feeling.

Mike What had you in mind?

Peter Flexibility.

Mike Oh, come on, I've bent over backwards –

Peter On *my* part. (*Beat.*) Some of what you said hit home, Mike. And I appreciate that new writing's the lifeblood and all that . . . so why don't I shift a little? OK. I think I can bury the young lady's past . . . I mean, even merchant bankers were young once but I'll need your help on the actual play. I mean, it's not at the final draft stage, I take it?

Mike No.

Peter Well then, see if you can't steer her away from the incest angle. Not totally, but . . . just make the point that people aren't too mad keen to fork out for that kind of thing.

Mike I'm sorry, but it's an important subject.

Peter Of course it is. But, it's a matter of taste. For example, *Fiddling About* would seem to be a singularly inappropriate title.

Mike It's ironic. The main character's a violinist.

Peter But, Mike, ask yourself the question: is it a funny subject? I'm a family man. I have two daughters. I don't think it's a funny subject.

Mike Not funny. Ironic.

Peter See if she won't consider changing it.

Mike I doubt very much if she will. Anyway, I won't ask her. (*Beat.*)

Peter You're budgeted eighteen K on this one, right?

Mike Right.

Peter If you're happy with that, then, I'll leave it to your judgement. I could double that budget, but I have too much respect for your artistic integrity to make you do something against your will.

Mike Thank you.

Peter We'll leave it to stand as your folly.

Mike What if it's a hit?

Peter Then I grovel. (*Pause.*) Which leaves us with Mister Murphy. (*Beat.*) Let me give it to you straight, Mike. If that play goes on, I pull out. And your first season will almost certainly be your last. (*Pause.*)

Mike Where's the much-vaunted flexibility on this one?

Peter Different kettle of fish. Nobody, but nobody, wants to be involved with something like that. We regard it as the unacceptable face.

Mike Because it's political?

Peter This goes way beyond politics. Whether you like it or not, those people are our enemies. Any apology, however muted, for what they do, is disgusting. And you can plead that he's not an IRA apologist until you're blue in the face. We wouldn't touch you with rubber gloves on. That's not a threat. It's a promise. (*Pause.*)

Mike So this is where it ends. 'Partnership. Creativity'. Whatever tacky buzzword you want to attach. It ends with you telling me, on behalf of your clients, on behalf of the government, what I can and can't produce. (*Beat.*) And this is going on all over the country. We've slimmed, trimmed, rationalised, whatever you want to call it, and now you twist the knife. Good people, committed people, actors who work for a hundred and sixty quid a week or less before tax, writers working for peanuts, people devoted to their industry being bullied and starved out of existence. I don't know why any of us are surprised. We watched them do it to coal, steel. They're doing it right now to education and health. All over the country there are little men like you, creating nothing, leeching your existence off the surplus, despising people who do something useful, something that counts. Obeying your political masters just as loyally as apparatchiks the world over. You want to see a *real* sneer? Look in the mirror. (*Beat.*) Still, when you've done your best to knock it all down, we'll come back and build it up again. Because that's what we do. You can't change that. (*He pours a drink and raises his glass.*) Right. I accept your terms. Eighteen peoples' jobs depend on me so now isn't the time to play Don Quixote. But don't expect me to like it. (*Beat.*) And don't expect me to like you. (*Beat.*)

Peter I'd hoped we could work together *and* be friends.

Mike (*laughing*) Forget it. I know the rules. Friendship isn't one of them. Be 'friends' with Philip Seymour. I'm nobody's tame aesthete. (*Beat.*)

Peter This is sad, Mike.

Mike No it's not.

Peter It is for me.

Mike It's a transaction. We'd be very silly to let sentiment interfere with that.

Peter I've told you how much I respect you . . .

Mike What do you know about respect? I've swallowed every principle I have to come here. I've listened to your triumphalist Tory crap and your secondhand selling pitch. I've let you mangle my season with your alternative light entertainers. I've promised to reject one of the best young writers in the country. In six months I'll smile and shake hands with a bunch of grinning zombies who made it all possible, and thank them for the privilege. (*Beat.*) And you know all that. And if you knew anything about respect, you'd throw me out. But you won't.

Peter No.

Mike No. Because that would be bad for business. (*Beat.*) So. Great doing business with you. (*He drains his drink, looks at his watch and stands.*)

Peter It's always great doing business.

Mike It must be. (*Beat.*)

Peter You need me. That's what you can't stand, isn't it? (*Pause.*) We'll get along fine. You'll see. I'm a sensitive guy. I have doubts sometimes. I cry. (*Pause.*) Well. Maybe you'll write a play about me. One day.

Mike I don't do farce.

Peter *suddenly laughs and raises his glass.* **Mike** *goes.*

Blackout